INTRODUCTION

Children everywhere delight at the approach of a locomotive. Locomotives have long been the most popular aspect of railroading. Is it the great power of these machines that fascinates us? Their sights and sounds? The feeling of the ground shaking as they roar by? A steam locomotive belching forth smoke and steam will always attract attention, and our fascination encourages us to learn more about these great machines. In nearly 200 years of locomotive production, countless variations have been produced. Some were experimental one-offs, others were mass produced in the thousands.

Steam locomotives ruled American rails for more than a century. The earliest were relative small curiosities, and later models were massive leviathans weighing more than 375 tons and capable of moving more than 10,000 tons. The roar of such machines was awesome, and their sight unforgettable. Nevertheless, despite decades of refinement steam locomotives remained inefficient. There had been some improvements, such as the use of compound engines and, in the second decade of the twentieth century, the widespread adoption of superheating. However, in general steam locomotives suffered as a comparatively poor means of converting fuel into motion.

Common Steam Locomotive Wheel Arrangements

The most common American method of classifying steam locomotives is the Whyte System. It was adopted in the early 1900s and replaced a host of unclear classification systems. The Whyte logic is simple. It designates locomotives by wheel arrangement, divided into three basic locations: leading, driving, and trailing. Each group is separated by a dash. A zero indicates the absence of wheels in one of the groups. For example, the American-type locomotive, which has four leading wheels, four driving wheels, and no trailing wheels, is designated as a 4-4-0, while the Atlantic type, which has four leading wheels, four driving wheels, and two trailing wheels, is designated as a 4-4-2. Locomotives such as Mallet Compound types and simple articulateds with more than one set of drivers and running gear count each grouping of drivers separately. *Old Maud*, Baltimore & Ohio's pioneer Mallet type with two sets of six driving wheels but no leading or trailing wheels is designated a 0-6-6-0. Locomotives without tenders, such as Forneys, that have built-in tanks are designated with a letter T following the wheel counts. A typical Forney type would be designated 0-4-4T. Most standard wheel arrangements have names. Early names were descriptive, such as the Ten-Wheeler, while later names often represented the railroad that first used the wheel arrangement. Several arrangements have more than one name; the best example of this is the 4-8-4, which is generally known as a Northern type, but also known by a host of other names, such Wyoming on Lehigh Valley and Niagara on New York Central.

Wheel arrangement	Whyte classification	Type	Wheel arrangement	Whyte classification	Type
<o00o	2-4-2	Columbia	<oo00000oo	4-8-4	Northern
<oo00	4-4-0	American	<o00000	2-10-0	Decapod
<oo00o	4-4-2	Atlantic	<o000000o	2-10-2	Santa Fe
<o000	2-6-0	Mogul	<o0000000o	2-10-4	Texas
<o000o	2-6-2	Prairie	<oo000000o	4-10-2	Southern Pacific
<oo000	4-6-0	Ten-Wheeler	<oo0000000o	4-12-2	Union Pacific
<oo000o	4-6-2	Pacific	<000 000	0-6-6-0	
<oo0000oo	4-6-4	Hudson	<o000 000o	2-6-6-2	
<o0000	2-8-0	Consolidation	<o0000 0000o	2-8-8-2	
<o00000o	2-8-2	Mikado	<o000 000ooo	2-6-6-6	Allegheny
<o00000oo	2-8-4	Berkshire	<o0000 0000oo	2-8-8-4	Yellowstone
<oo00000	4-8-0	Twelve-Wheeler	<oo000 00000oo	4-6-6-4	Challenger
<oo00000o	4-8-2	Mountain	<oo0000 0000oo	4-8-8-4	Big Boy

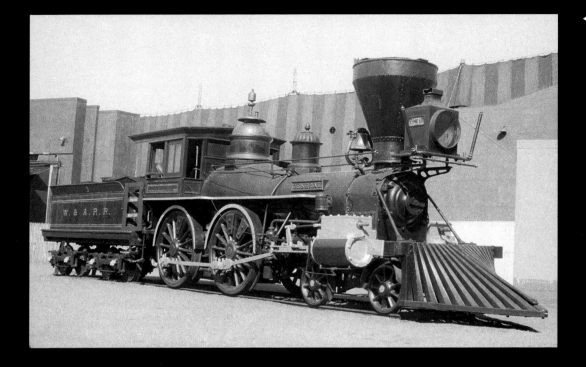

Beginning in the 1890s, railroads experimented with new forms of propulsion—electrics and internal combustion engines. In the early twentieth century, electrification seemed to be the way forward; in addition to being much more efficient, electric locomotives were much more powerful, accelerated faster, required less maintenance, and were much cleaner than steam. Several lines invested in expensive electrification schemes, but the high cost of electrical infrastructure, combined with general changes in the American economy, discouraged most roads from embracing electrification. In the meantime, many lines adopted self-propelled railcars for use in light passenger services and on branch lines. The most successful railcar designs blended internal combustion and electrical technologies. In the 1920s, further advances allowed for production of the first diesel-electric locomotives. Initially, the primary commercial application for these diesels was as slow-speed switchers, usually in areas where locomotive smoke was deemed objectionable. In the late 1920s and 1930s, further advances in diesel engine design—made possible by improved metallurgy and better fuel injection systems, and spurred by demand for marine applications—allowed for the development of compact, high-output diesel engines (in this sense "engine" refers to the component that powers the locomotive, rather than the locomotive itself). In the 1930s, General Motors entered the diesel business through the purchase of the Winton Engine Company and leading railcar producer Electro-Motive Company. In the mid-1930s, GM demonstrated the capabilities of diesel locomotive power while gradually refining and perfecting diesel engine designs. Streamlined passenger trains impressed the public, and diesel switchers made good commercial sense for yard work, but still the job of hauling heavy freight in that era remained the domain of tried-and-true steam locomotive designs.

Demonstrations of diesel locomotive potential fueled a final phase of steam development as traditional builders sought means to perpetuate this established technology. Yet when General Motors' Electro-Motive Company (renamed the Electro-Motive Division in 1940) debuted its extremely powerful and flexible model FT road diesel in 1939, steam was effectively finished. Not only did the FT equal the power of most heavy road locomotives, but also it did so with lower axle weight, substantially lower fuel cost, and a dramatically

Diesel Locomotive Wheel Arrangements

A different system than that used for steam locomotives is employed to denote the wheel arrangements of diesel and electric locomotives. For these locomotives, axles rather than wheels are represented. Since powered axles and unpowered axles do not follow the same pattern as steam locomotives, they must be represented in a different way; also, the groupings are based on trucks or otherwise connected sets of wheels (again, separated by hyphens). Under this system, letters indicate groups of powered axles—A for one axle, B for two, C for three, and so on. Numbers are used to indicate unpowered axles.

The most common type of diesel uses the B-B arrangement, which indicates two groups of two powered axles. Another common type was the A1A-A1A arrangement, in which there are two trucks, each with three axles but with only the outside axles powered. Such arrangements were necessary for adequate weight distribution.

Electrics use a variety of unusual wheel arrangements, often involving articulated frames. The Pennsylvania Railroad's famed GG1, for example, had a 2-C+C-2 arrangement.

lower maintenance bill. It was a powerful engine that could be used on just about any main line, and in many types service. The only impediments were its high initial cost and convincing an industry wedded to steam power to accept something entirely new. The FT and similar diesels demonstrated most of the advantages of electrification, but at much lower cost. Where wiring main lines had been deemed cost prohibitive, most railroads could justify the cost of buying diesel locomotives.

Although the established steam builders also began diesel development, General Motors had the edge. World War II interrupted the process. During the war, railroad traffic soared, while restrictions were imposed on locomotive acquisition. Military demands for vital equipment resulted in many railroads buying new steam as diesel engines, and electrical components were in high demand and very short supply. General Motors remained the primary supplier of road diesels, while the traditional locomotive builders, Alco and Baldwin, primarily constructed steam along with diesel switchers. In the meantime, GM refined its locomotive designs, while railroads that had bought GM diesels gained experience and were convinced of the superiority of the new technology.

After the war, most railroads planned for total dieselization. There were a few exceptions, such as Pocahontas coal haulers Chesapeake & Ohio, Norfolk & Western, and Virginian, that remained loyal to steam for a few more years. By the mid-1950s, even these lines recognized the superiority of diesels and began the conversion. In the postwar market, Alco and Baldwin offered diesels that emulated General Motors success, and engine-builder Fairbanks-Morse also entered the locomotive business by building diesel locomotives powered by its unusual opposed-piston marine engine. Over time, lower maintenance costs and higher reliability gave GM models the advantage in most areas.

The steam-to-diesel transition was the most colorful period in American locomotive history, with myriad new diesel models working alongside generations of steam. In 1960, the transition was virtually complete; by that time only Alco and EMD remained in the domestic locomotive market. The emphasis from then on was replacement diesels. General Electric entered the heavy diesel market during this new phase. GE was not a new player; it traditionally supplied electrical components, built heavy electrics and diesel switchers, and until 1953 was in partnership with Alco in production of domestic road diesel electrics. Its friendly days with Alco had ended, and in the 1960s it competed with both Alco and GM for market share. The typical road locomotive of 1959 was rated at just 1,800 horsepower, but by the late 1960s 3,000 to 3,600 horsepower was standard. Alco exited the business in 1969, while its Canadian affiliate Montreal Locomotive Works continued to build locomotives for a few more years, ultimately conveying its designs to Bombardier. In recent years, EMD and GE have been the primary suppliers of road-freight diesels, while smaller manufacturers have supplied switchers and passenger locomotives.

In the last two decades, desires for substantially more powerful freight locomotives with much greater pulling power (measured as tractive effort) resulted in development of three-phase alternating current traction systems. The first commercially successful three-phase AC diesel was EMD's SD70MAC, built in large numbers for Burlington Northern beginning in 1993. GE soon followed with its AC4400CW. Where EMD was the leading locomotive builder from the 1940s to the early 1980s, GE now has the dominant position. In 2005, General Motors sold EMD (now called Electro-Motive Diesel), and since 2010 it has been a division of Caterpillar's Progress Rail.

In recent years, environmental concerns have driven locomotive development, with new engines designed to produce lower greenhouse gas emissions and less noise while locomotives are built to provide a safer and more ergonomical workplace for railroaders. Today's most powerful road diesel locomotives are dramatically cleaner than postwar models, and they produce more tractive effort than even the largest, most powerful steam locomotive ever built. Straight electrics remain just a tiny portion of the market.

This book includes hundreds of photographs depicting a great variety of locomotives; it is organized by railroad rather than by era or manufacturer. A variety of different railroads have been profiled. Some are the large freight carriers of today, others the classic lines of yesteryear; also included are a number of smaller railroads and some of the leading passenger and commuter train operators. Even a big book such as this could not comprehensively cover the myriad lines that have served North America since railroading began, nor has any effort been made to cover each and every locomotive type. Rather, this book presents concise profiles listing interesting and relevant facts and details about locomotive fleets and individual machines. Fact bars highlight technical specifications of key types. Specifications such as weight, horsepower, and tractive effort are indices of the power potential of different models. In the diesel category, the word *transmission* refers to the means of delivering power to the wheels from the on-board diesel engine (sometimes called a prime mover). Until the advent of three-phase alternating current systems, most North American diesels used direct-current traction motors, although from the 1960s onward many locomotives used an alternator-rectifier system to produce DC for traction motors instead of a traditional DC generator powering traction motors. Since these locomotives still use DC motors, fact bars refer to them to as having DC electric transmissions to distinguish these diesels from those with modern three-phase AC-traction systems. A few diesels, such as imported Krauss-Maffei locomotives from Germany, used hydraulic torque converters instead of traction motors. These details, and many others, are revealed in the pages to come. Careful selection of locomotive photos and the detailed profiles are intended to enlighten, entertain, inform, and help put the great variety of North American locomotive fleets in logical historical context. Enjoy!

▲ Classic railroad fairs gave railroads the opportunity to display their newest and oldest locomotives to the public. On August 9, 1949, Bob Buck and Warren St. George of Warren, Massachusetts, toured the Chicago Railroad Fair, an event they would fondly recall for the rest of their lives. Here, they saw a Pennsylvania Railroad T-1 Duplex (left), New York Central Niagara No. 5500, and streamlined PRR GG1 electric, among other magnificent American locomotives. *Robert A. Buck*

1 AMTRAK

Traditionally, America's privately run railroads provided the public with passenger service. Decades of decline made continued operation of profitless passenger services untenable, so in 1971, to relieve railroads from their passenger obligations and preserve a skeletal passenger network, congress created the National Railroad Passenger Corporation (NRPC, subsequently known by the trade name Amtrak). Among Amtrak's stated goals were the following: "To provide financial assistance for and establishment of a national rail passenger system, to provide for the modernization of railroad passenger equipment, to authorize the prescribing of minimum standards for railroad passenger service." Railroads had the option of joining Amtrak and providing it with cash, equipment, or the equivalent, or staying out of it. Initially, 17 railroads signed contracts with Amtrak, and many contributed locomotives to Amtrak's fleet.

Inherited locomotives largely consisted of Electro-Motive E8s and E9s built specifically for passenger services in the late 1940s and early 1950s. There were some anomalies; Southern Pacific contributed a handful of FP7s. In the Northeast, Amtrak operated former

▼ Amtrak E8A No. 328 leads an eastward train at Rochester on March 8, 1975. This features Amtrak's early platinum mist and bloody nose livery of the early 1970s. Many of Amtrak's inherited E-units were well worn and tired after years of hard service, and they were soon replaced by SDP40Fs and later F40PHs. A few were rebuilt with head-end power and survived into the mid-1980s. *Doug Eisele*

▲ Amtrak began operations with an eclectic fleet inherited from the freight railroads. Among these were some former Pennsylvania Railroad GG1 electrics, of which only a few received Amtrak colors. Amtrak No. 924 rests at New Haven, Connecticut, alongside a specially styled Budd RDC built for New Haven Railroad that was originally part of a trainset assigned to the *Roger Williams*. *George W. Kowanski*

Penn Central electrified lines (New Haven–New York City–Philadelphia–Washington D.C., and Philadelphia–Harrisburg). These were the busiest and fastest lines. Venerable former PRR GG1s hauled most trains; these were fast, powerful, double-ended streamlined machines that had characterized PRR's electric operations for the previous three decades. Amtrak also inherited recently developed electric MP85 Metroliner multiple units and United Aircraft TurboTrains, modern federally funded high-speed trains designed to improve Northeast services. In 1976, Amtrak acquired a dozen former New Haven Railroad dual-mode FL9s from Penn Central. This fleet was modernized and paired down to six serviceable locomotives. All were assigned to Empire Corridor trains, where third-rail operation was required to reach New York City terminals.

In its early years, Amtrak had a need for new equipment that quickly resulted in purchase of a pair of five-car RTG turbo trains from French manufacturer ANF in 1972. Subsequently, Amtrak ordered seven more trains of similar design manufactured domestically under license by Rohr Industries in California. Originally, the RTG trains were based in Chicago and Rohr trains at Albany for Empire Corridor services. Amtrak's first new diesel locomotives were for 150 SDP40Fs, built by Electro-Motive between 1973 and 1974. The SDP40F, a six-axle/six-motor model, was adapted from the successful SD40-2 freight locomotive. Unfortunately, the SDP40F suffered from a series of high-profile derailments.

▶ Initially, United Aircraft TurboTrains operated as three-car sets. Amtrak increased this to five cars to increase capacity. However, while using futuristic designs, and popular with some riders, the TurboTrains were deemed unsuccessful. Amtrak withdrew them from regular service in September 1976, when new EMD F40PH diesels and Budd-built Amfleet was ready for service. *George W. Kowanski*

▼ Half of Amtrak's former FL9 fleet congregates at the old Albany-Rensselaer station on October 9, 1993. In the mid-1990s, GE Genesis dual-mode P32DM-ACs replaced Amtrak's FL9s, while allowing Amtrak to retire most of its turbo trainsets. *Brian Solomon*

FACTS

EMD F40PH/F40PHR
Wheel arrangement: B-B
Transmission: DC electric
Engine: 16-645E3
Horsepower: 3,000/3,200
Intended service: passenger
Number operated: 216
Years built: 1976–1989

Efforts to solve technical problems were inconclusive, and Amtrak ended up trading most of the SDP40Fs back to EMD for conversion into more satisfactory F40PHs. The final 18 locomotives were traded to Santa Fe in exchange for a batch of switchers and CF7s. Amtrak also ordered 25 specially designed P30CHs from GE. Built in 1974, these were the first locomotives with head-end power (HEP), which powered train heating and lighting from the locomotive and replaced antiquated steam-heat equipment.

The F40PH has been described as the engine that saved Amtrak. In essence, this was a cowl adaptation of the GP40-2. Introduced in 1976, the first units in Amtrak's 200 series

FACTS

GE DASH 8-32BWH

Wheel arrangement: B-B

Transmission: DC electric

Engine: 7FDL-12

Horsepower: 3,200

Intended service: long-distance passenger

Overall production: 20

Number operated: 20

Year built: 1991

were named to honor America's bicentennial. Ultimately, Amtrak bought 210 units from EMD, the last delivered in 1987. An additional group of six F40PHs were acquired second-hand from Ontario's GO Transit commuter agency, and they carried Amtrak numbers 410 to 415. Equipped with HEP, these were Amtrak's standard locomotive for most operations outside of electrified territory. In the 1990s, 21 of the car bodies were converted to unpowered cab-control cars for use in push-pull services.

Amtrak acquired 20 Dash 8-32BWHs (Amtrak designated them P32BHs) from General Electric in 1991. This model was based on Santa Fe's 500 series GEs, built in 1990. Most were initially assigned to western services. They were a prelude to more significant orders from GE in the form of the custom-designed Genesis models intended to replace the F40PHs. First were 44 800 series GE model Dash 8-40BPs (but known to Amtrak as P40s), built between 1993 and 1994. These were followed by more advanced 4,200-horsepower P42s, numbered 1 to 207, which entered production in 1996. In addition, 18 dual-mode P32AC-DMs were built to replace FL9s and 1970s-era turbo trains in Empire Corridor service. For new West Coast services, Amtrak acquired several fleets of EMD's streamlined F59PHi diesels in the 1990s.

For electric operations, in 1974 and 1975 Amtrak purchased GE's boxy E60 in two variations; seven E60CHs were equipped with steam heat, and 18 E60CPs were HEP

▲ Amtrak's 208 GE P42 Genesis (Nos. 1–207) diesels have been the staple of its long-haul intercity fleet since the late 1990s. The first batch of Genesis locomotives are the 800 series Dash 8-40BPs (which Amtrak designates as P40s). P42 No. 37 was nearly new when photographed eastbound at Mount Union, Pennsylvania, on October 11, 1997. *Brian Solomon*

FACTS

GE P42DC

Wheel arrangement: B-B

Transmission: DC electric

Engine: 7FDL-16

Horsepower: 4,200

Intended service: long-distance passenger

Years built: 1996–2001

◀ Amtrak P42 No. 142 leads the *Vermonter* to St. Albans, Vermont, at Palmer, Massachusetts, in October 2005. The Genesis models used this distinctively styled monocoque body. *Brian Solomon*

◀ Amtrak assembled a fleet of AEM-7s
using bodies crafted by Budd in
Philadelphia. The first was completed
in 1979, and Amtrak initially bought
47 of the compact, yet powerful electrics
to replace GG1s and some E60s on New
Haven–New York–Washington services.
Additional locomotives were acquired
later as wreck replacements. Amtrak
No. 946 was photographed in its
original livery at New Haven in 1989.
Brian Solomon

equipped. The model was intended to replace the GG1s but didn't perform as anticipated. As a result, Amtrak looked to European designs, settling on a variation of Sweden's Rc electric, adapted by EMD as the AEM-7. Originally, 47 were built, and they served as the backbone fleet for the Northeast Corridor. Additional units were later acquired. Amtrak's most recent straight electrics are 15 high-horsepower locomotives, designated HHP-8 and built by the Bombardier-Alstom consortium between 1999 and 2001. This are similarly styled to Bombardier Alstom's 20 high-speed trainsets built for *Acela Express* services between 1998 and 2000.

▲ Unique to Amtrak are its 20 custom-designed high-speed trainsets assigned to *Acela Express* services between Boston, New York, and Washington, D.C. These sophisticated electric trains incorporate Alstom's high-speed propulsion system and the Canadian-designed tilting system designed for VIA's LRC. They are allowed up to 150 miles per hour in revenue service on select tangent sections of main line between Boston and New Haven. *Brian Solomon*

2 ARKANSAS & MISSOURI RAILROAD

▲ Arkansas & Missouri's fleet of 14 secondhand C-420s represents more than 10 percent of Alco's total C-420 production. In 2012, the railroad continued to routinely assign five or more Alco diesels to its road freights, with the venerable C-420 being the most prominent and most common model. Five C-420s lead the southward freight near Monett, Missouri, on the afternoon of November 11, 2009. *Scott Muskopf*

▶ Lurking in the gloom adjacent to Arkansas & Missouri's Springdale offices are a group of the railroad's classic C-420s ready to begin the evening's work. *Brian Solomon*

Arkansas & Missouri began operations in September 1986 on former Frisco trackage acquired from Burlington Northern. Its main line runs 139 miles through the lush and mountainous Ozarks, between its connection with BNSF at Monett, Missouri, and Fort Smith, Arkansas. Locomotive shops and operations are centered in Springdale, Arkansas. Although primarily a freight-hauling short line, in 1990 A&M began a successful excursion service. The railroad is most famous for its immaculate all-Alco diesel fleet. As one of only a few remaining Alco-powered lines, A&M has to ensure its own parts supply. Over the last quarter century, A&M has collected Alco and Montreal Locomotive Works diesels from myriad lines, restoring some to service, while using others for parts. The backbone of its fleet is the C-420, a 2,000-horsepower four-motor model featuring a longer short hood than other century models. A&M's C-420s have come from many places, and the railroad's operation fleet is primarily represented by locomotives built new for Lehigh Valley, Lehigh & Hudson River, and Seaboard Air Line. A&M's fleet also consists four (of six) former Belt Railway of Chicago C-424s and some from Canadian Pacific. A sole former New York Central RS-32 routinely labors along with C-420s in road service. The oldest locomotive in A&M's fleet is a former Rutland Railroad RS-1; as of 2011, it was only locomotive not powered by Alco's 251-diesel engine, instead using Alco's prewar 539 prime mover. A half-dozen T-6 switchers work in local service. For a few years, A&M rostered a single former CP C-630, while it acquired several former CN M-636s for parts. So, more than 40 years after Alco exited the American market, A&M keeps the sights and sounds of Alco diesels alive on its daily trains.

◄ The C-420 was derived from Alco's 2,000-horsepower RS-32. Its longer short hood helps distinguish it from other Century series models. A&M's immaculate fleet of Alco-designed diesels continues to work more than four decades after the builder exited the domestic market. A&M C-420 No. 44 was built for Seaboard Air Line, later working for Seaboard Coast Line and Louisville & Nashville. *Scott Muskopf*

FACTS

ALCO C-420 (specification number DL-721A)

Wheel arrangement: B-B

Transmission: DC electric

Engine: 12-251C

Horsepower: 2,000

Intended service: general purpose road switcher

Overall production: 129

Years built: 1963–1968

3 ATCHISON, TOPEKA & SANTA FE RAILWAY

The Atchison, Topeka & Santa Fe began in Kansas in 1860 and grew to become one of the great American railway systems; it was the only steam-era company to directly connect Chicago with California. The extreme conditions imposed across Santa Fe's territory produced some unusual twentieth-century locomotive developments. Operations across Southwestern deserts encouraged utmost efforts to conserve water, while a dearth of coal on its western routes resulted in Santa Fe's pioneering of oil-fired steam locomotives. The road's almost fanatical interest in compound locomotives was in part a result of its desire to use less water; it embraced a full scope of compound types, including Baldwin's Vauclain and balanced compound designs. Early in the twentieth century's second decade, Santa Fe pushed the Mallet articulated concept to bizarre extremes, including high-driver 2-6-6-2s built with jointed boilers for fast passenger work and massive 2-10-10-2s for freight service. Despite these curiosities, most of its locomotives

▼ Santa Fe introduced the 2-10-2 in 1902. This was a specific adaptation to 10-coupled helpers working Raton Pass to ease reversing the big engine's downgrade; later 2-10-2s, such as No. 3847 photographed at Barstow, California, were intended for service as heavy freight haulers. *F. J. Peterson photo, Solomon collection*

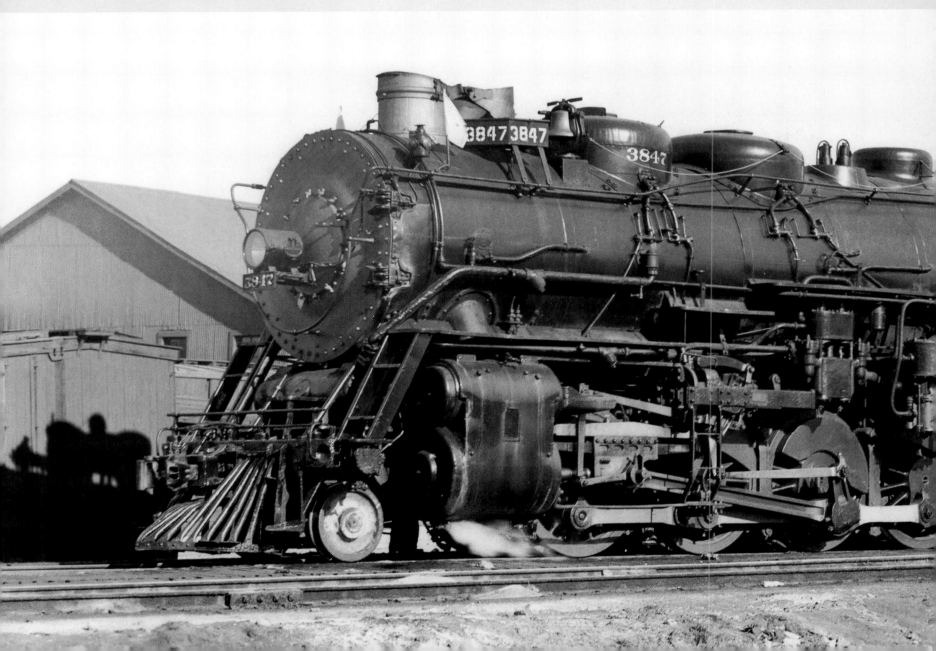

◄ Among the most impressive late-era steam locomotives were Santa Fe's Class 2900 4-8-4s. Thirty were built during 1943 and 1944, offering 300 pounds boiler pressure. They were capable of running more than 100 miles per hour. Here 2928 works with passenger-service FTs leading the *Chief* on Cajon Pass. *Paul Fredrickson photo, Solomon collection*

FACTS

ATSF CLASS 2900

Builder: Baldwin

Wheel arrangement: 4-8-4

Type: Northern

Cylinders: 28x32 in.

Drivers: 80 in.

Engine weight: 510,000 lbs.

Tractive effort: 66,000 lbs. (typical)

Intended service: mainline freight and
passenger service

Overall production: 30

Years built: 1943–1944

Santa Fe's first Northern was No. 3751, a pioneering Baldwin machine built in 1927. Fourteen of the class were built over the next two years. Although originally a consume burner in the 1930s, Santa Fe converted them for oil firing. At the end of steam operations, Santa Fe preserved many fine examples of its fleet, including No. 3751. In the 1980s, No. 3751 was operationally restored, and it occasionally works trips in home territory. On June 1, 2008, it is seen on the Surf Line at San Clemente, California, working its way to San Diego. *Brian Solomon*

▼ Working in an A-B-B-A set, Santa Fe freight service F3s lift an eastward freight over California's Cajon Pass on November 23, 1953. Santa Fe was one of several railroads with distinct fleets of freight and passenger service EMD F-units. Where the passenger Fs were painted in the famous warbonnet scheme, freight units wore the more conservative cobalt and yellow scheme. *Frank E. Meitz Santa Fe Railway*

were simple types. Santa Fe ultimately concluded, as did all American railroads (except Norfolk & Western), that the cost efficiencies offered by compounding were outweighed by higher maintenance. Many compounds were rebuilt as simples or scrapped. Santa Fe's last three decades of steam were typified by large, well-designed Baldwin types. Having already bought many 4-8-2s, in the late 1920s it embraced the 4-8-4 for general road service and continued to order these through World War II. Its 2900 series weighed in at more than 500,000 pounds, making them the heaviest 4-8-4s built. Its 4-6-4s were built for long-distance passenger work and boasted some of the longest steam runs in the United States. At the turn of the twentieth century, Santa Fe had pioneered the 2-10-2, originally using trailing wheels to aid reverse helpers downgrade on Raton Pass. In the 1930s, it ordered some of the most impressive 10-coupled engines ever built; its 5001-class 2-10-4s had 74-inch drivers, worked at 310 pounds boiler pressure, weighed 545,260 pounds, delivered 93,000 pounds tractive effort, and exhibited the largest piston thrust of any two-cylinder locomotive ever built.

Despite these late-era steam achievements, Santa Fe's water problems resulted in it being first in America to adopt road freight diesels on wide scale. In 1938, it had been among the first to buy E-units for fast passenger service. Then in the early 1940s, it invested in the largest fleet of EMD's pioneering FTs. These were assigned to desert service in Arizona and southern California. After World War II, Santa Fe bought hundreds of F-units for both freight and passenger service, as well as other types. Despite these early efforts, it was among the last western lines to complete dieselization.

In the late 1950s and 1960s, Santa Fe bought even more powerful road diesels, adding to its roster large numbers of EMD GP20s, SD24s, GP30s, GP35s, and SD45s,

as well as equivalent models from GE. In the late 1970s, Santa Fe encouraged development of cowl types, and it was the first and most enthusiastic buyer of FP45 and F45 models. To meet a need for fast high-horsepower diesels, Santa Fe continued to buy large numbers of four-motor models into the early 1990s. In the late 1980s, it pushed for development of the modern North American Safety Cab, and it was the only railroad to order GP60Ms and GE's Dash 8-40BW models, as well as EMD's cab-less GP60Bs. Its last new locomotives were six-motor types, including GE's Dash 9s and EMD's SD75s.

▲ None of these diesels were unique to Santa Fe, but no other line could produce such a collection of modern second-generation EMDs. These are as seen eastbound near Port Chicago, California, in November 1990. An SD40-2 with snoot nose section (intended for radio control equipment) leads GP60 No. 4032, SD45-2 No. 5709, and an F45. *Brian Solomon*

◀ Santa Fe was the only modern freight railroad to order four-motor high-horsepower locomotives equipped with North American Safety Cabs. Santa Fe reintroduced Leland Knickerbocker's classic warbonnet by repainting the FP45 in the late 1980s, but its first modern diesels in this super fleet scheme were EMD GP60Ms delivered in 1990. *Brian Solomon*

FACTS

EMD GP60M
Builder: EMD
Wheel arrangement: B-B
Transmission: DC electric
Engine: 16-710G
Horsepower: 3,800
Intended service: road freight
Number operated: 63
Year built: 1990

23

4 BALTIMORE & OHIO RAILROAD

Phineas Davis improved upon Peter Cooper's 1830 design, first constructing a prototype called the *York,* and later, with the help of Ross Winans, Davis constructed the *Atlantic*—the first of his successful Grasshopper types. It weighed approximately seven tons and featured a pair of vertical cylinders. It was nominally successful—about 20 similar locomotives were constructed at B&O's Mount Clare shops. Some served for six decades, finishing up on the Baltimore waterfront. A Grasshopper, identified as the *Atlantic,* entertains visitors to New York's 1939 World's Fair. *Horace W. Pontin photo, Solomon collection*

▶ Between 1929 and 1932, Baltimore & Ohio absorbed Buffalo, Rochester & Pittsburgh and Buffalo & Susquehanna as part of a greater effort toward railroad consolidation and B&O's ambitions to build a new main line across Pennsylvania. B&S operations remained isolated, and its locomotives were maintained at its Galeton, Pennsylvania, shops. B&O 2-8-0 No. 3104 Class E60 was former B&S No. 127. It is pictured at West Salisbury, Pennsylvania, on March 18, 1956. *Photographer unknown, Solomon collection*

FACTS

B&O CLASS EM-1
Builder: Baldwin
Wheel arrangement: 2-8-8-4
Type: Yellowstone
Cylinders: 4 @ 24x32 in. ea.
Drivers: 64 in.
Engine weight: 628,700 lbs.
Tractive effort: 115,000 lbs.
Intended service: road freight
Overall production: 30
Year built: 1944

Baltimore & Ohio's steam operations spanned the better part of 128 years. During most of that time, the majority of its operations were conducted with a variety of more or less ordinary locomotives. Yet B&O's fleet had some very notable distinctions, included a number of firsts, and exhibited more than its fair share of curiosities. On August 28, 1830, Peter Cooper demonstrated a diminutive, experimental domestically built locomotive on the B&O at Baltimore, which successfully hauled 13 tons at 4 miles per hour. Today known as the Tom Thumb, Cooper's unusual marine-engine design resulted in a generation of homegrown American locomotive technology on B&O. Most were constructed privately at the railroad's Mount Clare Shop—first by Phineas Davis, who built a small fleet of vertical boiler 0-4-0s called Grasshoppers (named for their unusual motion), and later by Ross Winans, who developed a variety of curious locomotives culminating with his famous 0-8-0 Camels (because of their humpback appearance) of the 1840s and 1850s. In the later nineteenth century, Mount Clare turned out more conventional locomotives, while B&O also bought many engines from commercial suppliers, typically 4-4-0s and 4-6-0s.

In June 1895, B&O made history by inaugurating America's first heavy mainline electrification with operations on its three-mile Baltimore Belt Line, including its new 1.25-mile city-center tunnel. Initially, B&O employed three General Electric steeple-cab locomotives. GE supplied boxcab electric locomotives between 1909 and 1912 and center-cab electrics in the mid-1920s. Electric operations were discontinued when diesels took over in the early 1950s. In 1904, B&O ordered from Alco the first articulated Mallet compound, an 0-6-6-0 No. 2400, named *Old Maud*, that set several important developmental

▲ The 4-4-4 wheel arrangement didn't enjoy widespread application in North America. Reading Company was first to try it in 1915 with a lone experimental. B&O's *Lady Baltimore* was the next singular attempt; its other nonstandard features included abnormally tall drivers (84 inches) and a water-tube boiler. Ultimately, Canadian Pacific had the best luck with two batches of 4-4-4s, locomotives it called the Jubilee type. *Photographer unknown, Solomon collection*

FACTS

B&O CLASS J-1 *LADY BALTIMORE*
Builder: B&O (Mount Clare Shops)
Wheel arrangement: 4-4-4
Cylinders: 17.5x28 in.
Drivers: 84 in.
Engine weight: 217,800 lbs.
Tractive effort: 28,000 lbs.; 35,000 lbs. with booster
Intended service: passenger
Overall production: 1
Year built: 1934

precedents. B&O continued buying articulated types, culminating with its order for 30 2-8-8-4 Yellowstones (Class EM-1) from Baldwin in 1944 and 1945. Ironically, at this late stage B&O preferred diesels, but it was encouraged by the War Production Board to buy steam. Yet B&O's own Mount Clare Shops kept busy during the mid-1940s churning out T-3 4-8-2s rebuilt from older types—the last of these was finished in 1948.

In the 1920s and 1930s, under the direction of B&O's chief of motive power, George H. Emerson, the Mount Clare shops experimented with progressive steam design by producing engines with novel features, including water-tube boilers, rotary valve gear, and lightweight reciprocating parts. Noteworthy were a lightweight 4-4-4 No. 1 named *Lady Baltimore* and a similar lightweight 4-6-4 No. 2 named *Lord Baltimore*. These efforts culminated with the pioneer Duplex type (featuring a 4-4-4-4 wheel arrangement on a rigid frame) that was designed in honor of Emerson.

In addition to its efforts to forward modern steam design B&O was also a diesel pioneer. In the 1920s, it bought one of the Alco-GE–Ingersoll Rand boxcab switchers and then experimented with an EMC prototype boxcab passenger diesel in 1935. In 1937 B&O bought EMC's first stand-alone streamlined passenger diesels, the *very* first of the E-unit line, models EA and EB. In the 1940s, B&O began more extensive dieselization, with large numbers of switchers from all the major builders, while a few EMD FTs came during World War II. After the war, it bought road-freight carbody-style diesels from Alco (FA/FBs), Baldwin (shark-nose models), and EMD F3s and F7s, as well as more passenger E-units. In the 1950s, road switchers dominated, with models from Baldwin, EMD, and a few from Fairbanks-Morse. B&O's final diesel acquisitions were standard high-horsepower models from EMD, including GP30s, GP35s, GP38s, and GP40s, as well as SD35s and SD40s. In the Chessie System era, new models included GP40-2s and SD40-2s.

Baltimore & Ohio F7A No. 4564 and a pair of GP30s are shown at Central Railroad of New Jersey's Communipaw engine facility in Jersey City, New Jersey, in March 1967. Although B&O sampled diesels from all the major builders in its early phases of dieselization, EMD products dominated in its final years. *George W. Kowanski*

On April 18, 1959, B&O E7A No. 1422 is at the front of a consist backing toward Washington Union Station. On the right is the Ivy City engine terminal where Pennsylvania Railroad GG1s and Richmond, Fredericksburg & Potomac Es have congregated. B&O No. 1422 was among the earliest E7s, built by EMD in 1945. The E7 remained in production until 1949, when it was succeeded by the E8. *Richard Jay Solomon*

5 BANGOR & AROOSTOOK RAILROAD

▶ Bangor & Aroostook operated some relatively ancient engines right to the end of steam; this Class D-3 4-6-0 had four decades of service behind it when George C. Corey caught it on the turntable at Greenville, Maine, in August 1951. Old No. 94 was still in pretty good shape at the time, although it had less than a year left. All the D-3s were off the roster by 1952. *George C. Corey*

▼ Bangor & Aroostook steam exhibited a tidy appearance. Typically, they were neat, used a balanced design, and were always well maintained. Consolidation 2-8-0 seen at Oakfield, Maine, in August 1939 was characteristic of its Alco freight power. *Robert A. Buck collection*

Bangor & Aroostook—known by its reporting marks BAR (to avoid confusion with other railroads using B&A initials)—enjoyed a virtual monopoly on rail service in northern Maine. It was content to rely upon 4-4-0s, 4-6-0s, and 2-8-0s for road services until the mid-1920s, when it bought a few 4-6-2s for passenger service and 4-8-2s for freight. A few more new 4-8-2s were bought in the 1930s and 1940s, and after World War II, BAR picked up five former New York, Ontario & Western engines, bringing its total fleet of 4-8-2s to 15. The railroad took pride in its locomotives, which displayed a tidy appearance fitting for a modern-day tourist railway; wheel tires and running boards were dressed in white paint and drivers and rods were kept immaculately clean.

In the late 1940s, BAR dieselized with classic EMD models, initially buying a pair of E7As for passenger service, eight F3As and four F3Bs for road freight, eight BL2 road switchers, and three NW2 switchers. Steam concluded operation in 1952. The railroad was quick to recognize

▲ Maine's Bangor & Aroostook bought one of the small fleets of EMD E-units—just two engines, Nos. 700 and 701, which it initially assigned to its well-run passenger service. On May 24, 1949, E7A was nearly brand new, while the lucky photographer had the thrill of visiting the cab courtesy of a sympathetic engine crew. After its passenger service ended, the railroad re-geared its E7s for freight, making it one of only a very few railroads to do so. *Robert A. Buck*

◄ Bangor & Aroostook preferred Ten-Wheelers to Pacifics; it owned just five 4-6-2s, all Class F, built by Alco in 1927, the last of which, No. 254, is pictured. The engineer gives the bell cord a lash as he moves No. 254 at Greenville on May 4, 1952. *Robert A. Buck*

FACTS

B&A CLASS F

Builder: Alco

Wheel arrangement: 4-6-2

Type: Pacific

Cylinders: 21x28 in.

Drivers: 69 in.

Engine weight: 237,000 lbs.

Tractive effort: 32,000 lbs.

Intended service: passenger

Overall production: 5

Years built: 1927

▲ On July 12, 1970, Bangor & Aroostook F3As, a BL2, and a GP38 are lined up at Northern Maine Junction. Years after most railroads traded F3s and BL2s back to EMD on more modern diesels, these old soldiers continued to work in northern Maine. Most were preserved after retirement. One of the BL2s now works in excursion service on New York's Saratoga & North Creek. *Jim Shaughnessy*

FACTS

EMD BL2

Wheel arrangement: B-B

Transmission: DC electric

Engine: 16-567B

Horsepower: 1,500

Weight: 226,405–246,065 lbs.
   (depending on options)

Tractive effort: 54,472–60,164 lbs.
   (depending on weight)

Intended service: branch-line road
   switcher

Overall production: 58 (plus 1 BL1
   demonstrator)

Years built: 1948–1949

advantages of EMD's road switchers and never bought more advanced carbody models, instead opting for GP7s in 1949 and GP9s in the 1950s. Among the anomalies in BAR's early diesel roster were five GE/Ingersoll Rand 660-horsepower switchers built for the New Haven Railroad and acquired secondhand. BAR's flashy *Aroostook Flyer* offered well-maintained passenger service, but by the early 1960s the money-losing service reached the end of the road.

After it discontinued passenger service, BAR made the unusual decision to re-gear its E7s for freight service. The experiment was short-lived; between 1966 and 1968, BAR ordered a fleet of GP38s, turning back its E7s in trade. The railroad's traffic peaked seasonally, and off-season it routinely leased its surplus motive power to other lines. BAR continued to operate its F3As and BL2s much later than other buyers of these models. In the early 1980s, BL2 No. 557 was restored to its as-built paint scheme and original road number and christened the *American Railfan*. Although the BL2s and most F3s were purged from the roster in the mid-1980s, many were sold to short lines and tourist train operations, so they have survived in various guises to the present day. However, BAR retained F3 No. 92 through the 1990s and later restored it to its attractive as-built livery and number. In the 1980s, to supplant aging 1940s-era models, BAR acquired some secondhand EMDs, primarily GP38 types. Despite changes in ownership culminating with its 1994 inclusion in the Iron Road network of lines in northern New England and eastern Quebec, BAR remained loyal to EMD four-motor types. In 2002, its roster included 21 GP38 variants (including remanufactured units) and eight GP7s (including rebuilt former Santa Fe units with low short hoods). During this final phase of operation, BAR locomotives were routinely mixed with other Iron Road lines, and little effort was made to keep road locomotives operating on their namesake lines. In 2003, the Iron Road network was sold to Rail World to become the Montreal, Maine & Atlantic.

◀ In Bangor & Aroostook's final years, Iron Road operated it as part of a northern New England and eastern Quebec network that also incorporated former Canadian Pacific lines west from Brownville Junction, Maine, run as Canadian American Railroad (CDAC). Motive power mixed freely between Iron Road railroads. On September 30, 1997, at Onawa, Maine, eastward GP38 No. 351, lettered for Bangor & Aroostook, led CDAC freight No. 902. *Brian Solomon*

6 BELT RAILWAY OF CHICAGO

Belt Railway of Chicago was built by the Chicago & Western Indiana in the 1880s. While its contemporary main line is only 28 miles long, it operates hundreds of track miles. BRC serves as a primary interchange for lines reaching Chicago. Key to its operation is Clearing Yard, a massive double-hump yard for classification of carload traffic. In addition, it performs switching services for online carload customers. As of 2011, BRC was owned by the six major North American railroads serving Chicago. Since BRC is an atypical railroad, it has had specialized locomotive needs, requiring locomotives with high-tractive effort and slow speed capabilities for hump services and transfer work, and also switchers and some road-freight units. At the time of World War I, it maintained more than 80 steam locomotives, primarily 0-6-0 and 0-8-0 switchers, along with some 2-10-2s with very low drivers; all were equipped with bunker-style tenders, allowing for better visibility working in reverse. BRC began dieselizing in the early 1930s, first with a GE-Ingersoll Rand 300-horsepower boxcab, followed by a few Alco high-hood switchers. During the 1940s, BRC bought more Alco switchers, a few Baldwins, and nine Alco RS-2 road switchers. Beginning in the late 1940s, the railroad emphasized EMD models, including model TR2 and TR4 cow-calf transfer diesels and various switchers and road switchers. It returned to Alco in the mid-1960s for six C-424s. BRC's current fleet consists of a few EMD SW1500s and MP15s, eight EMD GP38-2s, and a pair of remanufactured SD40-3s and five SD38-3s that work in hump service with yard slugs built from SD40/SD40-2 platforms. BRC's most recent motive power includes National Railway Equipment 2GS14B 1,400-horsepower twin gen-set low-emission locomotives.

▼ Belt Railway of Chicago operated America's most intact fleet of Alco C-424s through the late 1990s. Six of these 2,400-horsepower diesels worked in pairs on transfer runs and through moves on BRC's Chicago network. They were the last BRC Alcos; today, except for its NRE gensets, all of BRC's locomotives are EMD products. *Brian Solomon*

A pair of BRC GP38-2s works the hump at Chicago's Clearing Yard on July 1, 1995. BRC purchased six of this standard EMD 2,000-horsepower four-motor model in 1972, Nos. 490–495. Today, BRC's GP38-2 fleet consists of eight former Conrail units, Nos. 580–587. *Brian Solomon*

▼ Among EMD's more unusual models were semipermanently coupled cow-calf transfer diesels. Only one unit had a cab. BRC Nos. 502–514 were originally a drawbar-connected model TR4 rated at 2,400 horsepower. However, the two units were fitted with couplers and in later days were a TR4A and TR4B, as seen at Chicago's Clearing Yard in 1995. BRC no longer operates these classic transfer models. *Brian Solomon*

FACTS

EMD TR4

Wheel arrangement: B-B+B-B
(cow and calf)

Transmission: DC electric

Engine: 12-567B

Horsepower: 2,000 (BRC's units were later uprated to 2,400)

Weight: 493,880 lbs.

Tractive effort: 123,470 lbs.

Intended service: transfer freight

Number operated: two cow-calf sets

Year built: 1950

BNSF RAILWAY

BNSF was born from the 1995 merger of Santa Fe and Burlington Northern. The new railroad melded its predecessors' fleets together and acquired hundreds of new locomotives. Its preference for GE's DC-traction six motors for general freight is an outgrowth of Santa Fe's late-era motive power policies, while its preference for modern three-phase AC models for unit train (coal and other heavy commodities) services is a reflection of BN's policy that began in the early 1990s with its groundbreaking order for SD70MACs. In its first decade, BNSF's most common new locomotive model was General Electric's Dash 9-44CW (which BNSF classifies as C44-9W). By 2005, when GE introduced its Evolution Series, BNSF and its predecessor had acquired nearly 1,800 4,400-horsepower six-motor Dash 9 safety cab locomotives. Since that time, BNSF has bought fleets of GE ES44DCs for general freight, and GE ES44ACs and EMD SD70ACes for unit train services. In 2009, BNSF pioneered experiments with GE's ES44C4—a new AC-traction model employing A1A trucks—allowing for a modern six-axle four-motor model that had performance characteristics similar to GE's DC-traction Evolution locomotives. It has since bought more of this new type for intermodal service. GE's

▼ BNSF SD40-2s meet at speed along the former Burlington Mississippi River route at Alma, Wisconsin, in September 2000. As BNSF began repainting former BN and Santa Fe locomotives, many were treated to this orange and green livery inspired by classic Great Northern colors. In the 1980s, BN had one of the largest SD40-2 fleets. *Brian Solomon*

ES44C4 offers many of the advantages of AC traction but at a cost comparable to its older DC-traction models typically assigned to intermodal and general service.

In the 1990s, Santa Fe bought a pair of MK Rail's low-horsepower, low-emissions switchers that burned liquefied natural gas for work in emissions-conscious Los Angeles; BNSF has since acquired two additional units from UP. More significantly, in recent years BNSF has assembled a fleet of modern low-emission gen-set locomotives, using both National Railway Equipment and Railpower models, largely for terminal operations in California and Texas.

▲ BNSF's first decade saw many rainbow combinations of locomotives in a mix of predecessor liveries and newer schemes. On September 22, 1998, a westward freight on the former Santa Fe at Abo Canyon New Mexico has BNSF Dash 9-44CW No. 1015 leading a colorful mix of Santa Fe and BN diesels. *Brian Solomon*

FACTS

GE DASH 9-44CW

Wheel arrangement: C-C

Transmission: DC electric

Engine: 7FDL-16

Horsepower: 4,400

Intended service: general freight

Years built: 1993–2004

▲ BNSF EMD-built SD70ACe No. 9194 displays the railroad's latest livery, which includes the prominent BNSF underlined with an athletic swoosh. EMD's SD70ACe is a 4,300-horsepower locomotive with three-phase AC traction designed for heavy-haul applications. BNSF assigns these and other AC locomotives to unit train services, included loaded coal trains originating in Wyoming's Powder River Basin. *Brian Solomon*

◀ One of the advantages of AC-traction diesels is their ability to work at maximum throttle at very slow speeds for prolonged periods without damaging traction motors. In August 2011, BNSF SD70ACe No. 9222 and SD70MAC No. 9896, working as rear-end radio-controlled distributed power units, slug it out at less than five miles per hour with a loaded unit coal train near Decatur, Arkansas. *Brian Solomon*

▼ BNSF has invested in GE's most advanced design, the ES44C4, a six-axle four-motor variation of the Evolution series using a modern A1A-style truck. This offers tractive and braking effort equivalent to a six-axle ES44DC by using four AC-traction motors on the No. 1, 3, 4, and 6 axles. *Patrick Yough*

9 BOSTON & ALBANY RAILROAD

▲ Boston & Albany's master mechanic Wilson Eddy was famous for his unusual 4-4-0 design. Instead of the common wagon-top boiler with steam dome, Eddy used a straight boiler with a dry pipe (to gather steam). This and other novel features resulted in exceptionally good locomotives that were universally known as Eddy Clocks. Boston & Albany No. 217 was photographed with its crew at Palmer, probably in the 1880s. *Robert A. Buck collection*

Boston & Albany was created in the 1867 as a result of the union of the Western (of Massachusetts) and Boston & Worcester, lines that since 1841 had formed a through link between B&A's namesake cities. In its heyday, B&A was the principle link between southern New England and points west, and it connected with New York Central at Albany. In 1900, New York Central leased B&A, and while locomotives carried the New York Central name for about a dozen years, inept public relations by Central resulted in public furor that saw the B&A name restored to equipment until the end of the steam era.

Wilson Eddy, Western Railroad's master mechanic, had established a reputation as an expert locomotive builder, and since the 1850s he had built exceptional 4-4-0s at the railroad's Springfield, Massachusetts, shops. Eddy was a bit of a maverick, and his locomotives embraced some unusual features, including a straight boiler and dry pipe, instead of the more common wagon-top boiler with steam dome. Eddy's engines embraced a New England austerity: tidy and well balanced, yet nearly void of extraneous ornamentation. Eddy's Clocks, as they were known, were famous in their day for economical use of coal and for some notably fast runs. In addition to these home-built engines, the railroad also bought commercial locomotives. Eddy retired in 1880, and Arthur Underhill (formerly of the Boston & Worcester) succeeded him. Underhill also produced some impressive locomotive designs, known to enginemen by his name. In the late-nineteenth century, B&A operated some impressive 2-8-0s known to engineers as hogs and experimented with cross-compound designs, which because of their tendency to produce an uneven piston thrust at slow speed were known as "slam bangs."

In the twentieth century, B&A took its cues from New York Central. While it retained an element of independence, the contrast of B&A's graded line with New York Central's

Water Level Route resulted in more relevant demands for different types of motive power. The 4-4-2 made a fleeting appearance on B&A, with only five of the type assigned to the line. More significant was the railroad's early use of the Pacific. B&A continued to order Pacifics for two decades, and it was among a handful of railroads that assigned 4-6-2s to freight as well as passenger lines. Toward the end of steam, Pacifics worked local freights, especially on the B&A's East End. B&A's Boston suburban services, including circuit trains that used the meandering Highland Branch, were ideally suited to tank engines, and New York Central assigned several classes of these bidirectional locomotives; the last and largest were five Alco 4-6-6Ts built in 1928. Following the success of the 4-6-4 on New York Central's Water Level Route, 20 Hudsons were bought for the B&A, Class J-2, 10 built by Alco and 10 by Lima. These were fitted with slightly smaller drivers to better tackle B&A's grades.

▲ The last new passenger steam locomotives lettered for Boston & Albany were two orders of Class J-2 Hudsons. These were based on New York Central's successful J-1 design, but they were adapted for B&A's needs and used 75-inch drivers instead of 79-inch drivers that were better suited to graded operations. The first 10 (Classes J-2a and J-2b, Nos. 600–609) were built by Alco; the second order was from Lima (Class J-2, Nos. 610–619). On May 17, 1950, J-2a leads train No. 23 west at Warren, Massachusetts. *Robert A. Buck*

FACTS

B&A/NYC CLASS J-2a

Builder: Alco

Wheel arrangement: 4-6-4

Type: Hudson

Cylinders: 25x28 in.

Drivers: 75 in.

Engine weight: 353,000 lbs.

Tractive effort: 44,800 lbs. (52,320 lbs. with booster)

Intended service: express passenger

Overall production: 5 (plus 5 Class J-2bs and 10 Lima-built J-2cs)

Years built: 1928 (J-2a), 1930 (J-2b), and 1931 (J-2c)

◄ Boston & Albany was among a few railroads that routinely assigned 4-6-2 Pacifics to freight. On July 4, 1945, B&A No. 559 worked the Worcester–Palmer local freight at Palmer, Massachusetts. It was one of four B&A Class KL Pacifics built by Alco-Schenectady in 1912. *Robert A. Buck*

▲ Lima's famous Class A-1 2-8-4 Berkshires were synonymous with B&A's late-era freight operations. On September 16, 1945, A-1a No. 1414 pauses with a short westward freight at the water tanks in West Brookfield, Massachusetts, roughly midway between Worcester and Springfield. In the steam era, trains routinely paused here to take water. *Robert A. Buck*

FACTS

B&A/NYC CLASS A-1a

Builder: Lima

Wheel arrangement: 2-8-4

Type: Berkshire

Cylinders: 28x30 in.

Drivers: 63 in.

Engine weight: 389,000 lbs.

Tractive effort: 69,400 lbs. (81,400 with booster)

Intended service: heavy freight

Overall production: 25 (plus 20 A-1b and 10 A-1c)

Years built: 1926 (A-1a) and 1927–1930 (A-1b and A-1c)

▶ New York Central assigned three classes of 2-6-6-2 Mallet compounds to the Boston & Albany, totaling 13 locomotives. No. 1301 was of the first class, N-2b, built in 1912, and is here photographed at Beacon Park Yard, Alston, Massachusetts, before World War I. Subsequent classes were NE-2c and NE-2e, both built by Alco. *Stanley H. Smith photo, Robert A. Buck collection*

B&A was best remembered for its freight locomotives. While Central had assigned 2-6-6-2 Mallets, 2-10-2s, and large 2-8-2s, the most successful and influential type associated with the line was the 2-8-4, which was first tested by Lima on B&A's West End in 1925. Here, Lima's pioneer A1 2-8-4 demonstrated overwhelming superiority over previous types; not only could it haul more tonnage faster than a modern 2-8-2, but also the 2-8-4 did so by burning less fuel. New York Central placed three orders for Lima A-1s for B&A, and 55 engines were delivered between 1926 and 1930. They worked mainline freight until displaced by diesels in the late 1940s. While B&A had a token order of Alco high-hood diesel switchers lettered for the line, after World War II, with the introduction of road diesels, New York Central ended the practice of lettering new locomotives assigned to the B&A.

▲ Although more powerful locomotives were built for mainline freight, B&A's 2-8-0 Consolidations survived to nearly the end of steam operations on the line. Bob Buck photographed 2-8-0 Class G-16q No. 1052 at Woronoco, Massachusetts, on October 15, 1947. Built in 1912, it was among the newest 2-8-0s on B&A. *Robert A. Buck*

◀ After more than five decades of service with the Boston & Albany, veteran engineer Waldo "Baldy" Hunter rolls out of Warren, Massachusetts, on June 7, 1949, with 2-8-2 No. 1200 on his final trip. No. 1200 was an Alco-built H-5j Mikado from 1913. *Robert A. Buck*

▶ Boston & Maine's most famous locomotive is P4 Pacific No. 3713, seen here passing Ward Hill, Massachusetts, on April 20 1946. B&M's P4 gained public notice in the 1930s when the railroad sponsored a children's contest to name all 10 of them. Then, in 1956, B&M No. 3713 was the star of the railroad's final public steam run. Afterward F. Nelson Blount acquired it for the Steamtown collection. It was loaned to the Boston science museum for many years, where it sat as a static display outdoors. Presently, it is under restoration at Scranton, Pennsylvania. *John E. Pickett*

FACTS

B&M CLASS P-4

Builder: Lima

Wheel arrangement: 4-6-2

Type: Pacific

Cylinders: 23x28 in.

Drivers: 80 in.

Engine weight: 339,200 lbs.

Tractive effort: 40,900 lbs., plus 11,900 lbs. (with booster)

Intended service: passenger and fast freight

Overall production: 10

Years built: 1934 and 1937

n the late nineteenth century, Boston & Maine gobbled up its competitors, gradually dominating the heavily industrialized territory north and west of Boston. In the twentieth century, B&M invested heavily in its primary arteries—such as its Fitchburg route main line—installing heavy new bridges and, from the 1920s, modern Centralized Traffic Control. While mainline improvements allowed for heavier axle weights, branch lines and secondary main lines didn't benefit from such improvements and required smaller and lighter locomotives. This resulted in a disparity in B&M's locomotive fleet. Large, powerful modern steam was purchased for mainline work, while antique smaller engines survived for decades on secondary lines.

In the early twentieth century, B&M relied on 4-4-0s for most passenger services and continued to buy new engines of this obsolete type as late as 1910. For fast mainline runs, it acquired a fleet of 41 4-4-2 Atlantics, a few of which survived until after World

▲ At Fitchburg, Massachusetts, in 1941, photographer Dana D. Goodwin caught the first eastward trip of B&M's newest Mountains, Nos. 4115 and 4114; these new Baldwins were on their way from Troy, New York, to Boston. B&M bought 18 of these modern engines between 1935 and 1941, but in 1947, after being displaced by Electro-Motive diesels, B&M sent most of its 4-8-2s to the Baltimore & Ohio. Notice the modern features: boxpok drivers, lightweight rods, and smoke lifters at the sides of the boiler. *Dana D. Goodwin, Robert A. Buck collection*

▶ Although B&M ordered relatively modern big steam, it dieselized mainline operations early, which displaced its biggest steam locomotives. As a result, most of its last steam locomotives in regular revenue service were its relatively ancient Alco 2-6-0 Moguls. On February 23, 1954, B&M's Class B-15 2-6-0 No. 1478 marches out of Boston's North Station with an afternoon commuter train. *Robert A. Buck*

FACTS

EMC/EMD SW1

Wheel arrangement: B-B

Transmission: DC electric

Engine: 6-567/6-567A

Horsepower: 600

Weight: 198,000 lbs. (depending on options)

Tractive effort: 49,500 lbs. (depending on options)

Intended service: light switching

Years built: 1939–1953

War II, with one engine running into the early 1950s—decades after the type had fallen out of favor elsewhere. Many freight customers were served on light trackage winding through alleys, along the sides of canals, through back lots, and over small bridges, so the road required vast numbers of 0-6-0 and 0-8-0 switchers. Until 1916, road freights were largely the domain of 2-8-0s. As the demand for heavier freight took hold, B&M bought 2-10-2s, ordering 30 of the type from Alco between 1920 and 1923; in the late 1920s, it ordered 25 near copies of B&A's A-1 2-8-4 Berkshire, which B&M classed as T-1. Since these featured externally mounted Coffin feed-water heaters on the smokebox, the bell and headlight had an unusually low placement, resulting in a peculiar appearance. B&M's last new freight steam locomotives were 18 Baldwin-built 4-8-2s delivered between 1935 and 1941. Although B&M was late to adopt the 4-8-2 arrangement, its 4-8-2s were thoroughly modern engines with tall lightweight drivers, high-capacity boilers, multi-axle pedestal tenders, and elephant-ear smoke lifters. Its later passenger locomotives consisted of several classes of Pacific, a type first ordered in 1910. Its final Pacifics were 10 modern Lima-built Class P-4s delivered between 1934 and 1937. One of these magnificent engines, No. 3713, has been preserved. Despite various classes of modern steam, B&M may be best remembered for its fleet of 137 B-15 2-6-0 Moguls built by Alco in the early twentieth century. These versatile locomotives survived in service later than most modern types, laboring in Boston suburban services until replaced by Budd RDCs the mid-1950s.

Boston & Maine's Hoosac Tunnel operations were electrified between 1911 and the end of World War II; its electrics were near copies of New Haven's high-voltage AC box-cabs. B&M began sampling diesel switchers in the mid-1930s. Notably, it operated an EMC-powered diesel streamliner similar to Burlington's Budd-built *Zephyr*, initially assigned to the *Flying Yankee*—a Boston–Bangor service jointly run with Maine Central. B&M was among the first railroads to buy a large fleet of EMD's pioneering FT road diesel. After World War II, it rapidly dieselized mainline operations, ordering more EMD F- and E-units, along with BL2, GP7, and Alco's RS-2 and RS-3 road switchers. Numerous mass-produced EMD and Alco switchers were assigned to yards, industrial sidings, and branches. In the mid-1950s, B&M traded FTs back to EMD for a fleet of GP9s and turned back its handful of BL2s for GP18s. In the mid-1970s, 12 GP38-2s and 18 GP40-2s replaced aging first-generation models.

▲ In 1948, Bob Buck caught a pair of EMD FTs leading an eastward freight toward the Hoosac Tunnel's west portal. By 1945, B&M had enough diesels to retire its short Hoosac Tunnel electrification. B&M found the semipermanently coupled A-B FT sets restrictive; four units were often too much power, and two units were too little. To compensate, after World War II, B&M bought F2As to allow for three-unit A-B-A F-unit sets. *Robert A. Buck*

◄ Steam and diesel locomotives operating together was rare on Boston & Maine. In this early color view exposed about 1947, a new Boston & Maine F2A leads a steam locomotive with a long freight. EMD's F2 was an interim 1,350-horsepower model built before the 1,500-horsepower F3 entered regular production. Externally, F2As and early F3As are virtually the same. *Warren St. George, Robert A. Buck collection*

47

11 BURLINGTON NORTHERN

▶ Burlington Northern inherited SD9s from both Burlington and Great Northern, operating these stalwart EMD six-motors through its merger with Santa Fe in 1995. On January 13, 1994, a pair of SD9s delivering a transfer run to CP/Soo Line's Pigs Eye Yard passes Hoffman Avenue in St. Paul. Powered by EMD's successful 16-567C engine, the six-axle SD9 is unusual compared with its more common cousin: the four-axle GP9. *Brian Solomon*

▲ CB&Q's ad men wrote of its Mississippi River Line: "Where nature smiles 300 miles," yet although decades had passed since the last *Zephyr* graced these rails, freight continued to roll unabated. In September 1995—Burlington Northern's final month—C30-7 No. 5101 brought a grain train downriver on the right bank of America's greatest river. BN's fleet of GE's 3,000-horsepower C30-7s was the nation's largest. *Brian Solomon*

Burlington Northern was formed in 1970 from the merger of Chicago, Burlington & Quincy; Great Northern; Northern Pacific; and Spokane, Portland & Seattle and their affiliated lines, so BN's early years were characterized by a rainbow fleet of diesels inherited from these predecessors. In the 1960s, BN predecessors had shied away from EMD's 16-cylinder six-motor SD40, instead preferring high-horsepower four-motor units, General Electric models, and EMD's 3,600-horsepower 20-cylinder SD45. By the early 1970s, BN owned 172 SD45s along with similar EMD 20-cylinder 645-powered models, including eight SDP45s and 46 F45s. More SD45s came with the merger with Frisco in 1980. The honeymoon with 20-cylinder power ended with the 1970s oil crisis, and during the mid-1970s, BN bought vast numbers of 3,000-horsepower 16-cylinder SD40-2s, and ultimately it had one of the large rosters of this successful type. In the mid-1980s it disposed of 20-cylinder models. BN's established history with GE diesels, combined with rising fuel costs in the mid-1970s, encouraged BN to assemble a large fleet of U30Cs, followed by what became the largest domestic fleet of C30-7s.

BN inherited 10 GP50s, ordered by Frisco, but delivered to BN, and followed up with its own orders for an additional 53 GP50s, largely assigning these to intermodal services. In 1988, BN addressed a power shortage by contracting the rebuilding of GP30s and GP35s, which were redesignated GP39M, GP39E, and GP39V—depending on the company performing the rebuilding.

In the late 1980s, BN leased 100 new EMD SD60s on a "power by the hour" basis from EMD subsidiary Oakway (all painted in Oakway's sky blue and white rather than BN's Cascade green). A similar arrangement with GE resulted in 100 B39-8s lettered for GE's LMX subsidiary as assigned to intermodal service.

BN's first modern safety-cab locomotives were EMD SD60Ms, which entered service in early 1989. BN's desire to move heavy coal trains more efficiently resulted in it working with EMD in development of America's first heavy-haul AC-traction diesels. Following early 1990s trials using four SD60MAC prototypes, BN ordered hundreds of EMD's pioneer commercial AC-traction diesel for PRB coal traffic: the model SD70MAC.

▲ In the mid-1980s, BN experimented with fuel tenders to improve the range of road locomotives. On March 7, 1987, BN train No. 13, carrying double-stacked containers for the Pacific coast, works the former Burlington triple track west of Chicago at Highlands, Illinois. Spliced between a set of GP50s in the short-lived tiger stripe safety livery is a road service fuel tender. *Mike Abalos photo, courtesy of the Friends of Mike Abalos*

◄ In spring 1995, new EMD /SD70MACs dominated BN's Powder River Basic coal fleet. Using state-of-the-art three-phase AC traction, three SD70MACs could perform the same work as five SD40-2/C30-7s in coal service. BN's massive initial order for SD70MACs provided EMD with the capital incentive to refine AC-traction technology; today, most modern diesels use AC-traction systems. *Brian Solomon*

FACTS

EMD SD70MAC

Wheel arrangement: C-C

Transmission: AC electric

Engine: 16-710G

Horsepower: 4,000

Intended service: heavy freight

Years built: 1993–1995

Caltrain operates the most intensive railroad commuter service in California, providing a regular interval diesel-hauled service on the former Southern Pacific Peninsula line between San Francisco and San Jose (with less-frequent service beyond to Gilroy). Amtrak assumed operation of most long-distance passenger services May 1, 1971, but SP retained operation of its Peninsula suburban services, known as commutes. In the late 1970s, SP aimed to divest the commutes, so Caltrans stepped up by initially allocating local funding provided by local counties; equipment remained SP's, and SP continued as the contract operator. Between 1985 and 1988, the State of California replaced SP equipment with a new fleet—Japanese-built, stainless-steel bi-level push-pull equipment and EMD F40PH-2 (Nos. 900–919) diesel-electric locomotives lettered for Caltrain. Ironically, Caltrain's F40PH-2s were the last new locomotives delivered with SP's trademark full lighting package, which included headlights, oscillating headlights, and red oscillating lights. In 1987, the formation of the Peninsula Corridor Joint Powers Board set the stage for greater public agency involvement. In July 1992, Amtrak replaced SP as a contract operator. Ten years later, new Bombardier bi-level commuter cars debuted, followed by six new streamlined MotivePower Industries model MP36PH-3Cs (Nos. 923–928). In 2004, new equipment was assigned to *Baby Bullet* express train schedules. As built, Caltrain's F40PH-2s were built with head-end power (HEP) operated from the prime mover, a system that was deemed undesirable, so, beginning in the 1990s, Caltrain contracted MPI to overhaul them and install auxiliary CAT diesels to power HEP. In addition, Caltrain bought three F40PH clones from MPI (Nos. 920–922) in 1998. In the 2000s, Caltrain acquired a pair of former SP GP9s and a pair of MP15s for work train and switching service.

▼ In 1985, Caltrain supplied new equipment for San Francisco–San Jose commute services to replace aged Southern Pacific trains and locomotives. This included 20 EMD-built F40PH-2s that featured SP's classic full lighting. In addition to the as-built twin sealed-beam and oscillating headlights, during the 1990s ditch lights were added as pictured on locomotive No. 910 arriving at San Jose's Diridon station on November 4, 2003. *Brian Solomon*

▲ Caltrain improved and expanded San Francisco Peninsula services with its introduction of *Baby Bullet* express trains in 2004. These semiexpress trains make the San Francisco–San Jose run 25 to 30 minutes faster than typical all-stops services. For improved service, Caltrain bought six new MP36PH-3Cs, such as No. 926 (seen with a *Baby Bullet* at San Francisco in May 2008). *Brian Solomon*

FACTS

MotivePower Industries MP36PH-3C
Wheel arrangement: B-B
Transmission: DC electric
Engine: 16-645F3B
Horsepower: 3,600
Weight: 285,000–295,000 lbs.
    (depending on options)
Tractive effort: 85,000 lbs. (starting)
Intended service: push-pull
    commuter service
Years built: 2003–present

◄ The most unusual item on Caltrain's roster is this Budd-built SPV-2000; it serves as a track inspection vehicle. Previously, it worked for the U.S. Department of Transportation. In the 1970s, Budd designed the SPV-2000 as the successor to its successful rail diesel car. Although Amtrak and Metro-North operated a few cars, they proved troublesome mechanically and were deemed a commercial failure. *Brian Solomon*

► In the gloom of night, its safety valves hissing loudly, Canadian National 4-8-2 No. 6007 pauses at Strafford, Ontario, with a Toronto-bound passenger train. It's February 21, 1951, and the end is near for steam. CN was among the last in North America to work big engines on the main line. *Jim Shaughnessy*

FACTS

CN CLASS U-1-a

Builder: Canadian Locomotive Company

Wheel arrangement: 4-8-2

Type: Mountain

Cylinders: 26x30 in.

Drivers: 73 in.

Engine weight: 354,110 lbs.

Tractive effort: 49,590 lbs.

Intended service: dual service

Overall production: 37 (U-1a and U-1b)

Years built: 1923–1924

The financial collapse of several key Canadian railways at the time of World War I resulted in the creation of the government-owned Canadian National Railway. CN's predecessors had favored eight-coupled types for heavy freight and six-coupled types for passenger work. As a result, CN inherited 2-8-0s and some 2-8-2s, along with vast numbers of 4-6-0s—the most common type in Canada—as well as numerous Pacifics for passenger work. In the early 1920s, CN ordered more 2-8-2s for freight and large numbers of 4-8-2s for general service. It had also inherited a few freight service 2-10-2s and bought

▲ On January 12 1993, in a subzero freeze that typifies Montreal in winter, a pair of CN's venerable English Electric boxcabs leads an inbound morning suburban train at Val-Royal Station. Montréal Harbour Board bought these electrics in the mid-1920s, CN acquired them during World War II, and in the mid-1990s they were still on the move. Even older were the original General Electric boxcabs, some which dated to 1914, but also lasted into the 1990s. *Brian Solomon*

FACTS

ENGLISH ELECTRIC BOXCAB

Electric supply: 2,400 DC overhead

Wheel arrangement: B-B

Horsepower: 1,720 (as per manufacturer specification); 1,100 in later years

Engine weight: 221,760 lbs.

Tractive effort: 55,000 lbs. (starting)

Overall production: 9

Years built: 1925–1926

more in the 1920s, including 10 secondhand Boston & Albany Z-1s (displaced from B&A road service by Lima A-1 Berkshires). CN was early to adopt the 4-8-4 type, buying its first in 1927, only months after Northern Pacific's pioneer. CN initially and patriotically referred to 4-8-4s as Confederations rather than Northerns. Ultimately, it was the most enthusiastic 4-8-4 user; CN and its American subsidiary Grand Trunk Western bought more than 200 of the type—which became the largest 4-8-4 fleet in North America. Compared with many 4-8-4s in the United States, CN's 4-8-4s were lightweights; light axle loads enabled CN's 4-8-4s a wider range of routes than the heavily built 4-8-4s on other roads. Curiously, CN bought only five 4-6-4 Hudsons (for Montreal–Toronto express service), a notable contrast to its rival CP, which invested in 60 4-6-4s (and only two 4-8-4s). CN steam generally appeared clean and well maintained with whitewall wheels, white running boards, yellow numbers, polished brass, and its handsome maple-leaf logos on tenders.

Mainline electrification was unusual in Canada; one of the few examples was the product of Canadian National predecessor, Canadian Northern, which wired Mount Royal Tunnel and Montreal terminal operations during World War I, using a 2,400 DC overhead system. Three types of electric locomotives, plus a fleet of electric multiple units, worked these lines. The earliest locos were General Electric boxcab motors built between 1914 and 1916 and that served CN for the better part of eight decades. These were joined in the mid-1920s by English Electric box motors and by a handful of General Electric steeple cabs in 1950. The original electrification and rolling stock were replaced in the 1990s, with passenger operations conveyed to Montreal's suburban passenger agency.

▲ At Capreol, Ontario, on May 20, 1961, Canadian National SW1200 No. 7033 switches a old heavyweight sleeper fitted out as a rule inspection car. Typical of CN's General Motors switchers, No. 7033 is equipped with spark arrestors on engine exhaust stacks. End-cab switchers such as this one were designed for bi-directional operation. *Richard Jay Solomon*

Canadian National pioneered mainline diesel experiments in 1928 by testing a pair of Westinghouse diesel-electric passenger locomotives on transcontinental passenger runs. These massive oil-electrics bore a close resemblance to straight electrics of the period, featuring a 2-D-1+1-D-2 wheel arrangement. They were not successful, and so CN put off mainline dieselization until the early 1950s. Its regular operations were not fully dieselized until 1960.

CN spread road diesel acquisition over three builders. General Motors Diesel (EMD's Canadian affiliate) supplied freight and passenger F-units, large numbers of GPs, and specialized lightweight GMD-1 road switchers with A1A trucks for branches with light-axle loading. Montreal Locomotive Works supplied freight service FA/FBs and passenger service FPA-2/FPA-4s and a great variety of road switchers, many models specific to the Canadian market, including lightweight types on A1A trucks. In 1950, Fairbanks-Morse

▲ An eastward freight passes Bay View Junction, Ontario, on October, 12 1956. Leading a pair of Fairbanks-Morse/Canadian Locomotive Company C-liners is S-1 Class 2-8-2 No. 3456. Many of CN's F-M diesels barely outlasted the steam locomotives they were intended to replace. By contrast, many GMD and MLW diesels bought at the same time labored for decades, with a few serving right to the present day. *George C. Corey*

▶ Brand-new Canadian National SW1200 No. 1294 displays the railroad's attractive green and gold paint scheme at Montreal's Turcot Yard on May 4, 1958. As on most of its GM switchers, CN specified EMD's Flexicoil trucks instead of the more common AAR-style trucks typical of EMD-designed switchers. This locomotive had a 62:18 gear ratio designed for 65 mile-per-hour maximum operation. Lurking beyond the SW1200 is one of CN's Fairbanks-Morse C-liners. *Richard Jay Solomon*

▶ In the 1990s, CN bought SD70I and SD75I models from EMD. Both types use EMD's WhisperCab—also known the isolated cab since it was isolated from the under frame and so was designated by the letter I. While mechanically SD70I and SD75Is were nearly identical, the SD75 delivered slightly greater output—4,300 horsepower versus 4,000 horsepower—largely as result of control software modification. CN SD75I No. 5720 leads a mixed consist on BNSF in June 2004. *Brian Solomon*

FACTS

EMD SD75I

Wheel arrangement: C-C
Transmission: DC electric
Engine weight: 398,000 lbs.
Tractive effort: 175,000 lbs. (starting based on 33 percent adhesion)
Engine: 16-710G3C
Horsepower: 4,300
Intended service: road freight
Years built: 1996–1999

bought the Canadian Locomotive Company. Using its Kingston, Ontario, plant F-M supplied diesels for Canadian lines. CN took a fair sampling of F-M-designed models, including C-liners, and four- and six-motor road switchers. Compared with GMD and MLW models, these had relatively short lives. CN's diesels in the 1950s were dressed in a classic elaborate olive and yellow livery with gold and black trim. This gave way to a much simplified black, white, and orange in the 1960s.

High-horsepower models from GMD and MLW followed in the 1960s. In the 1970s, CN began ordering locomotives with wide-nose safety cabs—two decades before this style became the standard in the United States. CN continued to buy Alco-derived locomotives into the 1980s, which by that time were built by Bombardier. These included the four-motor HR-412 (a variation of the M-420 devised by MLW in the early 1970s) and six-motor HR-616, which featured a tapered cowl body. In the 1980s, new cowl six-motor models were a peculiarity of CN's preference; it bought customized Canadian models from EMD (SD50F and SD60F) as well as General Electric's similarly tailored Dash 8-40CM. In the 1990s, CN refrained from the trend toward AC-traction models, ordering Dash 9s from GE with specialized cab styles and fleets of EMD SD70Is and SD75Is. In the 2000s, it represented the last major holdout for heavy freight service DC-traction types, buying ES44DCs from GE and SD70M-2s from EMD.

▲ Canadian National Dash 9-44CW No. 2637 leads a pair of SD75Is at Montreal in October 2004. CN remains the last large holdout for traditional direct-current traction, heavy-haul freight diesels. The other heavy haul carriers have largely embraced three-phase AC traction. *Brian Solomon*

14 CANADIAN PACIFIC RAILWAY

▲ On August 28, 1958, Canadian Pacific Class G-2 4-6-2 No. 2583 leading the eastward *Scoot* pauses along the shore of Moosehead Lake at Greenville, Maine. CP had hundreds of Pacifics that worked its lines through the 1950s. *Richard Jay Solomon*

In its early years, CP adopted a relatively uniform locomotive fleet. While it had a large number of engines, relatively few were of unusual design then. The *Yale*, CP No. 1, was a secondhand Virginia & Truckee 2-6-0 built by the Union Iron Works in San Francisco in 1869. It was among locomotives bought by a CP construction contractor. Initially, CP focused on fleet expansion with new 4-4-0s for both freight and passenger work. Although it bought many engines from commercial builders, as early as 1883, CP built its own engines at company shops in Montreal. By the late 1880s, heavy traffic required larger types; the 4-6-0 was adopted as CP's new standard, and over the next quarter century CP acquired nearly 1,000 of this type. It remained the most prevalent engine on CP for decades, although it was largely relegated to branches and secondary services when larger types displaced them from mainline work.

Canadian Pacific had the largest North American roster of 4-4-4s; the first five were 1936 products of Alco's Montreal Locomotive Works and were near-cousins to Milwaukee's Class A Atlantics of 1935. More numerous were 20 built by Canadian Locomotive Company in 1937 and 1938. Of the notable differences, the Alco/MLW engines featured the drive rod coupled to the forward drivers, while CLC's engines, such as this one, couple drive rods to trailing drivers. *CP photo, Solomon collection*

In the early twentieth century, CP adopted the 4-6-2 Pacific for mainline passenger service and 2-8-2 Mikado for heavy freight; its first 4-6-2 came in 1906, and CP continued to order the type until 1948. The Mallet articulated wasn't used in Canada, the sole exception being six CP 0-6-6-0s built between 1909 and 1911 for helper service. These were short-lived and rebuilt after a half-dozen years as 2-10-0s. CP also bought 2-10-2s, and beginning in 1929, it invested in a fleet of 2-10-4 Selkirks for mountain service. In the 1920s and 1930s, CP adopted the 4-6-4 Hudson for long-distance passenger trains and ultimately became one of the greatest 4-6-4 operators with 65 of the type. Most famous were its semi-streamlined Royal Hudsons—named because in 1939 two of this class hauled King George VI and Queen Elizabeth on their Canadian tour (so Royal Hudsons were decorated with embossed crowns). Peculiar to CP, were its 4-4-4 Jubilees built in mid-1930s for light and relatively fast work on branch passenger trains.

▲ Most famous of all Canadian locomotives were the Royal Hudsons. Not only were these excellent performing locomotives and attractively streamlined, but they earned their place in public imagination when members of their class hauled Royal specials in 1939. *CP photo, Solomon collection*

▲ In September 1949, Canadian Pacific 4-6-4 No. 2822 makes a spectacular departure from North Bay, Ontario. Notice the embossed crown on the side of the engine identifying this as one of the Royal Hudsons. *J. William Vigrass*

FACTS

CANADIAN PACIFIC CLASS H1e

Builder: Montreal Locomotive Works

Wheel arrangement: 4-6-4

Type: Royal Hudson

Cylinders: 22x30 in.

Drivers: 75 in.

Engine weight: 365,400 lbs.

Tractive effort: 45,300 lbs. (plus 12,000 lbs. with booster)

Intended service: express passenger

Overall production: 5

Year built: 1940

CP bought an experimental 600-horsepower diesel in 1936 (No. 7000), yet it didn't begin serious diesel acquisition until the late 1940s and only moved to dieselize its mainline operations in the 1950s. In the mid-1940s, it acquired some American-built diesels, including Alco and Baldwin switchers; later it bought a few Alco RS-2s and three EMD E8As for international service. During the 1950s, CP bought large numbers of four-motor covered wagon models from EMD's Canadian builder, General Motors Diesel, but also from Alco's Canadian affiliate Montreal Locomotive Works and Fairbanks-Morse's Canadian Locomotive Company. By the late 1950s, CP preferred road switchers from these builders, and in the 1960s, it emphasized high-horsepower types. Although it bought a large number of General Motors SD40s, it also supported MLW, buying C-424s, C-630/M-630s, and M-636s. In the 1970s, it focused on the GMD/EMD SD40-2 as its primary freight locomotive, continuing to prefer the new SD40-2 and its derivatives into the late 1980s—well after EMD introduced its more powerful Super Series models. In the mid-1990s, CP switched to General Electric as its primary supplier, buying hundreds of AC4400CWs, followed by ES44ACs. It also sampled more than 60 of EMD's convertible 4,300-horsepower SD90MACs and four of its as-built 6,000 SD90MAC-Hs. Other additions have included locomotives inherited through its Soo Line affiliate and acquisition of Delaware & Hudson.

The SD40-2 was Canadian Pacific's standard road freight locomotive of the 1970s and 1980s. CP No. 6007 was photographed at Binghamton, New York, on October 12, 2003, where it was working on the former Delaware & Hudson. Although the ranks of SD40/SD40-2s have been culled as modern GEs have gradually taken over, many of these old horses continue to work CP rails. *Brian Solomon*

◄ Canadian Pacific M-630 No. 4571 leads a symbol freight past St. Martins Junction, north of Montreal, on January 11, 1993, when the temperature was just above zero Fahrenheit. CP continued to buy Alco-design six-motor models longer than railroads in the United States, operating a few into the mid-1990s. A few survive on American short lines. *Brian Solomon*

FACTS

Montreal Locomotive Works M-630
Wheel arrangement: C-C
Transmission: DC electric
Engine: 16-251E
Horsepower: 3,000
Intended service: road freight
Overall production: 67
Years built: 1969–1972

▲ Central Railroad of New Jersey's G3 Pacifics contrasted with its army of archaic-looking camelbacks. The narrow-grate, large-boiler firebox intended for bituminous coal was a well-proportioned design featuring a prominent Elesco feed-water heater. In the 1930s, Pacific No. 833, dressed in royal blue, leads CNJ's famed *Blue Comet*. *Photographer unknown, Solomon collection*

FACTS

CNJ CLASS G3s

Builder: Baldwin

Wheel arrangement: 4-6-2

Type: Pacific

Cylinders: 26x28 in.

Drivers: 79 in.

Engine weight: 333,830 lbs.*

Tractive effort: 52,180 lbs.*

Intended service: passenger

Overall production: 5

Year built: 1928

*Based on CNJ Class G4s of 1930.

Central Railroad of New Jersey, like its close affiliate Reading Company, was an anthracite road with heavy freight traffic and an intensive suburban service, and only a few long-distance passenger trains. In the late nineteenth and early twentieth century, it assembled an impressive fleet of anthracite burning camelbacks in the 0-6-0, 0-8-0, 2-8-0, 4-4-0, 4-4-2, and 4-6-0 wheel arrangements. Unusual were its camelback 4-8-0s. CNJ continued to run camelbacks right to the end of its steam operations in 1954—years after most other lines had given up on this distinctive type. CNJ was among only a few American roads to operate bi-directional suburban tank engines, a type popular in Britain (as in Thomas the Tank) but rare in the United States. The railroad was slow to embrace twentieth-century types with radial trailing trucks, but in 1918, while under USRA control, CNJ finally adopted 2-8-2s for freight and 4-6-2s for express passenger service. Its most famous Pacifics were five Baldwin-built Class G3s. Delivered in 1928, these featured prominent Elesco feed-water heaters across the smokebox; three were painted blue for the exclusive *Blue Comet* service between Jersey City and Atlantic City. Another five came in 1930, Class G4s.

In 1925, CNJ bought a 300-horsepower diesel-electric boxcab switcher produced by a consortium of Alco, GE, and Ingersoll Rand. No. 1000 was assigned to isolated waterfront trackage on the Bronx, and it has been deemed America's first commercially successful diesel. For more than a decade, this pioneer was an anomaly in CNJ's fleet; then in the late 1930s and early 1940s, the railroad bought a variety of commercial diesel switchers from Alco, Baldwin, and EMD. After World War II, CNJ took an abnormal approach toward

▲ CNJ's Schleppo the Tank was virtually unknown compared with its famous British cousin. No starring roles for this engine! CNJ bought 20 Baldwin 2-6-2T suburban tank engines between 1902 and 1903 (Nos. 200–219). All were scrapped by the end of World War II. *Photographer unknown, Solomon collection*

◀ The principal markets for the first diesels were isolated switching operations in New York City where steam locomotives were frowned upon; the first commercially built locomotive was sold to Central Railroad of New Jersey, becoming No. 1000. This spent its entire career working waterfront track in the Bronx. *Vintage postcard, Solomon collection*

FACTS

CNJ No. 1000

Builder: Alco-GE–I-R

Wheel arrangement: B-B

Transmission: electric

Engine: I-R six-cylinder

Horsepower: 300

Weight: 120,000 lbs.

Tractive effort: 30,000 lbs.

Intended service: yard switching

Overall production: 1

Year built: 1925

▲ Leave it to Central Railroad of New Jersey, one of the few railroads to embrace bi-directional steam tank locomotives in the United States, to be the only major railroad in the country to order twin-cab streamlined diesels for suburban services. Its fleet of Baldwin double-enders was like no other. *J. R. Quinn collection, via Solomon collection*

mainline dieselization. Instead of standardizing on a few models, it sampled a great variety of diesels from all the commercial builders while assigning locomotives to specific services much in the way it had assigned steam power. In addition to common models such as EMD GP7s and F3s, and Alco RS-3s, it bought a variety of Baldwin road switchers and model DR 4-4-1500 carbody types.

Unique to CNJ were two orders for three Baldwin double-cab baby-face carbody diesels, model DRX 6-4-2000s, delivered between 1946 and 1948 for suburban services. These were America's only streamlined double-cab diesel-electrics. Like many Baldwin road diesels, they suffered from poor reliability and were out of service within a decade. From Fairbanks-Morse, CNJ bought 1000-horsepower switchers, as well as 1,500- and 1,600-horsepower four-motor road switchers. Then in the mid-1950s, it took two orders of F-M six-motor 2,400-horsepower Train Masters. For heavy freight work, it bought Alco's six-motor 1,600-horsepower RSD-4s and RSD-5s. Although the line was in financial straits by the 1960s, it bought a dozen each of EMD SD35s for freight and special-order GP40Ps for suburban passenger work. In addition, it acquired nine former B&O SD40s. When CNJ was absorbed by Conrail, most of its diesels went to scrap, except for its most modern engines and the commuter service GP7s—some of which served NJ Transit into the 1980s.

◀ Central Railroad of New Jersey sampled diesels from all the major builders, making its small fleet among the most diverse in the United States. Fairbanks-Morse H-15-44 road switcher No. 1508 leads a commuter train over New Jersey's four-track Bayonne Bridge in March 1961. *Richard Jay Solomon*

▼ In its final years, CNJ painted locomotives bright red and white, which contrasted with its older olive and mustard livery that had been used since the mid-1950s. Shortly before Conrail absorbed the railroad on April 1, 1976, CNJ's westward ES-99 (Elizabethport, New Jersey, to Scranton, Pennsylvania) passes Cranford Junction, New Jersey, with SD40 No. 3067 in the lead. Both this locomotive and its sister (trailing) were built for B&O and later transferred to CNJ. *George W. Kowanski*

16 CENTRAL VERMONT RAILWAY

▲ South of Palmer, Massachusetts, the Central Vermont ascends State Line Hill, a 1.27 percent climb through Monson, Massachusetts. The top of the grade is reached at the Massachusetts–Connecticut border. On a brisk February 17, 1952, CV 2-8-0s, Nos. 462 and 468, charge upgrade across Route 32 in South Monson on their way south toward the state line. All of Central Vermont's 2-8-0s were assigned the 400 series number block. *Robert A. Buck*

FACTS

CV CLASS T-3-a

Builder: Alco

Wheel arrangement: 2-10-4

Type: Texas

Cylinders: 27x32 in.

Drivers: 60 in.

Engine weight: 419,000 lbs.

Tractive effort: 76,800 lbs. (at 62.6 percent cutoff), plus 13,100 lbs. (with booster)

Intended service: road freight between St. Albans and Brattleboro

Overall production: 10

Year built: 1928

Central Vermont was controlled by Canada's Grand Trunk Railway, and in the 1920s, when GT became GTW under the newly created Canadian National Railways, CV became part of the CN system. Although it retained its individual identity, its locomotives shared a family resemblance and common numbering with CN. Among the characteristics of CV steam were external feed-water heaters, commonly the Elesco and Coffin types, mounted on the front of the smokebox. During the early years of the twentieth century, prior to CN control, CV assembled a fleet of 36 freight service Alco-Schenectady-built 2-8-0s. Some of the early engines were delivered as compounds, but these were soon converted to simple operation.

CV also had seven similarly proportioned Alco 4-6-0s. In 1928, Alco built 10 modern 2-10-4 Texas types for the line. These were CV's heaviest and most powerful engines, and notably the heaviest steam locomotives in New England, but they were also the lightest 2-10-4s ever built (which says as much about New England railroading as it does 2-10-4 design). Weight restrictions precluded operation south of Brattleboro, Vermont, where CV's 2-8-0s soldiered on until the end of steam in 1957. Passenger services were handled by three Baldwin 4-6-2 Pacifics and four Alco 4-8-2 Mountains, while gas-electric railcars provided local service until the mid-1940s. Until the 1930s, CV kept a few old 4-4-0s handy to pinch hit when the unreliable gas-electrics failed.

CV gradually phased out steam, and during the transition various CN/GTW road diesels worked CV road freight trains. In the mid-1950s, CN's Fairbanks-Morse C-liners and Montreal Locomotive Works–built FA/FB cabs regularly worked CV through freights. In the late 1950s, EMD's GP9s were assigned to CV and served as the backbone of its road fleet for the next 30 years. CV's original GP9s (Nos. 4923–4929) were equipped with steam boilers for passenger operations. These featured the torpedo boat air reservoir configuration with roof-mounted air tanks. Later, GP9s with dynamic brakes were assigned to CV—although this feature was not used on CV in later years. Beginning in 1965, CV GP9s were

▶ Duluth, Winnipeg & Pacific No. 3604 was one of several RS-11s assigned to CV in the 1970s and 1980s. Later, it was painted in CV's attractive green and yellow livery. It is seen with GP9 No. 4927 working an industrial siding at Brattleboro, Vermont, in the early 1980s. In the late 1980s, New York–based Genesee Valley Transportation bought CV No. 3604, and it survives today on GVT's short-line system as No. 1804. *Dennis LeBeau*

▶ In the late 1970s, CV adopted this colorful green and yellow livery for its locomotives, which replaced the bland CN-inspired black and orange paint. In February 1989, CV GP9 No. 4549 and a GP9 loaned from Grand Trunk Western work near Dublin Street in Palmer, Massachusetts. *Brian Solomon*

FACTS

EMD GP9*

Wheel arrangement: B-B

Transmission: DC electric

Engine: 16-567C

Horsepower: 1,750

Weight: 245,270 lbs.

Tractive effort: 44,000 lbs.
    (continuous)

Intended service:
    general purpose

Overall production: 4,000+

Years built: 1954–1963 (U.S.
    production ended in 1959)

*Specifications based on
    CV Nos. 4547–4557.

augmented by a fleet of Alco RS-11s (Nos. 3600–3614) that variously worked for CV and CN's Duluth, Winnipeg & Pacific affiliate. Initially, these were lettered for DW&P and were gradually repainted and relettered for CV. These RS-11s rode on Canadian-built Dofasco trucks. When RS-11 No. 3609 was destroyed in a wreck in 1979, the railroad acquired a replacement from Norfolk & Western, and this was assigned the same number. The second, No. 3609, was distinctive because it was equipped with dual controls and a different arrangement of air-intake vents. The RS-11s were favored on CV's short St. Albans, Vermont–Palmer, Massachusetts, intermodal train named the *Rocket* (after its 1930s fast freight). The reincarnated *Rocket*, began in the 1970s as a short caboose-less train with just a two-man crew. In 1985 and 1986, a pair of RS-11s were repainted in metallic green for Palmer-based Quaboag Transfer and assigned to Quaboag's version of the *Rocket*, which primarily carried flatbed truck bodies with loads of lumber. Also on CV's diesel roster were a handful of switchers, a few Alco S models, and three EMD SW1200s. Of the Alcos, S-4 No. 8081 survived the longest, working into the mid-1980s. In later years, this was painted red and white and worked at Franklin, Connecticut, for K&L Feeds, one of CV's on-line shippers.

During the final decade Grand Trunk Western service, its locomotives were regularly assigned to CV, while CN road units often operated on through freights. Ultimately, CV's GP9s and RS-11s were superceded by GP38s leased from GTW. CN sold CV's route to RailTex in 1995 for operation as New England Central (NECR), but CV's locomotives were not part of the transaction and NECR acquired its own fleet of GP38s.

▲ November 7, 1993, finds a trio of CV lettered GP38s working northward, crossing the Conrail diamond at Palmer, Massachusetts. In CV's last years, GP38s leased from Grand Trunk Western prevailed on the south end, while road freights from St. Albans to Palmer tended to operate with locomotives from the CN pool. *Brian Solomon*

CHESAPEAKE & OHIO RAILROAD

▲ Chesapeake & Ohio converted four of its once-handsome all-business F-19 Pacifics into bizarrely shrouded Hudsons that proved to be among the heaviest of their type. A fifth Pacific was converted as a 4-6-4, but mercifully without stainless-steel shrouds. C&O No. 490 was resting between assignments at Cincinnati Union Terminal on August 10, 1947. Today, it is displayed at the Baltimore & Ohio Railroad Museum in Baltimore. *J. R. Quinn collection, via Solomon collection*

Chesapeake & Ohio locomotives followed an exceptional twentieth-century developmental path. The railroad was a pioneer user of the 4-6-2 Pacific (adopted in 1902, just weeks after Missouri Pacific did) and the pioneer for the 4-8-2 Mountain (1911). Later it left a remarkable legacy of outstanding late-era steam designs. Many of C&O's late-era types shared a characteristic countenance typified by a large-diameter boiler, high-mounted Elesco feed-water heater, smokebox-mounted pairs of cross-compound air pumps, a high-mounted bell, and a low-set headlight. C&O is noted for its articulated designs; it pushed these types to new limits: first with its H-7 2-8-8-2 simple articulateds in 1923 and 1924, and then with the massive H-8 2-6-6-6 Alleghenies of 1941. In 1949, it took 10 new 2-6-6-2 Mallets from Baldwin, a design three decades out of date, which proved to be Baldwin's last domestic steam. Modern passenger steam included some very heavy Pacifics and America's heaviest Hudsons, along with some excellent late-built dual-service 4-8-4s. Uncharacteristic in appearance for C&O were its 40 Class T-1 2-10-4 Texas types, which were derived from Erie's S-class 2-8-4s. Peculiar in every regard were C&O's three immense streamlined Baldwin-Westinghouse steam-turbine electrics of 1947 and 1948.

Coal-hauling C&O delayed initiating dieselization until the late 1940s. It sampled Alco road switchers, including several six-motor types, and it bought several orders of Baldwin six-motor types. However, it emphasized EMD models, ordering switchers, E7s, and F7s, followed by vast fleets of GP7s and GP9s. Unusual were SD18s built in 1963 that rode on recycled Alco tri-mount trucks. C&O's late-era diesel fleet was typified by EMD four-motor road switchers, a fair-sized fleet of SD40s, and a variety of General Electric models, beginning with the U25B. C&O's fleet was blended with Baltimore & Ohio's and Western Maryland's in the Chessie System era. In the 1980s, it was melded into CSX.

▲ The 2-6-6-6 Allegheny was among the heaviest reciprocating locomotives ever built. In 1953, one of the massive machines rolls through Mount Carbon, West Virginia. Two have been preserved, one in Baltimore and the other at Dearborn, Michigan, but neither has worked since the 1950s. *J. R. Quinn collection, via Solomon collection*

FACTS

C&O CLASS H-8

Builder: Lima

Wheel arrangement: 2-6-6-6

Type: Allegheny

Cylinders: 4 22.5x33 in.

Drivers: 67 in.

Engine weight: 724,500 lbs.*

Tractive effort: 110,200 lbs.

Intended service: road freight

Overall production: 60

Years built: 1941–1948

*This official figure was less than the actual
    weight, which was later reported as
    778,000 lbs.

◀ Chesapeake & Ohio committed to complete dieselization later than most railroads, and though it operated a variety of curiosities, its transitional fleet was dominated by standard EMD models, especially the ever-common GP9 (of which it had more than 200). C&O No. 6236 had seen nearly three decades of hard service before it was photographed at B&O's Cone Yard in East St. Louis on July 27, 1984. *Scott Muskopf*

18 CHESSIE SYSTEM

Chessie System was created in February 1973 as a holding company for Chesapeake & Ohio, Baltimore & Ohio, and Western Maryland—three closely affilatiated railroads. For observers, Chessie System presented a new image with a characteristic 1970s flair; beginning in 1972, locomotives were painted with bright yellow body, vermilion and blue striping, and large stylized Chessie kitten on the front. C&O was the dominent line, and while the kitten was new on locomotives, this insignia had been C&O's symbol for decades; plus, the railroad had been known informally Chessie for many years. The Chessie System was a principle component of CSX, created in 1980, yet retained its distinctive image and operational independence until 1986. Under Chessie, locomotives retained sublettering for component lines, but in practice, most locomotives might be used anywhere on the network, with the exception of C&O's GEs, which tended to remain in home territory.

B&O's primary contribution to Chessie was its fleet of EMD four-motor road switchers; 1950s-era GP7s and GP9s; 1960s-era GP30s, GP35s, GP38s, and GP40s; and late-era GP40-2s. B&O had been an early buyer of six-motor models and continued buying these models, which ranged from SD7s to SD40s. C&O's fleet was similar to B&O's, with large numbers of EMD road switchers. Unusual to C&O were its 19 SD18s that recycled Alco tri-mount trucks and 20 GP39s, powered by turbocharged a 12-cylinder 645 engine rated at 2,300 horsepower. C&O also operated a sizeable fleet of GE U-boats that included the pioneering U25B, as well as U23Bs, U30Bs, and six-motor U30Cs. Western Maryland's fleet of Alco RS-3s and FA/FB cabs were being retired in the early 1970s. A few of its EMD Fs struggled into the Chessie era, while its pair of BL2s lasted in Hagerstown hump service until the early 1980s. WM's GP7s, GP9s, GP35s, GP40s, SD35s, and SD40s represented the majority of its contribution to the Chessie fleet. In the 1970s, Chessie System added many more GP40-2s and SD40-2s to B&O's fleet, with some GP40-2s assigned to C&O, followed by GP15Ts and GE B30-7s assigned to C&O in the early 1980s. Early in the CSX era, an order for 144 SD50s, built 1983 and 1985, was divided between Chessie System and the CSX component Seaboard System. After 1986, new locomotives were delivered in CSX paint.

◄ Freshly painted GP15T No. 1518 leads a Chessie System freight at North Harvey Junction at Blue Island, Illinois, on April 30, 1984. GP15Ts represented the majority of this variation on EMD's GP15 model built during 1982 and 1983. All of the GP15 models used recycled components, while GP15T was distinguished by its use of a turbocharged engine. *Mike Abalos photo, courtesy of the Friends of Mike Abalos*

FACTS

EMD GP15T

Wheel arrangement: B-B

Transmission: DC electric

Engine: 8-645E3

Horsepower: 1,500

Intended service: road switcher

Number operated: 25

Overall production: 28

Years built: 1982–1983

19 CHICAGO & NORTH WESTERN RAILWAY

▲ In this classic scene in 1951, Chicago & North Western's Pacific No. 614 takes water from the tank at Madison, Wisconsin. Steam locomotives were thirsty machines, and a wise engineer took water whenever it was available. If boiler water was allowed to get too low, the engine was at risk of a boiler explosion. *John Gruber*

Chicago & North Western Railway dated to the mid-nineteenth century and grew to become one of the largest networks radiating west from Chicago. In the C&NW fold was the Omaha Road (trade name for the Chicago, St. Paul, Minneapolis & Omaha Railway). Although C&NW operated a variety of larger types, its freight steam was personified by its R/R-1-class 4-6-0 Ten-Wheeler, a versatile locomotive of classic proportions. C&NW had 325 R-1s, making these by far the most numerous type of any C&NW steam locomotive and among the railroad's longest lived steam. For passenger services, C&NW emphasized the 4-4-2 in the first decade of the twentieth century, but after 1910 it preferred the Pacific. Noteworthy were three Baldwin 4-6-2s built for operation on the Omaha Road that were the heaviest Pacifics on record. Also very heavy were C&NW's 35 Class H Baldwin 4-8-4s bought for dual service in 1929; these weighed nearly half a million pounds. North Western's most modern steam was its streamlined Alco-built 4-6-4 Hudsons; these were patterned after Milwaukee Road's famous F7 streamliners and actually more numerous. Although Milwaukee's *Hiawatha* service engines received better press, C&NW had nine locomotive to Milwaukee's six.

▲ A triple-headed freight thunders up Radner Hill, north of Peoria, Illinois, on May 31, 1941. In the lead is C&NW Class J-4 2-8-4 No. 2810, one of 12 built by Alco's Dunkirk Locomotive Works in 1927. At the time of delivery, they were the railroad's most powerful engines. Triple heading trains with steam was expensive; unlike with diesels, each locomotive required its own two-man crew. *J. R. Quinn collection, via Solomon collection*

◄ The most common type of steam locomotive on Chicago & North Western was the R-1. A jack of all trades, these versatile engines labored around the system for five decades. In December 1955, No. 894 drills the yard at Baraboo, Wisconsin. From pilot to tender coupler, the R-1 measured 67 feet, 10.25 inches. *John Gruber*

FACTS

C&NW CLASS R-1

Builders: Alco and Baldwin

Wheel arrangement: 4-6-0

Type: Ten-Wheeler

Cylinders: 21x26 in.

Drivers: 63 in.

Engine weight: 149,500, lbs.

Tractive effort: 30,900 lbs.

Intended service: general freight

Overall production: 325

Years built: 1901–1908

Just after 1 p.m., on July 17, 1958, a visit to Chicago & North Western's engine facilities in Chicago finds a good selection of contemporary diesels. At the left are E7s and E8s, next over is a long row of EMD road switchers with GP9 No. 1716 at the front, and a set of F7s is to the right. At the far right lurks a ubiquitous Alco S switcher. *Richard Jay Solomon*

C&NW had early experience with road diesels as a result of its participation in movement of Union Pacific's streamlined *City* trains. In the 1940s, C&NW invested in an eclectic array of switcher models from Alco, Baldwin, EMD, Fairbanks-Morse, and Whitcomb. Although mainline dieselization emphasized standard EMD models, including various E- and F-units, GP7s and GP9s, and Alco and F-M road switchers, C&NW also sampled a great variety of unusual early models, including the unique Baldwin DR-6-2-1000—a curious half-diesel/half-baggage car using the nonstandard A1A-3 wheel arrangement, a lone Alco DL109, and a pair of FM's so-called Erie-built cab units. C&NW developed an early enthusiasm for six-motor types, buying Baldwin DRS 6-6-1500s and AS-616s, Alco RSD-4s and RSD-5s, F-M H-16-66 Baby Trainmaster, and EMD SD7 and SD9s. In the 1960s, C&NW's fleet was augmented with its acquisition of Minneapolis & St. Louis, Chicago Great Western, and other lines.

In addition to SD40s inherited from CGW, C&NW placed its own orders with EMD for GP30s, GP35s, SD40s, and SD45s, as well as an order for seven GE U30Cs. In the 1970s and 1980s, EMD GP38-2s, GP50s, SD38-2s, SD40-2s, SD50s, and SD60s dominated its new locomotive purchases, yet it also acquired a variety of secondhand locomotives, including Union Pacific E-units for suburban service, Norfolk & Western high-hood Alco C-628s for ore service, Conrail GP40s and SD45s, and Rock Island GP7s. In the late 1980s, it turned to General Electric as its primary supplier, buying Dash 8 and Dash 9s and a few AC4400CWs before merging with Union Pacific in 1995. In its final decade, C&NW favored high-horsepower six-motor types, tending to assign its newest locomotives to coal trains originating in Wyoming's Powder River Basin. These trains operated over Union Pacific lines to the Omaha gateway.

◄ Every railroad had its trademark quirks, and one of C&NW's was a preference for a nose-mounted locomotive bell, as seen on SD40-2 No. 6842. Some of these locomotives survive in Union Pacific's fleet today. *Brian Solomon*

FACTS

EMD SD40-2
Wheel arrangement: C-C
Transmission: DC electric
Engine: 16-645E3
Horsepower: 3,000
Intended service: road freight
Overall production: 3,900+
Years built: 1972–1986

▼ Chicago & North Western had been a loyal EMD customer from the late 1960s until the mid-1980s; however, it turned to General Electric for Dash 8s in the late 1980s and continued to buy GE models until it merged with Union Pacific. Shortly before merger, C&NW considered EMD's 5,000-horsepower SD80MAC, and what an interesting sight that would have made. In May 1995, a Dash 8-40C works south of Bill, Wyoming. *Brian Solomon*

FACT BAR

CB&Q FLEET STATISTICS
Years of operation: 1855–1970
Steam locomotives: 475 (c. 1952)
Diesel locomotives: 521 (c. 1952)*
Electric locomotives: 0
Electric multiple units: 0
Gas-electric railcars: 3 (c. 1952)
*Includes early EMC streamliners.

Among the anomalies of CB&Q's early twentieth-century steam fleet was pioneer adoption of the 2-6-2 Prairie type. This stemmed from a sole Baldwin experimental 2-4-2 that it initially bought for fast passenger service in the 1890s. However, the 2-4-2 proved an unusual type that was more popular with toy train builders than real railroads. However, in 1900, CB&Q expanded 2-4-2 into the more practical 2-6-2 Prairie type and then assembled a fleet of 420 2-6-2s primarily for freight service. Simultaneously, it bought 4-4-2 Atlantics for fast passenger work (many were compounds). It was an early user of 2-10-2s, buying them as early as 1912 for drag freights. It also perpetuated the 4-4-0 after this design had largely fallen out favor on most lines. During the second decade of the twentieth century, CB&Q's West Burlington Shops rebuilt more than 100 4-4-0s for branch-line work. CB&Q's late-era steam included 2-10-4s and impressive O-5-class 4-8-4s—the last of which were railroad-built in 1940. Another of its standard freight types was the older Class O-1 to O-4 2-8-2 Mikados. Its small fleet of Hudsons worked express passenger service; two were awkwardly styled with bulky stainless-steel shrouds to pinch hit for EMC diesels.

A large user of gas-electric railcars, CB&Q was an ideal customer for EMC's first diesel train. And in 1934, it made railroad history with its EMC-powered, Budd-built diesel-electric *Zephyr* streamliner. This demonstrated the practicality of the diesel for high-speed service while helping to establish General Motors' Electro-Motive Corporation (Electro-Motive Division after 1940) as a credible locomotive builder. In the mid-1930s, CB&Q bought a fleet of EMC *Zephyrs* and later was among early buyers of the EMC/EMD's E-units and FT diesels. After World War II, CB&Q completed dieselization with EMD products. In the late 1950s, it bought EMD's high-hood early turbocharged models SD24 and GP20. During the 1960s, it sampled GE's high-horsepower models, along with the latest offerings from EMD.

▶ Chicago, Burlington & Quincy O-5a No. 5625 blasts under a signal bridge supporting classing lower quadrant semaphores at Somonauk, Illinois, in September, 1941. A year after this photo, No. 5625 was experimentally fitted with rotary poppet valves in place of conventional piston valves. In the late 1950s, Burlington revived O-5A No. 5632 for excursion service. It worked for a few years entertaining thousands who may have never known big steam. While this popular machine was unfortunately scrapped, other examples survive.
Robert A. Buck collection

◀ Portrait of power. In the mid-1950s, Burlington M-4 2-10-4 No. 6323 charges west toward Galesburg, Illinois, with a mile of freight at its drawbar. Burlington's 18 2-10-4 Texas types were an anomaly in Midwestern freight operations; the majority of railroads in the region preferred more conservative types. *John E. Pickett*

FACTS

CB&Q CLASS M-4
Builder: Baldwin
Wheel arrangement: 2-10-4
Type: Texas
Cylinders: 31x32 in.
Drivers: 64 in.
Engine weight: 512,110 lbs.
Tractive effort: 90,000 lbs.
Intended service: heavy freight
Overall production: 18
Years built: 1927–1929

▼ Burlington was one of Electro-Motive's best customers. It bought the first diesel streamliner, followed by a whole fleet of similar trains, and then bought FTs too. EMD's LaGrange, Illinois, plant was on CB&Q's main line, and so EMD often worked with Burlington to test new diesels. CB&Q was a natural customer for both of EMD's first turbocharged models, the six-motor SD24 and four-motor model GP20 (pictured). *Robert A. Buck*

21 CHICAGO, MILWAUKEE, ST. PAUL & PACIFIC RAILROAD

▶ Among Milwaukee Road's early locomotives was this classic 4-4-0 American, No. 14. It thought to have been built in 1856 and scrapped about 1888, and it was representative of the highly ornamented locomotives from the wood-burning era. *John W. Gaylord, Solomon collection*

Milwaukee Road was an ambitious Midwestern granger with an extensive system that by 1909 reached all the way to Puget Sound. Its early years were characterized by hundreds of 4-4-0s working both freight and passenger trains. In the twentieth century, it was a maverick and made its mark on American railroading by doing things its own way. While its late-era streamlined speedsters for *Hiawatha* service eclipsed every other locomotive it ever operated, Milwaukee should also be remembered for its significant fleet of nearly 200 2-6-2 Prairies, many built at the railroad's Milwaukee, Wisconsin, shops. In 1909, it expanded this design into its first 2-8-2s, and this type became the backbone of its freight fleet, with 500 of them in service across its system. For passenger service, Milwaukee acquired several classes of 4-6-2 Pacifics, ultimately owning 125 of the type. In 1929, it ordered 4-6-4s from Baldwin and then 4-8-4s to very similar design.

In the wake of Burlington's high-speed diesel-powered *Zephyr*, Milwaukee introduced its own high-speed streamliners, but it also reached very high speeds using highly refined steam rather diesels. In 1935, it worked with Alco in development of a 4-4-2 type with 84-inch drivers that was America's first as-built shrouded steam locomotive for service on

Milwaukee's super-fast *Hiawatha*; a total of four were built and numbered in single digits (Nos. 1–4) to reflect their importance to the company. They were capable of hitting 120 miles per hour with lightweight passenger trains. *Hiawatha*'s success demanded longer consists, and Milwaukee returned to Alco for six streamlined 4-6-4s. These remain among the finest locomotives to have ever graced American rails. Milwaukee continued to buy new steam, with additional orders for 4-8-4s: 40 Class S-2s built by Baldwin between 1937 and 1940 and 10 World War II Class S-3s built by Alco.

FACTS

MILWAUKEE ROAD CLASS F7

Builder: Alco

Wheel arrangement: 4-6-4

Type: Hudson

Cylinders: 23.5x30 in.

Drivers: 84 in.

Engine weight: 415,000 lbs.

Tractive effort: 50,300 lbs.

Intended service: fast passenger

Overall production: 6

Year built: 1938

◀ Milwaukee A1 Atlantic No. 2 was only about a year old when it was photographed marching out of Chicago with the *Hiawatha* bound for Milwaukee and the Twin Cities. Built for speed, these steam locomotives routinely hit speeds of 110 miles per hour and faster. The A1s were very modern steam power featuring all-welded firebox construction, Boxpok cast-steel drivers, hollow driving axles, a cast-steel engine bed, and alloyed steel main rods. *Seaver photo, Jay Williams collection*

FACTS

MILWAUKEE ROAD EP-2 BI-POLAR

Builders: Alco and GE (Alco mechanical; GE electrical)

Electric supply: 3,000 volts DC

Wheel arrangement: 1B-D+D-B1

Horsepower: n/a

Engine Weight: 521,200 lbs.

Tractive effort: 114,500 lbs. (starting)

Intended service: passenger

Overall production: 5

Year built: 1919

▶ With Fairbanks-Morse's Beloit, Wisconsin, factory on-line, Milwaukee was among F-M's best customers and proved among the last major railroads to work F-M diesels. Two H 12-44s switch the east end of Milwaukee's Savanna, Illinois, yard on October 20, 1978. *John Leopard*

To reduce operating costs on its transcon, Milwaukee contracted GE to supply 3,000-volt direct-current overhead electrification on two sections of its recently completed Pacific Extension. Electric operations commenced in 1915 and reached their zenith in 1927. Initial motive power came from jointly built GE and Alco Class EF-1 boxcabs. These were built in 1915 and featured the highly unusual 2-B-B+B-B-2 wheel arrangement, while measuring 112 feet long. Similar were Class EP-1s assigned to passenger services. In 1919, GE built five massive electrics, Class EP-2s, that featured three-piece articulated bodies in an 1-B-D+D-B-1 arrangement. These distinct machines where known as the Bi-Polars, a name that reflected the type of twin-pole traction motor design. To demonstrate their power, Milwaukee staged a tug of war; it pitted a Bi-Polar electric against a massive 2-6-6-2 Mallet compound and a conventional 2-8-0. The electric won. Today, a surviving Bi-Polar E-2 is displayed at the Museum of Transportation in Kirkwood, Missouri. Among, Milwaukee's later electrics were 10 Westinghouse boxcabs, while its very last electrics were 12 streamlined double-cab GEs delivered in 1950. These had been built for Russia, but Cold War politics intervened. They were known colloquially as Little Joes in honor of Soviet dictator Joseph Stalin.

Milwaukee bought road passenger diesels before World War II, taking a pair of DL109s—which used styling by Otto Kuhler, who helped streamline Milwaukee's steam—and a pair of EMD E6s, both types for *Hiawatha* service. It wasn't shy when it came acquiring diesel switchers and bought from all the major builders, including 44-ton models from GE, Whitcomb, and Davenport. It was keen on road freight diesels too, making repeat orders for EMD's pioneering FT, delivered between 1941 and 1945. After the war, Milwaukee was magnanimous in its distribution of road diesel orders. While its roster was a virtual catalog of standard EMD products, it also favored Fairbanks-Morse, whose Beloit, Wisconsin, plant Milwaukee served. Where many railroads sampled F-M's opposed-piston models,

▲ Milwaukee sampled Fairbanks-Morse's powerful diesels with passenger gearing for *Hiawatha* service. These were powered by F-M's opposed-piston diesel and assembled in 1946 and 1947 by GE at its Erie, Pennsylvania, works. Leading the *Afternoon Hiawatha*, F-M 12A is seen at Milwaukee, Wisconsin, on August 10, 1949. The F-M's fluted front end was styled specifically for Milwaukee Road. *Robert A. Buck*

FACTS

F-M "ERIE-BUILT" A-UNIT (Specification Nos. Alt. 100.3 and Alt. 200.3)

Wheel arrangement: A1A-A1A

Transmission: DC electric

Engine: 10-cylinder opposed-piston

Horsepower: 2,000

Weight: 327,000 lbs.*

Tractive effort: 55,600 lbs.*

Intended service: depended on gearing

Overall production: 83

Years built: 1945–1949

*Based on Milwaukee Road 12A.

▲ Milwaukee Road E8A No. 36C in fresh armour yellow paint leads a suburban train north of Chicago Union Station in June 1961. Union Pacific shifted its transcontinental passenger business from Chicago & Northwestern to Milwaukee Road in the 1950s, leading Milwaukee to adopt UP's colors for its passenger power. *Richard Jay Solomon*

Milwaukee bought a full range of F-Ms, including 1,000-horsepower switchers, both Erie-built 2,000-horsepower and 1,600-horsepower C-liner-style carbody models, and various road switchers. From Alco, Milwaukee sampled the common RS-3, but also the light-axle load RSC-3 (for work on very light branch lines) and six-motor RSD-5s. Baldwin wasn't neglected, as Milwaukee bought its relatively successful AS-616 six-motor road switcher.

In the 1960s, Milwaukee sampled GE's 2,500-horsepower U25B and EMD's ever more powerful road switchers. It bought a few SD45s and ordered five FP45s, 3,600-horsepower units powered by the 20-cylinder 645 engine (the FP45 was a model better known for service on the Santa Fe Railway). More high-horsepower GE models followed in the late 1960s and early 1970s. Peculiar to Milwaukee were 10 SDL39s—a specialized lightweight six-motor locomotive designed to replace the RSC-3s. Milwaukee's finances stalled in the 1970s; a fleet of SD40-2s represented the bulk of its new freight locomotives from EMD, while 15 F40Cs were funded by Chicago-area's Northwest Suburban Mass Transit District for commuter service. Milwaukee's inability to buy enough new power resulted in numerous older types, including F-units and F-M switchers, surviving in freight service longer than on most other roads. Milwaukee was reorganized in 1980, drastically scaling back operations. In 1985 it merged with Soo Line, yet locomotives struggled in faded Milwaukee paint for another decade.

◀ Only Santa Fe and Milwaukee Road bought EMD's FP45. While Santa Fe got almost three decades of service from their units, Milwaukee's were gone after a little more than 10 years. On March 5, 1980, Milwaukee FP45 No. 2 and SD45 No. 13 lead train 399 at Clinton, Iowa. The two 20-cylinder diesels produced 7,200 horsepower between them. *John Leopard*

▼ A Milwaukee Road "Little Joe" electric E78 leads three SD40s and two other units at Idaho's St. Paul Pass in August 1972. By the early 1970s, Milwaukee's pioneering direct-current electrification was in its sixth decade and the infrastructure was showing its age. By that time, it was only operating a couple of through freights daily on its Pacific Extension. *Robert A. Buck*

▲ Rock Island 2-10-2 No. 3019 was spic and span as it went for a spin on the Silvis, Illinois, turntable on October 21, 1939. One of the Quad Cities, Silvis was the location of an important Rock Island back shop and an operational focal point. *John E. Pickett*

FACTS

ROCK ISLAND CLASS N-78

Builder: Alco

Wheel arrangement: 2-10-2

Type: Santa Fe

Cylinders: 30x32 in.

Drivers: 63 in.

Engine weight: 405,000 lbs.

Tractive effort: 77,800 lbs.

Intended service: freight

Overall production: 35

Years built: 1918–1925

In the steam era, flatland Rock Island offered few surprises as its steam fleet largely mirrored national developmental trends, with the notable exception of articulated types (which Rock avoided completely). In its early days, 4-4-0s predominated. In the late nineteenth century and early twentieth century, Rock sampled various compound types, especially Baldwin's famed Vauclain compound (of which it bought 22 by 1900), and later, it used some of Baldwin's patented balanced compounds. Like most other lines, Rock didn't embrace compounding on a wide scale, and the majority of its locomotives remained simple types. In the twentieth century, its freight power advanced from 2-8-0 to 2-8-2 and 2-10-2. For passenger service, Rock progressed from 4-6-0 to 4-4-2 and 4-6-2. Relatively early, it adopted the 4-8-2 Mountain as a passenger engine, while its late-era steam was typified by well-proportioned, high-drivered Mountains and one of America's largest fleets of dual-service 4-8-4 Northerns.

In contrast to its conservative steam policy, Rock Island had an early interest in diesels, which produced one of the most unusual and diverse fleets in the Midwest. Prior to widespread commercial diesels, Rock operated a sizeable fleet of internal combustion railcars, including many EMC products. In 1937, EMC built Rock a fleet of six model TAs; these 1,200-horsepower locomotives were custom styled for the *Rockets* streamliners and built to unique specifications. While technologically similar to the early E-units (each TA was powered by 16-cylinder Winton 201-A diesel and used related electric components),

the TAs were distinctive from the Es because of their single engine and B-B wheel arrangement (Es used twin engines and the A1A-A1A arrangement). More significantly, in 1940, Rock Island urged Alco to expand the design of its basic switcher into a flexible road diesel; the result was the first road switcher (later known as model RS-1). These were the first of a type that within a decade grew to become the most popular diesel arrangement in the United States. By the late 1950s, it had become the dominant type. Also in 1940, EMD built a pair of flat-front half baggage car/half locomotive model EBs (derived from the E-unit) for service on the Colorado Springs section of its *Rocky Mountain Rocket*.

FACTS

EMC TA

Wheel arrangement: B-B
Transmission: DC electric
Engine: Winton 201-A
Horsepower: 1,200
Intended service: streamlined passenger
Overall production: 6
Years built: 1937

◀ Of the larger railroads, only Rock, Southern Pacific, and Spokane, Portland & Seattle bought Alco's center-cab 1,500-horsepower model C-415. Alco built just 26, and Rock Island took 10 units, Nos. 415–424. This view of Rock No. 417 at Blue Island, Illinois, on March 15, 1980, symbolizes the railroad's sad state in its final days. *John Leopard*

▶ This engine lineup at Blue Island, Illinois, on July 18, 1958, exemplifies a colorful eclectic period of Rock Island's dieselization. Here we find two Alco RS-3s (one in the lively Route of the Rockets passenger scheme), an EMD BL2, and an FP7. *Richard Jay Solomon*

▲ A pair of Rock Island FA-1s leads two EMD GPs with a long freight in August 1966. Rock Island bought a fleet of Alco-GE FA/FB-1s in 1948. To solve difficulties with these locomotives, Rock Island sent them to EMD for rebuilding between 1954 and 1957, at which time they were repowered with EMD's 567BC and 567C diesels. *Robert A. Buck*

Rock Island also embraced a variety of standard EMC and Alco models before World War II, including early E-units, a lone Alco DL103, and a variety of switchers. After the war, it dieselized rapidly, again favoring Alco and EMD, buying a mix of common and unusual models. It bought BL2s, Fs, and Es from EMD, as well as more RS models along with FA/FB cab units from Alco. Among the unusual small diesels owned by Rock were Davenport-built models, including a group of 30-ton six-wheel side rodders built between 1938 and 1941, several 44-ton switchers, and a pair of 1,000-horsepower center cabs built in 1950. It also sampled Whitcomb's small switchers. Rock Island took an interest in EMD's lightweight trains of the late 1950s, initially buying one with Talgo cars for its *Talgo Jet Rocket* and ultimately inheriting all of the progressively styled Aerotrains, which finished their days in Chicago suburban service. In the 1960s, Rock bought U25Bs, U28Bs, and U33Bs from GE; center-cab C-415s from Alco; and GP18s, GP35s, and GP40s from EMD. Although destitute in the 1970s, Rock added EMD GP38-2s and SD40-2s and GE U30Cs to its fleet. The railroad was liquidated in 1980, and its locomotives were sold to lines across the nation.

▲ In August 1978, Rock Island U33B No. 199 belches black smoke as it accelerates westward with symbol freight ARRO at Bureau, Illinois, on its Chicago–Omaha main line. Rock operated a number of GE Universal series U-boat models, including 42 of its pioneering 2,500 U25B (built between 1963 and 1965). The U33B was built between 1967 and 1970, and it delivered 3,300 horsepower. One hundred thirty-seven were built, of which the Rock took 25. *John Leopard*

◄ Rock Island's myriad paint schemes gave it one of the most colorful diesel fleets in the Midwest. In its final years, Rock adopted a sky blue and white livery that contrasted sharply with its previous red and yellow paint. GP7 No. 4533 and a pair of U25Bs rest at Inver Grove Heights, Minnesota, in August 1978. After Rock was liquidated, Chicago & North Western acquired many of its GP7s, while some U25Bs were bought by Maine Central. *John Leopard*

23 CONRAIL

▲ In Conrail's early years, it struggled with a ragtag fleet of under-maintained locomotives inherited from its bankrupt predecessors. In December 1979, this U25B working a ballast train at Warren, Massachusetts, was experiencing inadequate engine aspiration, likely the result of a failed turbocharger. In the early 1980s, Conrail retired all of its U25B/U25Cs in favor of more reliable motive power. *Doug Moore*

ongress created the Consolidated Rail Corporation (Conrail) to stave off decay in Northeast railroading. As a result, on April 1, 1976, Conrail assumed operations of Central Railroad of New Jersey, Erie–Lackawanna, Lehigh & Hudson River, Lehigh Valley, Penn Central, Reading Company, and these railroad's affiliated lines. Fresh blue paint gradually covered the fading liveries of the failed railroads. Conrail inherited a vast and myriad collection of poorly maintained locomotives. In addition to a virtual catalog of EMD products, an armada of GE U-boats, a ragtag army of Alcos, and former Penn Central electrics made Conrail's fleet the most diverse in the nation. Initially, new power consisted of a quartet of GE U36Bs (originally ordered by Auto Train) and a small fleet of U23Bs (ordered during Conrail planning, they were among Conrail's first new locomotives). However, in 1977 following injection of massive federal grants, new power began arriving on Conrail en masse with fleet of 141 GE B23-7s, 10 C30-7s, and hundreds of EMD GP40-2s, SD40-2s, and 100 GP15-1s (which incorporated recycled components from older GPs).

▲ Conrail's 141 General Electric B23-7s were among its first new locomotives. Built between 1977 and 1979, these were used to replace numerous aged and poorly maintained machines inherited from predecessor roads. Some units, such No. 1925 pictured at Peekskill, New York, in July 1989, had pilot profiles contoured to accommodate third rail in New York electrified territory—so indicated by the yellow outline. *Brian Solomon*

▲ Unique to Conrail were 50 C30-7As (Nos. 6550–6599); in place of the common 16-cylinder 7FDL, these used GE's 12-cylinder 7FDL diesel to deliver 3,000 horsepower with better fuel economy. Initially, the C30-7A fleet was based at Selkirk Yard (south of Albany, New York), and those locomotives were largely used on the steeply graded former Boston & Albany main line. On May 28, 1997, a quartet of the classic GEs work east of Palmer, Massachusetts. After Conrail was divided, some of its C30-7As were sold to operations in Estonia and Brazil. *Brian Solomon*

FACTS

GE C30-7A
Wheel arrangement: C-C
Transmission: DC electric
Engine: 7FDL-12
Horsepower: 3,000
Intended service: road freight
Overall production: 50
Year built: 1984

Despite new locomotives and lots of government money, Conrail initially failed to check declines in Northeast railroading. As its traffic tapered off, and the general economy slowed down, its older locomotives were stored or scrapped. First to be thinned from the fleet were EMD E- and F-units, along with old and unusual Alco models. The onset of recession in the early 1980s accelerated the process. Electric operations were discontinued, while hundreds of older EMD switchers, GPs, most of the SD45 fleet, the remainder of the Alcos, and most of the older GEs were sidelined. By 1984, long-dead lines at yards in Selkirk, New York; Enola and Altoona, Pennsylvania; Collinwood, Ohio; and elsewhere spoke volumes of the state of Conrail's fleet.

Although the economy recovered, new management stabilized Conrail, and its traffic levels eventually returned, very few of these stored old horses ever served the line again. Some were sold off to other railroads, many powering the numerous short lines created by Conrail spin-offs. Rather than revive the hoards of tired and inefficient diesels stored at its yards, Conrail focused on its more reliable types while opting to buy new fleets of more efficient locomotives. In 1983 and 1984, GE supplied high-horsepower B36-7s and C30-7As, along with 10 preproduction C32-8s (designed to test GE's new Dash 8 technology in road service). EMD produced a fleet of 3,500-horsepower SD50s. In the mid-1980s, Conrail preferred GE models and added C36-7s, C39-8s, and Dash 8-40Cs for heavy freight,

The 3,000-horsepower GP40 was well suited to fast freight operations on the Water Level Route; New York Central was first to order this popular type. On January 11, 1988, Conrail GP40 No. 3199 roars west on the former New York Central main line near Macedon, New York. *Brian Solomon*

Four years after Conrail's 1976 April Fool's startup, many Conrail locomotives continued to roam the system in Penn Central paint. GP30 No. 2191 was a regular on the Boston & Albany route—its New York Central heritage evident by the lack of dynamic brakes. Although the locomotive body features a dynamic brake blister above the engine compartment, it doesn't have the necessary electrical equipment, grids, vents, or cooling fans. *Doug Moore*

An SD60M leads an eastward intermodal train approaching a red signal at Palmer, Massachusetts, on January 11, 1998. Early safety cabs featured a three-piece windshield arrangement; later locomotives used the more attractive two-piece design, as seen on Conrail No. 5502. *Brian Solomon*

and a fleet of hot-rod 4,000-horsepower Dash 8-40Bs to join its existing B36-7s and EMD GP40-2 in 70-mile-per-hour piggyback services.

Conrail picked up three EMD SD60 demonstrators in 1986 and then ordered a small fleet in 1989 to augment its SD50s. In 1990, Conrail received its first GE Dash 8-40CWs, its first locomotives to feature the recently introduced North American Safety Cabs. This popular model dominated acquisitions over the next few years. Conrail also acquired safety cab–equipped SD60Ms from EMD, and in the mid-1990s it bought both EMD-built units and EMD kits (assembled at Altoona and designated SD60I because they feature the isolated cab to reduce engine noise.) In 1995, Conrail bought the only fleet of 5,000-horsepower SD80MACs, which were painted in an attractive new paint scheme that featured a white front and lighter blue body, augmented by stylized lightening bolts on the cab sides to distinguish them as alternating current traction locomotives. Initially 28 were bought, followed by EMD's pair of demonstrators. Conrail's successful transformation of Northeast railroading led CSX and Norfolk Southern to buy and divide the property. As Conrail was being dissected, its final locomotives were delivered: SD70MACs to be conveyed to CSX after breakup and conventional cab SD70s built to NS specifications.

▼ Conrail's 30 SD80MACs, built between 1995 and 1996, were the largest and most powerful locomotives to serve the railroad. Each measured 80 feet, 2 inches long; weighed approximately 430,000 pounds fully serviceable; and delivered 185,000 pounds starting tractive effort. In February 1999, a pair of SD80MACs and a GE B23-7 work west near Palmer, Massachusetts. *Brian Solomon*

FACTS

EMD SD80MAC
Wheel arrangement: C-C
Transmission: Three-phase AC electric
Engine: 20-710G3
Horsepower: 5,000
Intended service: heavy freight
Number operated: 30
Overall production: 30
Years built: 1995–1996

24 CSX

▶ CSX Transportation began painting locomotives in 1986 using this blue and gray scheme, as seen on this Chessie System GP30 in July 1988. Between 1988 and 1998, CSX converted many older four-motor Electro-Motive diesels—mostly GP30s and GP35s—into road slugs. The engines and related equipment were removed and replaced with ballast, and external features, such as radiators grilles and most air-intakes and fans, were removed and blanked up. *Brian Solomon*

FACTS

GE B36-7
Wheel arrangement: B-B
Transmission: DC electric
Engine: 7FDL-16
Horsepower: 3,600
Intended service: fast freight
Overall production: 222
Years built: 1980–1985

CSX was created in 1978 as a holding company for Seaboard Coast Line (and its affiliates) and Chessie System. While the railroads were grouped under this new banner in 1980, the old images prevailed for a few more years. In 1983, SCL components were consolidated as Seaboard System, and then in 1986, CSX Transportation was created as part of a corporate restructuring that ended the Chessie System and Seaboard System images. The first CSXT-painted locomotives appeared in April 1986. Initially, CSX applied blue and gray paint to locomotives, but after a few years this gave way to an austere of all gray (of a slightly lighter shade) with blue lettering—a livery described by observers as the "stealth scheme," in allusion to the 1980s-era U.S. Air Force F-117A stealth fighter. In the 1990s, this was improved upon by addition of a bright yellow patch at the ends of the locomotive and then a more elaborate blend of royal blue and yellow that minimized the effect of the gray body. This revised scheme dominated for a decade until replaced in the early 2000s with a new more somber livery, reminiscent of the C&O image in 1960s, that uses a dark blue body with mustard gold ends and lettering.

CSX inherited a potpourri of diesels from its component railroads, the newest being fleets of SD50s ordered during the early CSX era and delivered in Chessie System and

▼ In its first decade, many CSX locomotives continued to display heritage paint while a wide variety of models from predecessors roamed its network. In October 1993, a former Seaboard System SD40-2 and CSX SW1500 sail across the Potomac River near Magnolia, West Virginia, on the old Baltimore & Ohio. *Brian Solomon*

On February 20, 2004, CSX No. 8785 (former Conrail SD60M) and No. 8737 (former Conrail SD60I) work south on the former Atlantic Coast Line main line near the Virginia–North Carolina state line. These display the 1990s "bright future" and 2000s "dark future" liveries, as they are known to many observers. CSX inherited hundreds of locomotives from Conrail in 1999. *Brian Solomon*

CSX bought a pair of former Amtrak F40PH-2s (CSX Nos. 9992 and 9993) to work its executive office car trains. On June 17, 2004, a CSX special graces the rails of the former C&EI near Grant Park, Illinois. CSX No. 9992 was originally Amtrak No. 390, one of 30 Amtrak units sometime classified as an F40PHR because it incorporated components from SDP40Fs returned to EMD in trade. *Brian Solomon*

Seaboard System paint. In 1989, CSX turned to General Electric as its primary supplier, placing successive orders for GE's very successful 4,000-horsepower Dash 8-40C; by the end of 1990, CSX had 147 of them, Nos. 7500–7646. It followed up with repeated orders for the safety cab variation, Dash 8-40CW (Nos. 7650–7917). CSX often uses its own designations instead of those applied by builders and identifies its Dash 8-40CWs as CW40-8s. Later versions were delivered with early Dash 9 features, although they retained key elements of Dash 8 design, resulting in confusion as to the appropriate model designation; CSX

identified unit Nos. 9000–9052 as CW44-9s. In 1990, CSX acquired 20 4,000-horsepower four-motor Dash 8-40Bs from New York, Susquehanna & Western—locomotives it had helped finance when NYS&W was designated operator of the Delaware & Hudson.

CSX's interest in modern three-phase AC traction led to its massive investment in GE's AC4400CW, a strategic move that encouraged the manufacturer in its commercial refinement of AC technology for heavy-haul applications. GE delivered the first AC4400CWs to CSX in 1994. Although similar in appearance to late-era Dash 8/Dash 9s, AC4400CW can be distinguished by the large box on the fireman's (left) side of the locomotive used to house inverters. These became most common model on CSX's modern roster (Nos. 1–173, 201–599, and 5101–5122). Between 1996 and 2000, CSX also received 117 AC6000CWs (Nos. 600–699 and 5001–5016)—massive 6,000-horsepower AC-traction diesels. CSX's AC6000CW represent the majority of GE's domestic production (Union Pacific acquired the minority of domestic production; additional locomotives have been to lines in Australia). In 1997, after more than a decade since its last major order, CSX returned to Electro-Motive for 25 SD70MACs. It followed up with more in 2003 and 2004, and these later SD70MACs featured angled rear radiators to accommodate increased radiator capacity for improved greenhouse gas emissions. In 2004 and 2005, CSX added to its roster a fleet of 20 SD70ACes, EMD's model that supplanted the SD70MAC. More numerous are its modern fleets of GE Evolution diesels in both AC and DC versions. The 1999 split of Conrail resulted in infusion of many former Conrail diesels into CSX's fleet, including a share of the unusual 5,000-horsepower SD80MACs.

▲ Six-motor AC-traction General Electric safety cab diesels have dominated CSX's road fleet for more than a decade. Among the newest are GE model ES44ACs, units CSX classifies as ES44AHs. On the evening of August 20, 2010, a pair of clean CSX ES44ACs leads westward intermodal freight Q161-20 at Buffalo, New York. *Brian Solomon*

FACTS

GE ES44AC
Wheel arrangement: C-C
Transmission: three-phase AC electric
Engine: GEVO-12
Horsepower: 4,400
Weight: 415,000 lbs.
Tractive effort: 198,000 lbs. (starting)
Intended service: heavy freight
Years built: 2004–present

25 DAKOTA, MISSOURI VALLEY & WESTERN RAILROAD

▲ Dakota, Missouri Valley & Western's SD50Fs, Nos. 5418 and 5439 (former Canadian National), work a westbound plow extra west of Lehr, North Dakota, on December 28, 2010. Although Santa Fe was first to order modern cowl dieses, Canadian railroads were the primary buyers of cowl-type locomotives in the 1980s. *Chris Guss*

▶ North Dakota winters make for a harsh operating environment. DMV&W GP40-2L (GP40-2W) No. 9442 leads a local at Falkirk, North Dakota, on a bright and sunny Groundhog Day in 2009. This local is day putting its train together for the run northward on former Soo Line trackage to Max, North Dakota. *Chris Guss*

High plains regional railroad Dakota, Missouri Valley & Western began operations in 1990, and today operates freight on 522 miles of Soo Line secondary routes in Montana, North Dakota, and South Dakota. Since start-up, DMV&W has relied upon a small fleet of secondhand EMD diesels. Its early years were characterized by turbocharged four-motor models, mainly GP20s and GP35s. In recent years, the railroad has augmented its fleet with GP40-2Ls—an adaptation of the successful GP40-2 built for Canadian National with the Canadian-style safety cab—and a variety of six-motor models. It has three Wisconsin Central SD45s, placing it among the last operators of the once this once-popular 20-cylinder 3,600-horsepower road diesel, and five former CN SD50Fs—an unusual cowl variation of the SD50 known colloquially as Draper Tapers as a nod to CN's William L. Draper, who adapted the cowl body with a tapered section to improve visibility. Sixty of these distinctive locomotives were built for CN between 1985 and 1987. This body style was also applied to the SD40-2F, SD60F, and C40-8Ms. Among DMV&W's most recent acquisitions are seven KCS SD40-3s (the "-3" designation reflects upgrading and modification with solid-state electricals and microprocessor control.) In late 2011, DMV&W operated 34 locomotives, with five leaving as trade-in's for the KCS SD40-3s in early 2012.

◄ SD50F No. 5408 is parked south of McKenzie, North Dakota, on September 25, 2011. Dakota, Missouri Valley & Western operates five of 60 SD50Fs built for Canadian National in the mid-1980s. This was one of several models built with the so-called "draper taper" cowl body style that allows for better rear visibility from the operator's cab. *Chris Guss*

FACTS

EMD (LONDON, ON) SD50F

Wheel arrangement: C-C

Transmission: electric

Engine: 16-645F

Horsepower: 3,600

Intended service: road freight

Number operated: 5

Years built: 1985–1987

26 DELAWARE & HUDSON RAILWAY

▲ This is one of four unusual high-pressure experimental locomotives built by D&H at its Colonie Shops (near Waterford, New York). Three were 2-8-0s, one a 4-8-0; these aimed to improve the thermal efficiency of the steam locomotive. *J. R. Quinn collection, via Solomon collection*

▶ At first glance, locomotive No. 604 looks like something found on one of Britain's imperial railways, yet it is in fact a Delaware & Hudson Pacific. The combination of a wide firebox and smoke lifters was unusual, and D&H's had conservative styling preferences that tended to add a foreign hint to its late-era steam. *Robert A. Buck collection*

Delaware & Hudson was one of America's pioneer railroads, beginning as an industrial tramway designed to augment a canal in the movement of anthracite from Pennsylvania mines to East Coast markets. It's noteworthy for its pioneer interest in steam power. Under the direction of John B. Jervis, D&H imported four British-built engines and was the first American railroad to test steam in service. On August 8, 1829, D&H made a public trial of Foster, Rastrick & Company–built *Stourbridge Lion* at Honesdale, Pennsylvania. Unfortunately, it was found the imported engines were ill suited to D&H's light track, and they were not used as intended.

Over the following decades, D&H developed into a full-fledged mainline railroad, remaining as a primary anthracite hauler into the twentieth century. Its late nineteenth-century steam was characterized by anthracite burning camelbacks, with 4-4-0s and 4-6-0s working passenger trains, 0-6-0s for switching, and 2-8-0s as the mainstay of its freight fleet. In the twentieth century, years after other lines moved toward 2-8-2s, 2-10-2s, and superpower types, D&H remained loyal to the 2-8-0 Consolidation. It moved away from the camelback arrangement and expanded the capacity of its engines, rebuilding many to modern standards. During the mid-1920s and early 1930s, D&H used the 2-8-0 as basis for very progressive home-built high-pressure compounds with water tube boilers. This unusual effort culminated with a 4-8-0 built in 1933. In 1910, D&H experimented with an Erie Railroad 0-8-8-0 and later ordered 13 from Alco. Where Erie's engine was a curious anthracite-burning camelback, D&H's 0-8-8-0s used the conventional single-cab arrangement. In the 1940s, D&H embraced modern steam design, acquiring a fleet of 40 4-6-6-4 Challengers for freight service and 15 4-8-4s for dual freight and passenger service. D&H's late-era commitment to steam was short-lived; most of these engines were out of

▲ Delaware & Hudson's 15 Alco 4-8-4s, bought during the height of World War II for dual service, served for just a decade. In May 1952, 4-8-4 No. 308 makes for a majestic sight leading a southward freight at Plattsburgh, New York. Just a few years later, D&H returned to Alco to replace the steam locomotives it had just bought. *Jim Shaughnessy*

FACTS

D&H CLASS K-62

Builder: Alco

Wheel arrangement: 4-8-4

Type: Northern

Cylinders: 24.5x32 in.

Drivers: 75 in.

Engine weight: 447,200 lbs.

Tractive effort: n/a

Intended service: road freight and
passenger

Overall production: 15

Year built: 1943

▶ Unlike most American railroads that dieselized with EMD switchers, E- and F-units, and GPs, Delaware & Hudson turned exclusively to Alco. And despite serving as a test bed for Alco's early cab units—the ill-fated 244-powered Black Maria—it only bought switchers and four-motor road switchers. In April 1952, a pair of black and yellow RS-2s pauses at Mechanicville, New York, with the southward *Laurentian*. *Jim Shaughnessy*

▼ Delaware & Hudson bought 15 1,800-horsepower RS-36s from Alco in 1963. No. 5015 displays a nonstandard experimental paint scheme at Mechanicville, New York. On the right, a set of nearly new U30Cs makes a set off. In the mid-1960s, D&H shifted locomotive purchases from Alco to its one-time partner-turned-competitor General Electric. Where Alco had been a weak player in its final years, by the 1980s, GE had grown to become America's foremost locomotive builder. *Jim Shaughnessy*

service within a decade. D&H's last steam run occurred in summer 1953, by which time it had returned to Alco for a fleet of road switchers.

D&H's dieselization was atypical. Not only did it begin late, but also it relied exclusively on Alco. And despite testing the ill-fated Black Maria carbody-style cab units in the late World War II period, it only bought new switchers and road switchers. Initially, these were painted in a spartan black with golden yellow lettering. In the 1960s, D&H changed its paint scheme to the popular blue and gray lightening stripe, while it continued to purchase from Alco, with an order for RS-11s in 1961 (including six high-hood units originally ordered by New York Central), RS-36s in 1963, and culminating with C-628s in 1964 and 1965. In 1966, it turned to GE for U30Cs while sampling EMD's 3,600-horsepower SD45.

More new GEs followed in the form of U23Bs and U33Cs. In 1967, D&H bought four former Santa Fe Alco PAs for passenger service, and then in the mid-1970s it briefly operated a pair of former New York Central Baldwin RF-16 Sharks in local freight service. D&H expanded its reach in 1976 with extensive trackage rights over Conrail, which resulted in acquisition of former Lehigh Valley Alco C-420s and EMD GP38-2s, and Reading Company EMD GP39-2s. In addition, it acquired a small fleet of GE-rebuilt C-424s (redesignated C-424M and downgraded to 2,000 horsepower), while contracting with Morrison-Knudsen to rebuild some RS-3s with 251 engines and low short hoods. The PAs, Sharks, C-628s, and U30Cs were sold in the late 1970s. Guilford Transportation operated D&H between 1984 and 1988, followed by the New York, Susquehanna & Western between mid-1988 and D&H's ultimate purchase by Canadian Pacific in 1990. By that time, very few of D&H's locomotives remained on the property; its operations were largely handled by CP's fleet and leased locomotives.

▲ D&H acquired four former Santa Fe PAs in the late 1960s, at a time when other PA-owning lines were sending this attractive model to the scrap heap. D&H dressed them in an attractive blue and silver livery, patterned on Santa Fe's warbonnet. D&H Nos. 17 and 19 work Amtrak's *Adirondack*, crossing D&H's Mohawk River Bridge at Cohoes, New York, on the run from Montreal to Albany–Rensselaer (where a Amtrak will take over for the run to Grand Central). *George W. Kowanski*

FACTS

ALCO PA-1

Wheel arrangement: A1A-A1A

Transmission: electric

Engine: 16-244

Horsepower: 2,000

Weight: 317,900 lbs.

Tractive effort: 33,600 lbs.

Intended service: passenger

Number operated: 4 (acquired from Santa Fe in 1967)

Overall production: 170 (excludes PA-2 and PB units)

Years built: 1946–1950

27 DELAWARE, LACKAWANNA & WESTERN RAILROAD

► Extraordinarily unusual in the annals of American steam is this semi-streamlined Lackawanna 4-4-0. Built in the early twentieth century as a camelback, it was part of small batch of 4-4-0s that DL&W rebuilt as end-cab locomotives. In the late 1930s it was fitted with skirting and shrouds as seen in this rare photograph. *Robert A. Buck collection*

Known as "The Road of Anthracite," Lackawanna was historically synonymous with hard coal. Not only was it a leading producer and hauler, but also until the eve of World War I, it preferred anthracite as locomotive fuel. It operated legions of camelback 4-4-0s, 2-6-0s, 4-6-0s, 2-8-0s, and 4-8-0s in road service, as well as camelback 0-6-0s and 0-8-0s switchers. Later anthracite burners included freight-service 2-8-0s and passenger-service 4-6-2s with a single-cab arrangement but necessarily wide firebox grates. Beginning with a purchase of 2-8-2 Mikados in 1912, DL&W began the shift to bituminous coal. Its later 4-6-2s were bituminous burners. In the mid-1920s, DL&W embraced Alco's three-cylinder concept; it ordered two fleets of 4-8-2s—one for road freight, the other for passenger service. In 1927, DL&W made an early purchase of the new 4-8-4 wheel arrangement, which it designated as the Pocono, rather than the more common Northern. Its early 4-8-4s were bought for passenger service; additional 4-8-4s, delivered in 1934, were dual-service engines. DL&W's last new passenger steam engines were a quintet of thoroughbred 4-6-4 Hudsons delivered in 1937 for express passenger service. The railroad experimented with early boxcab diesels, and in the 1930s it acquired several models of commercially built diesel switchers. In fact, it was among Electro-Motive Corporation's first switcher customers. After World War II, the railroad dieselized rapidly and road steam was finished in the early 1950s, with the final run occurring in 1953. Road diesels began with its World War II EMD FT fleet, followed by large numbers of F3 and F7s for freight service, and E8s for passenger work. Alco RS-3s worked suburban services and local freight. DL&W also bought EMD GP9s and Fairbanks-Morse H-16-44, and H-24-66s—the famed 2,400-horsepower six-motor Train Master. DL&W's primary locomotive shop at Scranton, Pennsylvania, is the nucleus for today's Steamtown National Historic Site.

◄ Delaware, Lackawanna & Western was one of a few railroads in the mid-1950s that bought F-M's 2,400-horsepower Train-Master largely for suburban passenger service. Locomotive No. 858 is seen accelerating away from the train shed at Hoboken Terminal. In later years, these F-Ms worked freight. *Richard Jay Solomon*

◄ Lackawanna began serious dieselization with EMD FTs and F3s. June 20, 1948, finds F3A No. 659 waiting at Scranton to shove an eastward freight to Mount Pocono. At the left is an A-B-B-A set of FTs. *John E. Pickett*

FACTS

EMD FT

Wheel arrangement: B-B

Horsepower: 1,350 (arranged in 2-, 3-, and 4-unit sets)

Engine weight: 115,800 lbs. (A-B set)

Tractive effort: 462,600 lbs.

Intended service: heavy freight

Years built: 1939–1945

▲ A pair of Rio Grande K-37 2-8-2s barks loudly, tackling the 4 percent ascent of Cumbres Pass on August 16, 1952. Between 1928 and 1930, Rio Grande's Burnham Shops transformed 10 standard gauge 2-8-0s into narrow gauge K-37 2-8-2s. D&RGW No. 497 is a survivor and among the 2-8-2s residing on the Cumbres & Toltec Scenic Railroad. *John E. Pickett*

Narrow Gauge Steam

Denver & Rio Grande began operations with a three-foot gauge Baldwin 2-4-0, named *Montezuma*. During in its early years, 12 Baldwins covered all of D&RG's needs: four 2-4-0s for passenger trains and eight 2-6-0s for freight service. It ordered a single double-end Fairlie type in 1873 named *Mountaineer*, assigned as a helper on La Veta Pass. As D&RG grew, it required large types. While it ultimately embraced standard gauge and added the word Western to its name, some of its narrow gauge lines remained in operation into the late 1960s. In 1877, it began buying large numbers of Baldwin 2-8-0s for freight service. Where early narrow gauge locomotives were essentially scaled-down versions of standard gauge types, in 1903, Baldwin built a new powerful narrow gauge type by adapting the 2-8-2 for D&RGW. These were Class K-27, popularly known as Mudhens. These employed outside frames and outside counterweights and crankpins. In total, 15 were built; originally Vauclain compounds, they were later converted to simple operation. In 1923, D&RGW bought another 10 outside-frame 2-8-2s from Alco, Class K-28, followed by 10 more Baldwins, Class K36. The last D&GRW narrow gauge steam locomotives were 10 2-8-2s converted by the railroad's Burnham Shops from standard gauge 2-8-0s and designated Class K-37. Today, some of D&RGW's narrow gauge Mikados remain as popular tourist attractions on the Durango & Silverton and Cumbres & Toltec Scenic preserved lines.

◀ Rio Grande K-36 2-8-2 No. 485 works the Monarch Branch on August 15, 1954. Baldwin built 10 K-36s for Rio Grande in 1925; they were the final group of new narrow gauge locomotives. Scrapped in 1955, old No. 485 was the unlucky sister. All the other K-36s have survived in tourist service. *John E Pickett*

FACTS

D&RGW CLASS K-36

Builder: Baldwin

Wheel arrangement: 2-8-2

Gauge: 36 in.

Cylinders: 20x24 in.

Drivers: 44 in.

Engine weight: 187,100 lbs.

Tractive effort: 36,200 lbs.

Intended service: narrow gauge general service

Overall production: 10

Year built: 1925

◀ Former Rio Grande K-27 Mudhen No. 463 takes water at Cresco Tank on the climb from Chama, New Mexico, to Cumbres Pass. Cumbres & Toltec Scenic uses former Rio Grande 2-8-2s to haul its popular tourist passenger trains between Antonito, Colorado, and Chama. *Brian Solomon*

Standard Gauge Steam

The popularity of D&RGW's narrow gauge engines has overshadowed its standard gauge steam, yet it employed a variety of impressive locomotives. Typical for the period, 4-6-0s and 2-8-0s dominated D&RGW in the early years of its standard gauge operations. These were augmented in the twentieth century's second decade by 2-8-2s and 2-10-2s. More noteworthy were heavy freight service 4-8-2s built in 1924 and some unusual three-cylinder dual-service 4-8-2s built in 1926 by Baldwin (noteworthy, since Alco was the primary driver of three-cylinder designs). For its mountain grades, Rio Grande embraced articulated design beginning in 1909 and 1910 with 2-6-6-2 Mallets; 2-8-8-2 Mallets followed in 1913 with even more bought in the early 1920s. Unusual were 10 2-8-8-2 simple articulateds built in 1927. These briefly held title of "world's largest" but were soon usurped by Northern Pacific's Yellowstone. More of these were built in 1930. Rio Grande adopted the 4-6-6-4 Challengers for fast freight service in 1937. Where Alco had pioneered this type a year earlier for Union Pacific, D&RGW turned to Baldwin for its 4-6-6-4s. More followed during World War II. The last batch of six Rio Grande 4-6-6-4s were Alco-built to UP specifications, but they only briefly worked on D&RGW before being transferred to the Clinchfield. Other articulateds worked by Rio Grande were a fleet of compact 2-6-6-0 Mallets inherited with its purchase of Denver & Salt Lake; also some former 2-6-6-2 and 2-8-8-2s were acquired secondhand to ease the World War II traffic crunch. In 1929, the railroad bought 10 4-8-4s for passenger service, followed by five modern 4-8-4s in 1937.

▶ In 1953, Bob Buck had the privilege to sit in the cab of 2-8-8-2 No. 3613 and later to take its photograph on the turntable at Grand Junction, Colorado. Rio Grande's mountainous operations were well suited to the 2-8-8-2 arrangement, and the railroad acquired several classes of both Mallet and simple types. The first were 16 Alco Mallets of 1913, while the last were 10 Alco simples, Class L-132 built in 1930, to which No. 3613 belonged. *Robert A. Buck*

FACTS

D&RGW CLASS L-132
Builder: Alco
Wheel arrangement: 2-8-8-2
Type: Simple-articulated
Cylinders: 4 @ 26x32 in. ea.
Drivers: 63
Engine weight: 665,000 lbs.
Tractive effort: 131,800 lbs.
Intended service: heavy freight
Overall production: 10
Year built: 1930

▶ In 1937, Denver & Rio Grande Western bought 10 Baldwin-built 4-6-6-4 Challengers (Nos. 3700–3709) for fast freight service on its western end. Five more came during World War II (Nos. 3810–3814). The last were five Alco-built 4-6-6-4s (Nos. 3800–3805) patterned after UP's successful design and also delivered during the war. Notwithstanding the Alco 4-6-6-4's otherwise popular design, DRGW was unhappy and conveyed them to the Clinchfield after the war. *Robert A. Buck collection*

On the evening of October 2, 1959, first-generation EMDs idle in the Alamosa, Colorado, yard. Close inspection will find the dual-gauge tracks still in place, and, narrow gauge steam still using this trackage alongside diesels (it would continue for the next decade). Ironically, the GP9s and FTs pictured are long gone, but most of the DRG&W narrow gauge Mikados are in use on tourist railways today. *Jim Shaughnessy*

An American classic: Rio Grande F3s lead the eastbound *California Zephyr* at Grand Junction, Colorado, in August 1953. Rio Grande bought FTs during World War II and followed up after the war with F3s, F7s, and finally F9s. Its last A-B-B F9 set survived in regular service into the 1980s as power for the *Rio Grande Zephyr*—the railroad's pocket streamliner, a vestige of the old *CZ* that had been canceled back in April 1970. *Robert A. Buck*

Diesels

D&RGW began dieselization in the early 1940s by acquiring switchers from Alco, Baldwin, EMD, and GE (followed by a few Fairbanks-Morse units in 1948). Road units were initially EMD Fs, beginning with 24 sets of A-B-B-A FTs, followed by orders for F3s, F7s, and a handful of F9s. It sampled Alco's passenger diesel in 1947, buying four PAs and a pair of PBs, then five RS-3s in 1951. In the mid-1950s, it bought EMD road switchers, including six-motor SD7s and SD9s. In 1961, it imported three Krauss-Maffei high-horsepower diesel hydraulics, but it found these unsatisfactory and sold them to Southern Pacific. From that point forward, all its diesels were EMD products. Between 1961 and 1964, D&RGW traded back its early Fs for GP30s and GP35s; later some of its F7s were traded in for GP40s. Also added in the 1960s were batches of SW1000s and SW1200s (10 each). In 1967 and 1968, it received 26 3,600-horsepower model SD45s, which it retained in as-built condition longer than any other railroad. Between 1974 and 1980, it bought 73 SD40T-2 Tunnel Motors that employed the revised airflow pattern devised for high-altitude operation on SP. Its final new diesels were 17 SD50s, followed by three GP60s (acquired after D&GRW was controlled by SP interests). D&RGW didn't join Amtrak in 1971, and for a dozen years it continued to operate its *Rio Grande Zephyr* with its surviving F9A and a pair of F9Bs.

◄ An anomaly in Rio Grande's diesel fleet were three H-15-44s, Nos. 150–152. As World War II production wound down, F-M looked to develop civilian markets for its high-output submarine engine, so entered the locomotive market. No. 151 works with a yard slug at Grand Junction, Colorado, on August 20, 1953. *Robert A. Buck*

FACTS

Fairbanks-Morse H-15-44
Wheel arrangement: B-B
Transmission: DC electric
Engine: 8-cylinder opposed-piston diesel
Horsepower: 1,500
Weight: 240,900 lbs.
Tractive effort: 72,270 lbs.
Intended service: road switcher
Number operated: 3
Overall production: 30
Years built: 1947–1949

▼ By the late 1980s, Rio Grande's SD45s represented the largest unmodified 20-cylinder fleet operated by an original owner in the United States. A pair of SD45s near Kyune, Utah, climbs toward Soldier Summit in September 1989. *Brian Solomon*

29 DULUTH, MISSABE & IRON RANGE RAILWAY

Duluth, Missabe & Iron Range was a U.S. Steel road created in the early 1930s as a consolidation of the Duluth & Iron Range and Duluth, Missabe & Northern, and finally formalized by merger in 1937. DM&IR inherited a variety of 2-8-0s, 2-8-2s, 2-10-2s, 2-8-8-2s, and switchers from its components, and it routinely exchanged locomotives with the other U.S. Steel roads. As a conduit for iron ore, it was famous for running extraordinarily heavy freights. Its late-era steam is best remembered by three types: 18 Baldwin-built 2-8-8-4 Yellowstones delivered between 1941 and 1943, 18 2-10-4s acquired from sister road Bessemer & Lake Erie, and unusual 0-10-2s acquired from Union Railroad. The railroad resisted dieselization for decade longer than most American railroads, and while it acquired a few diesel switchers in the early 1950s, and a lone RDC for passenger services, it refrained from investing in road diesels until 1956. As a result, it skipped buying early types and moved directly to high tractive–effort six-motor models that were well suited for its heavy, slow-speed applications. Between 1956 and 1960, it bought a significant fleet of EMD SD9/SD18s, along with six Alco RSD-15s. Some of the EMD units enjoyed four decades of service, with a few rebuilt with low short hoods as SD-Ms, but the Alco models were shifted to B&LE in 1964. In early 1970s, DM&IR began acquiring EMD's 2000-horsepower SD38, and later SD38-2s. Between 1973 and 1976, it operated 10 former Union Pacific Alco C-630s before selling them to the Cartier Railway in Quebec. In the mid-1990s, DM&IR upgraded its six-motor fleet with 20 SD40-3s, rebuilt by VMV Paducah from SD40T-2s, SD45T-2s, and SD45-2s. In 2004, CN acquired the line, finally merging it into its Wisconsin Central affiliate at the end of 2011.

▼ On March 20, 1992, a pair of DM&IR SD9s works across a wooden trestle at Calumet, Minnesota. The moderate horsepower six-motor SD9 was ideal for many of DM&IR runs, and the model survived on the line for more than four decades. *John Leopard*

▲ This photo exemplifies the majesty of the steam locomotive. In the mid-1950s, DM&IR 2-10-4 No. 700 leads a loaded ore train across a steel trestle. DM&IR's modern Texas types were acquired from sister U.S. Steel road Bessemer & Lake Erie. *John E. Pickett*

FACTS

DM&IR CLASSES F-4 TO F-7

Builders: Alco and Baldwin

Wheel arrangement: 2-10-4

Type: Texas

Cylinders: 31x32 in.

Drivers: 64 in.

Engine weight: 524,440 lbs.

Tractive effort: 96,700 lbs.

Intended service: heavy freight

Years built: 1937–1945 (acquired from B&LE in 1951)

▲ DM&IR preferred 2,000-horsepower SD38/SD38-2s for slow-speed heavy service. These locomotives are designed for high-tractive effort applications rather than high-horsepower applications. Where the 3,000-horsepower SD40/SD40-2 models are powered by a turbocharged 16-645 diesel, the SD38/SD38-2 models use the same block but are aspirated with a Roots supercharger. On July 17, 1991, DM&IR No. 204, leading an empty train for the Minntac plant, passes Mountain Iron, Minnesota. *John Leopard*

30 ERIE LACKAWANNA RAILWAY

▲ A pair of former Erie diesels leads the eastward *Pocono Express* (Binghamton–Jersey City) as it pauses under wire on the former DL&W at Dover, New Jersey, in May 1964. Up front is EL E8A No. 828, one of 14 built for Erie in 1951; trailing is a former Erie Alco PA still wearing Erie Railroad green and gold. *Richard Jay Solomon*

In 1960, longtime rivals Erie Railroad and Delaware, Lackawanna & Western merged in a desperate effort to salvage their traffic and stave off bankruptcy by saving money through route and facilities consolidation. Both lines had dieselized rapidly after World War II, and like most American railroads, they had completed the process by the mid-1950s. Combined, the two roads had a wide variety of first-generation diesels. Both roads' fleets featured large numbers of EMD E, F, and GPs, as well as myriad Alco switchers and road switchers. Erie contributed a fleet of Alco FA/FB and PA cab units and Baldwin road switchers, along with curiosities such as Lima-Hamilton switchers. Lackawanna's Fairbanks-Morse units added further diversity to the mix of heritage locomotives. Initially, Erie Lackawanna adopted a paint scheme similar to Erie's late-era livery, but it soon settled upon an attractive adaptation of Lackawanna's gray and maroon with yellow stripes. Some locomotives, such as Erie's PAs, operated for a number of years in their old paint, and one former Erie Alco switcher survived until Conrail without evidence of EL on its body.

On June 9, 1968, a pair of Erie Lackawanna (former Erie) Alco PAs and an E-unit worked an excursion between Hoboken, New Jersey, and Binghamton, New York. EL was one of a few railroads that assigned its PAs to freight service before they were retired. *George W. Kowanski*

Erie Lackawanna SDP45 No. 3664 and U36C No. 3328 roar west with NY-99 on the former Erie main line near Erwins, New York, on October 16, 1975. EL wanted avoid refueling on long runs between Chicago and East Coast yards, and in 1969, it bought SDP45s (Nos. 3635–3668) because the longer frame allowed for a larger fuel tank. In 1972, it bought 13 SD45-2s with extra-large tanks for the same reason. *Bill Dechau, Doug Eisele collection*

FACTS

EMD SDP45

Wheel arrangement: C-C

Transmission: DC electric

Engine: 20-645E3

Horsepower: 3,600

Intended service: road freight and/or passenger*

Number operated: 13 (not equipped with steam generators)

Overall production: 52

Years built: 1967–1970

*When equipped with a steam generator for passenger car heat.

▲ In spring 1963, Erie Lackawanna Alco RS-2 No. 950 leads a suburban train along Main Street in Passaic, New Jersey, shortly before EL discontinued the line. EL favored RS-2s for suburban service because of their excellent acceleration. *Richard Jay Solomon*

The new company bought a variety of high-horsepower models, ordering U25Bs and later U33Cs from GE, and C-424s and C-425s from Alco (the latter model was built on an EL's special request to match the 2,500-horsepower output of GE's U25B). From EMD, EL ordered GP35s, followed by several orders for 20-cylinder six-motor models. In addition to SD45s, it bought SDP45s (with extra-large fuel tanks to run the length of the main line without need to stop for a top up). Purists might argue that EL's SDP45s were really just SD45s on a longer frame, since the P in the designation indicated the model carried a steam generator and EL's SDP45s never had this equipment. In the 1970s, most American lines opted for EMD's 16-cylinder 3,000-horsepower SD40-2, but EL retained its 20-cylinder preference and ordered SD45-2s (also with large fuel tanks). It was one of only a few lines to buy GE's 3,600-horsepower U36C, which externally appeared nearly identical to the U33C. Similar were U34CHs paid for by the New Jersey Department of Transportation and assigned to EL passenger services radiating from New Jersey's Hoboken Terminal. These diverted a portion of output for head-end power (HEP) for train heating and lighting. They were delivered in adaptation Erie Lackawanna livery, using blue and silver with both EL heralds and NJDOT logos.

EL struggled financially, but moved an impressive volume of freight on its main lines, including high-priority intermodal trains for United Parcel Service. Although EL retired its Alco cab units and most of its more eclectic diesels, it retained many EMD Es and Fs until its inclusion in Conrail in 1976. Before Amtrak's 1971 startup, EL had discontinued all passenger services, except for its Cleveland- and New Jersey–based suburban services. To make use of surplus passenger E8s, it re-geared them for freight service. These seemed to perform reasonably well in flatland running but faired poorly on more heavily graded lines. Most EL cab units, along with many Alco RS-3s, were sidelined when Conrail took over. Two E8As survived longer than the others, and one remains to this day: former Erie No. 833 became Conrail No. 4022, which was later shopped and made into Conrail's executive locomotive. A few years ago, it was restored into its as-built Erie livery.

▲ Most of EL's E- and F-units were worn out by the time Conrail assumed operations on April 1, 1976. While most were sent to scrap, two E-units soldiered on, initially working in Cleveland suburban service and later transferred to operations on New Jersey Transit's New York & Long Branch. Conrail No. 4014 shows its EL heritage at Cleveland, Ohio, on December 24, 1976. *Jim Marcus, Doug Eisele collection*

◄ On June 10, 1973, EL SD45 No. 3624 and GP35 No. 2584 roll westward past the company shops at Hornell, New York. In front of the shops rests an E8A, NW2 No. 441 (former DL&W No. 461) and GP7 No. 1243 (former Erie Railroad). Hornell was an important town on the old Erie Railroad. In addition to locomotive shops, this was a division point, the junction between Chicago and Buffalo routes, and the location of an important freight yard. *R.R. Richardson, Doug Eisele collection*

31 ERIE RAILROAD

► Many of Erie's steam locomotives could be characterized by brute functionality. Erie's Mikado No. 3097 was under steam at Meadville, Pennsylvania, in the late 1940s. Positioned awkwardly atop the smokebox is an Elesco feed-water heater. Pipes and hoses draped indiscriminately across the boiler contribute to its business-like look. *J. William Vigrass*

▼ Erie's April 29, 1945, public timetable proudly displays artwork of both its modern steam and new EMD FT diesels. Erie initially assigned FTs to freight on the difficult district between Meadville, Pennsylvania, and Marion, Ohio, where a saw-tooth grade profile made for tricky train handling. *Solomon collection*

In the nineteenth century, Erie Railroad was made famous by large locomotives and financial scandal. Until 1880, the railroad's six-foot gauge was the broadest in the United States. The best remembered of all Erie's engines were its early twentieth-century behemoths built for helper service on Gulf Summit. In 1907, Alco built the only Mallet camelbacks on record, three massive 0-8-8-0s, to shove on the back of heavy freights. These were bettered in 1914, with Baldwin's development of gargantuan 2-8-8-8-2 Triplexes. Of the three monster locomotives, best known was *Matt H. Shay*. While immensely powerful, these machines ran out of steam quickly, which limited their usefulness.

Fantastic as they were, the massive articulated compounds were by no means representative of Erie steam. Rather, 2-8-0s more commonly served for decades as standard freight power—in both conventional cab and camelback arrangements. In 1911, Erie adopted the 2-8-2 Mikado; then during World War I, it developed a fondness for 10-coupled types for freight service, buying fleets of 2-10-0 Decapods and 2-10-2 Santa Fes. In the late 1920s, Erie embraced the 2-8-4 Berkshire, placing orders for the type from all three major builders (Alco, Baldwin, and Lima). These powerful machines were among the most handsome engines to work Erie rails. It was never a major passenger road; Erie's meandering main line missed most major population centers, and the few big cities served tended to be reached by its secondary lines and were better served by other trunk lines. In 1905, Erie adopted the Pacific as its preferred passenger engine and continued buying new Pacifics into the 1920s. These served until diesels took over after the war.

Road diesels included fleets of Alco FA/FBs and PAs, EMD E and Fs (beginning with World War II–era FTs), as well as armies of road switchers, including both four- and six-motor models from Baldwin. In 1960, Erie's fleet was melded with Lackawanna's.

Erie Railroad

ONE OF AMERICA'S RAILROADS—ALL UNITED FOR VICTORY

Buy War Bonds and Stamps

▲ The U.S. Railroad Administration controlled American railroads during World War II and set standard designs for locomotive production. A 2-10-2 Santa Fe type with a long boiler and low drivers was designed for heavy freight service. No. 4218 was built in 1919 by Alco's Brooks (at the location of Erie's former Dunkirk, New York, Shops). It was northbound at Carbondale, Pennsylvania, leading freight in 1948. *John E. Pickett*

FACTS

ERIE CLASS R-3

Builder: Alco

Wheel arrangement: 2-10-2

Type: Santa Fe **Cylinders:** 30x32 in.

Drivers: 63 in.

Engine weight: 380,000 lbs.

Tractive effort: 74,000 lbs.

Intended service: heavy freight

Overall production: 25

Year built: 1919

▲ For more than three decades, Alco's S model switchers were a common sight on many American railroads. Built in 1952, Erie S-4 No. 529 was unusual only because it survived in company paint for more than a decade after the Erie Lackawanna merger of 1960. It was seen at Meadville, Pennsylvania, on August 18, 1971. This locomotive has been featured as a popular HO-scale model. *Doug Eisele*

32 GENESEE & WYOMING RAILROAD

▲ Genesee & Wyoming No. 46 is one of two MP15DCs bought new from General Motors' Electro-Motive Division in 1980—when the railroad was still just a short line connecting Salt Mines at Retsof with the P&L Junction near Caledonia, New York. It is seen working P&L Junction in May 1989. The MP15DC was EMD's late-1970s switcher model and G&W's were delivered in the model's final production year. *Brian Solomon*

FACTS

EMD MP15DC

Wheel arrangement: B-B

Transmission: DC electric

Engine: 12-645E

Horsepower: 1,500

Intended service: multipurpose

Overall production: 246

Years built: 1974–1980

The Genesee & Wyoming Railroad was formed in 1899. In its first eight decades, it served as a 14-mile short line primarily handling rock salt mined at Retsof, New York. In the steam era, 2-6-0s, 2-8-0s, and switchers dominated its roster. It was dieselized by 1945, initially relying on GE 80-ton switchers. In the 1950s and 1960s, it acquired Alco switchers and RS-1s. During the 1980s, G&W began to expand operations, first by acquiring additional trackage for its original operation and then by establishing new short lines and acquiring existing short lines. G&W's 1980s diesel additions consisted primarily of a pair of MP15DCs, a SW1500, two former New York Central GP38s, and three former Delaware & Hudson Alco C-424Ms (rated at 2,000 horsepower)—one of which was wrecked at P&L Junction in Caledonia, New York, when it was struck by runaway freight cars. Expansion gradually dwarfed its original operation. In 1986, G&W created Rochester & Southern to operate former CSX trackage between Rochester and Salamanca, New York. Initially, this began operations with former New York Central GP40s acquired from Conrail and a pair of former Southern Pacific SW1200s. Other early G&W short-line expansion included a cluster of former SP branches operated as Louisiana & Delta primarily with former Santa Fe CF7s and as then Buffalo & Pittsburgh on additional former CSX trackage in New York and Pennsylvania. B&P's roster had included a mix of secondhand EMD models, including GP9s, GP38s, GP40s, and SD45s. In 2010, B&P introduced a pair of modern, low-emission gen-set locomotives. By 2012, G&W Industries operated more than 60 railroads in North America, Europe, and Australia, with locomotives as varied and diverse as the multifaceted patchwork history of its many lines.

▲ Rochester & Southern's pair of former Southern Pacific SW1200s works cab to cab at Rochester's Brooks Avenue Yard on December 4, 1988. Telltale SP features include the full lighting package: oscillating headlights, red oscillating lights, and twin sealed-beam headlights. *Brian Solomon*

▲ Louisiana & Delta was one of G&W's first expansion properties and began operations of former SP branch lines in Louisiana's bayou country during the mid-1980s. Its fleet was largely made up of former Santa Fe 1,500-horsepower CF7s painted in G&W corporate orange, yellow and black, and lettered for L&D. *Brian Solomon*

▼ On April 3, 2011, Buffalo & Pittsburgh No. 462 is the first of four former Southern Pacific SD45s leading train SIJB at East Salamanca, New York. Buffalo & Pittsburgh was formed in 1988 as a Genesee & Wyoming subsidiary; today it is a 368-mile regional freight railroad comprised of the former Buffalo, Rochester, & Pittsburgh south of Machias, New York; the old Pittsburg & Shawmut; and the former PRR's Low Grade Secondary and Philadelphia and Erie main line between Saint Mary's and Erie, Pennsylvania. *Patrick Yough*

33 GO TRANSIT

Originally the marketing name for Government of Ontario Transit, today GO Transit is a division of Metrolinx, the agency tasked with coordination of public transport in the Toronto–Hamilton, Ontario, region. GO Transit began heavy rail suburban services in 1967, using a progressive model that has exemplified modern commuter rail practice. Its original locomotive fleet consisted of eight GP40TCs, a head-end power-equipped GP40 variation specially designed and built for GO Transit by General Motors Canada. In the 1970s, GO expanded its fleet with 11 GP40-2Ws (Nos. 700–710) operated in push-pull fashion with HEP control cars converted from old FP7s (originally Ontario Northland and Milwaukee Road units). In the early 1980s, GO acquired seven former Rock Island GP40s (Nos, 720–726) that were paired with HEP cars rebuilt from former Burlington Northern F7Bs. In 1978, GO bought six F40PHs (Nos. 510–515), which provided head-end power (HEP) using an alternator powered by the prime mover. In the late 1980s, GO completely reequipped its fleet; it worked with GM in the design of the F59PH (a modern Canadian wide cab–equipped cowl-style passenger locomotive), and between 1988 and 1994, it standardized its fleet with 45 of this distinctive model (numbered in the 520 to 564 block). Beginning in 2007, GO reequipped again, buying streamlined MotivePower Industries MP40PH-3Cs (Nos. 600–646). Rated at 4,000-horsepower, these are substantially more powerful than older models and intended to singly work 12-car bi-level trainsets. A few of the F59PH's have been retained, although many have been sold as GO Transit placed new MP40PH-3Cs in traffic.

▼ In the 1970s and early 1980s, GO saved money by rebuilding old F-units into head-end power cars. As a result, GO was able to assign unmodified freight locomotives to commuter trains, which was cheaper than buying custom-built passenger locomotives. GO Transit's GP40 No. 721 (former Rock Island) and F7B HEP powercar No. 801 rest at Toronto's North Bathurst Yard in May 1985. *Brian Solomon*

▼ Since 2007, GO Transit has bought an all-new fleet of MotivePower Industries MP40PH-3Cs to replace the 1980s-era F59PHs. During the transition period, it was possible to see both types working passenger consists. On the evening of June 11, 2010, MP40PH-3C No. 635 and F59PH No. 552 shove a long suburban set west from Toronto Union Station. *Brian Solomon*

FACTS

MotivePower Industries MP40PH-3C
Wheel arrangement: B-B
Transmission: DC electric
Engine: 16-710G3B
Horsepower: 4,000
Weight: 285,000–295,000 lbs.
    (depending on options)
Tractive effort: 85,000 lbs. (starting)
Intended service: push-pull
    suburban passenger
Years built: 2007–present

▲ On February 8, 2010, GO F59PH No. 541 leads a push-pull consist at Bathurst Street on approach to Toronto Union Station. In the late 1980s and early 1990s, GO Transit replaced most of its older locomotives with a uniform fleet of F59PHs. GO worked with General Motors in engineering this model specifically for push-pull suburban services with HEP. *Brian Solomon*

▶ Among the least discussed mainline electrification in America was Great Northern's second Cascade electrification, using a relatively conventional 11,000-volt single-phase AC system, installed in the late 1920s with completion of the second Cascade Tunnel (9.1 miles long). A pair of heavy GN boxcabs leads a freight in Washington state in the early 1950s shortly before GN discontinued electrification in favor of diesel operations. *John E. Pickett*

FACTS

GN CLASS Y ELECTRIC

Builders: Alco and General Electric

Wheel arrangement: 1-C+C-1

Engine weight: 518,250 lbs.

Tractive effort: 102,645 lbs. (later locomotives 105,150 lbs.)

Intended service: freight

Overall production: 8

Years built: 1927–1930

reat Northern was James J. Hill's well-planned foray across the high plains to reach Puget Sound. It was the core of his western railroad empire that later included GN's rival Northern Pacific, along with Chicago, Burlington & Quincy. Like the railroad itself, GN's twentieth-century steam was built for business, characterized by high-capacity Belpaire fireboxes (a boxy type with ample heating surface that was popular in Europe but did not enjoy widespread use in North America). Late-era GN steam tended to feature bulky air pumps mounted on the firebox. Early in the twentieth century, GN bought Baldwin balanced-compound 4-4-2 Atlantics for passenger service. Center cylinders powered forward drivers with a crank axle, and outside cylinders powered rear drivers with main rod connections. GN was an early proponent of Mallet compounds for road service and was first in the continental United States to buy them from Baldwin. It acquired some very unusual articulated types, including nonstandard 2-6-8-0s. In the 1920s, it bought simple 2-8-8-2s. GN was also well known for its impressive 4-8-2 Mountain types; the earliest were built in 1913, more came in the 1920. Then in 1929 and 1930, GN bought two batches of handsome 4-8-4 Northerns.

In 1911, Great Northern electrified its first Cascade Tunnel with a General Electric three-phase AC overhead system. When GN completed the second Cascade Tunnel, it reelectrified using a more standard single-phase, high-voltage AC system.

During World War II, GN operated GE massive steam-electric turbines (originally built for Union Pacific) in heavy freight service between Spokane and Wenatchee, Washington. More significant were its EMD FTs, some bought to handle vital Montana copper traffic during 1943. After the war, GN dieselized predominantly with EMD products, buying a few E7s and large numbers of F-units. It remained loyal to this carbody type longer than many lines and as result bought many F9s. From Alco, it bought road switchers and a few sets of FA/FB road units. In the 1960s, it was first to adopt the 3,600-horsepower SD45, and it was keen on the corresponding cowl model, F45. In 1970, GN merged with its long-time affiliates to become Burlington Northern.

▶ On the icy afternoon of February 7, 2004, Guilford SD45 No. 681 leads an eastward freight at Gardner, Massachusetts. Originally Norfolk & Western No. 1771, this one of several former Norfolk Southern high-hood SD45s acquired by Guilford in late 1987. In 2004, it was one of the last 20-cylinder EMDs operating in the region; it has since been withdrawn. *Brian Solomon*

▼ Freshly painted C-424M No. 74 rests near the Fitchburg, Massachusetts, scale track on August 21, 1987. Built in 1963, as Erie Lackawanna No. 2414, this Alco Century diesel went to Conrail in 1976 and then was one of several C-424s rebuilt by General Electric at Hornell, New York, in 1980. Output was reduced from 2,400 horsepower to 2,000 horsepower. *Brian Solomon*

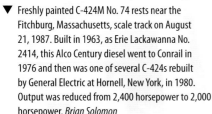

Guilford Transportation Industries assumed operations of Maine Central in 1981, Boston & Maine in 1983, and operated Delaware & Hudson from 1984 to 1988. Later GTI was renamed Guilford Rail System, and in 2006 it was again renamed Pan American Railways.

In its early years, Guilford operated with locomotives inherited from its component lines. These included Maine Central's EMD and Alco switchers and EMD GP7s, GP9s, and GP38s; General Electric U18Bs (bought new in the 1970s); former Rock Island GE U25Bs (among the last of their kind in heavy freight service); Boston & Maine's EMD switchers and road switchers (GP7s, GP9s, GP18s, GP38-2s, and GP40-2s); D&H's eclectic fleet of Alco road switchers; plus GE U23Bs and U33Cs; and EMD GP38s and GP39s. During the mid-1980s, GTI acquired surplus EMD and GE road switchers at bargain prices from various lines, allowing them to retire or sell many of the inherited locomotives. Additions included former Conrail GP40s, U33Bs, and U33Cs in 1985 and 1986; a few former Detroit Edison SD40s and a sole U30C; former Illinois Terminal SD39s in 1986; and a fleet of former Santa Fe SD26s. These were followed by some former Norfolk Southern high-hood SD45s and a sole former Western Maryland SD35 in 1987.

In the 1990s, more secondhand EMD diesels were acquired, largely GP40s and GP35s, both of the common low short hood and uncommon high short hood varieties. In 2000, 20 former Canadian National GP40-2Ls joined the Guilford fleet as the most modern engines on the roster and the only wide-cab locomotives to wear Guilford's charcoal and orange livery. Although few of the four-motor GEs survived into the early 2000s—largely confined to operations on the Maine Central—Guilford/Pan Am operations in the last decade have been characterized by one of the more unusual fleets of EMD road-switcher models. Since 2006, many locomotives have been repainted in Pan Am blue and white. Recent acquisitions have included 20 rebuilt six-motor types based on EMD's SD40 configuration, plus a pair of historic former Canadian National FP9s for the company's executive train.

◄ Pan Am GP40-2L No. 511 with local RJ-1 works former Boston & Maine trackage at North Hoosic, New York, on July 27, 2010. In 2000, Guilford bought 20 former Canadian National GP40-2Ls with the unusual Canadian safety cab. These are among the newest units on the Pan Am system. *Brian Solomon*

FACTS

GM DIESEL (LONDON, ON) GP40-2L

Alternate designations: GP40-2W and GP40-2WL

Wheel arrangement: B-B

Transmission: DC electric

Engine: 16-645E3

Horsepower: 3,000

Intended service: road freight

Number operated: 20

Overall production: 278 (estimate)

Years built: 1973–1976

▼ In 2006, the Pan Am Railways image began supplanting Guilford Rail System. On July 11, 2011, the westward EDMO (East Deerfield, Massachusetts, to Mohawk Yard in Schenectady, New York) growls through Buskirk, New York, on the former B&M main line. Leading is SD40-2 No. 600 wearing the latest shade of Pan Am blue. *Brian Solomon*

36 GULF MOBILE & OHIO RAILROAD

▲ In June 1961, Gulf, Mobile & Ohio F3A No. 882B leads an eastward passenger train at Joliet, Illinois. This attractive GM&O livery was among the most elegant diesel-era scheme in the Midwest. *Richard Jay Solomon*

FACTS

EMD F3A
Wheel arrangement: B-B
Transmission: DC electric
Engine: 16-567B
Horsepower: 1,500
Intended service: general service
Overall production: 1,111
Years built: 1945–1949

Gulf Mobile & Ohio was assembled in the 1930s from parallel Mobile & Ohio and Gulf, Mobile & Northern systems, and their merger in 1940 formalized earlier affiliations. Between 1945 and 1947, GM&O acquired the old Chicago & Alton system. GM&O never bought a new steam locomotive, and most of its inherited steam was fairly antiquated. However, GM&N had bought Alco-powered diesel streamliners built by American Car & Foundry in the 1930s (assigned to its *Rebel* services). In the early 1940s, GM&O focused locomotive purchases on Alco, buying S-1 and S-2 switchers, RS-1 road switchers, and three DL-109s road diesels. After World War II, there was little reason for G&MO to consider perpetuating its steam fleet, and GM&O opted for complete dieselization. It returned to Alco for FA/FB road freight diesels (its FA cabs were the first built and featured a slightly different headlight/nose grill arrangement than later examples). It also bought three Alco PAs for passenger service and a fleet of RS-2s. Unique to GM&O was a lone 1,500-horsepower cab unit built by Ingalls Shipbuilding in 1946. From Baldwin, it sampled a pair of baby-face DR-6-4-2000s, and from EMD it bought a fleet of F3s and F7s. It also inherited EMD E7s and a pioneer EMC boxcab from the Alton. GM&O bought all of its second-generation diesels from EMD, acquiring fleets of GP30s and GP35s in the early 1960s, SD40s in 1966, and finally GP38s, GP38ACs, and GP38-2s between 1969 and 1972. GM&O and Illinois Central merged in 1972 to form Illinois Central Gulf, and for a decade many GM&O diesels retained their old numbers and paint.

▲ Seen at Chicago's Glenn Yard in January 1983, more than a decade after merger with Illinois Central, former Gulf Mobile & Ohio GP35s still retained their old paint and numbers. GM&O was among several railroads in the 1960s that bought new EMDs featuring recycled AAR-style trucks from old Alcos received in trade. *Mike Abalos photo, courtesy of the Friends of Mike Abalos*

◀ Brightly painted No. 907 was brand new when photographed in August 1966; it was one 21 new SD40s built for the railroad that year. GM&O later acquired a sole former EMD demonstrator model SD40X. Much of the GM&O network was parallel with Illinois Central. The two railroads merged as Illinois Central Gulf in 1971, forming Illinois Central Gulf. Gradually over the next decade and a half, ICG dismembered most of the old GM&O trackage. *Robert A. Buck*

37 HURON & EASTERN RAILWAY

By Chris Guss

▲ Rail America GP9 No. 1471, working in corporate paint with Minnesota Northern reporting marks, and former Canadian National GP40-2L No. 9712 lead the Elkton, Michigan, local heading toward Deckerville, Michigan, on October 10, 2008. *Chris Guss*

Huron & Eastern Railway was the first railroad owned by the Rail America conglomerate (created in 1986). Today, the railroad includes properties acquired through the acquisitions of the Central Michigan and Saginaw Valley railroads in 2004. Over the years, these lines have had a colorful collection of vintage diesels, but things have changed quickly. During recent years, Rail America has culled most of the most unusual models.

Motive power for the original Huron & Eastern consisted of a collection of former Santa Fe, B&O, and C&O GP7s and GP9s, while the Central Michigan, which began operations in 1987, opted for six former Missouri Pacific GE-built U23Bs. Saginaw Valley started operations with a secondhand SW9 and SW1200. During the 1990s, Huron & Eastern phased out GP7s and GP9s, replacing them with GP38-2s. Meanwhile, Central Michigan purchased more secondhand General Electric models, including three former B30-7A cabless units, one former Burlington Northern B30-7 and two former BNSF C30-7s.

As of 2012, the Huron & Eastern fleet consisted of Minnesota Northern GP9 No. 1471, HESR GP40-2L (GP40-2W) No. 9712, and GP38AC Nos. 8802 and 8804. It also was home to the following Rail America GP38-2s: Nos. 3865, 3866, 3867, and 3868, lettered for HESR; No. 3852, lettered for New England Central (reporting marks NECR); and Nos. 3826 and 3838, both lettered for Central Oregon & Pacific (reporting marks CORP). While B30-7 No. 5492 and C30-7 Nos. 5086 and 5175 were still operating as of early 2012, it is understood these locomotives were also for sale.

Rail America retired the three cab-less B30-7s along with the remaining two U23Bs in late 2011, leaving just three GE units in 2012. When they go, it will end 25 years of General Electric on short lines in the region. Also, one of the Saginaw Valley's two switchers left the property in 2011, with the other anticipated to go soon.

▲ A former Burlington Northern C30-7 works as Huron & Eastern No. 5086 on the northward Durand, Michigan, turn near Burt, Michigan, in October 2008. It was one of two former BN/BNSF GE-built C30-7s on this colorful Michigan short line. *Chris Guss*

FACTS

GE C30-7
Wheel arrangement: C-C
Transmission: DC electric
Engine: 7FDL-16
Horsepower: 3,000
Intended service: heavy freight
Overall production: 783 (not including
    units built for export)
Years built: 1976–1986

◀ Huron & Eastern No. 9712 switches at Sebewaing, Michigan. The GP40-2L (sometimes described as a GP40-2W) model was built in Canada. Most were delivered to Canadian National between 1974 and 1976. *Chris Guss*

Known as the Main Line of Mid-America, Illinois Central is among the best remembered of all American railroads. Yet its traffic flow was anomalous; where the tide of American freight and passenger business tended to travel east–west, IC largely ran along a north–south axis. In the nineteenth century, neither IC, its mainline locomotives, nor its locomotive development was unusual. At the turn of the twentieth century, the railroad slipped into the lore of railroading when engineer John Luther Jones—better known as Casey—changed assignments. In those days, enginemen were routinely assigned to specific locomotives. Casey had been working a 2-8-0 (No. 638, according to some sources), but he gave this old goat up for a flashy assignment with a high-driver 4-6-0, No. 382. Casey was trying to make up time leading the southward *New Orleans Special*—colloquially "the Cannon Ball"—with this fated engine when he crashed into the back of standing freight at Vaughn, Mississippi.

Although IC remained loyal to the 2-8-0 for freight work nearly to the end of steam, it progressed to larger types for new acquisitions. It adopted the 2-8-2 in 1911, the 2-10-2 in the early 1920s, and the 2-8-4 Berkshire in 1926. Impressed with the 2-8-4, it even bought Lima's famous A-1 that had successful demonstrated on the Boston & Albany in 1925. Yet the 2-8-4 didn't prove entirely satisfactory on IC, and IC made a variety of modifications to them over the years. IC was among twentieth-century American railroads that built and rebuilt many of its own engines, and after 1929 it ceased buying steam from commercial manufacturers altogether. Among its home-built adaptations was the conversion of a 2-8-4 into America's only freight service 4-6-4.

IC's passenger steam followed the usual early twentieth-century progression from the 4-4-2 to 4-6-2, and in the 1920s it chose the 4-8-2. There it stopped. IC never embraced the 4-8-4, nor did it adopt the 4-6-4 as a passenger locomotive. Another of IC's curious conversions was the adaptation of 4-4-2s with low drivers for freight service. By comparison, other railroads simply scrapped 4-4-2s or cascaded them into suburban traffic, when they were no longer suited to passenger work.

▼ Illinois Central built and rebuilt many locomotives at its Paducah, Kentucky, shops. One of IC's most unusual transformations was creation of this freight service 4-6-4 Hudson from 2-8-4 Berkshire No. 7038. Precious few railroads considered the 4-6-4 arrangement for hauling freight; IC No. 1 remained a one-of-a-kind experiment. *Robert A. Buck collection*

FACTS

IC 2-4-4T
Builder: Rogers Locomotive Works
Wheel arrangement: 2-4-4T
Cylinders: 16x22 in.
Drivers: 56.5 in.
Engine weight: 107,600 lbs.
Tractive effort: 11,862 lbs.
Intended service: suburban passenger
Years built: 1880–?

Among IC's notable locomotive anomalies were its Chicago suburban engines; these included several varieties of tank engines, including one of the only mainline fleets of Forneys. By the time the city of Chicago demanded IC electrify suburban services (fully wired in 1926), IC's suburban fleet was notably antique, with many engines having served for more than four decades. One of these engines, a particularly ancient 2-4-4T (No. 201), has been preserved and is now displayed at the Illinois Railway Museum in Union.

▲ Illinois Central's classic passenger scheme adorns an E7A and E8A pair working a northward passenger train at Centralia, Illinois, on July 24, 1958. IC's E fleet began with prewar E6s and ran through to the E9 built in the early 1960s. Some of IC's most modern Es were bought with trades on the oldest units. *Richard Jay Solomon*

Before World War II, IC experimented with boxcabs, unusual and very heavy transfer types, and an EMC- and Pullman-built streamliner named *Green Diamond* that was similar to Union Pacific's early articulated diesel streamlined trains. Despite early interest in diesels, IC retained steam longer than most of its neighbors and didn't begin intensive mainline dieselization until the 1950s. It bought E-units for passenger work beginning with the prewar E6 and continuing right up to the E9, but it never acquired new F-units. Instead, IC's freight dieselization favored EMD switchers and road switchers. In the 1960s, it sampled EMD six-motor types, which included the SD40A with extra-large fuel tanks, along with GE U30Bs, U33Cs, and a small fleet of Alco C-636s. It merged with Gulf, Mobile & Ohio in 1972 (becoming Illinois Central Gulf), which melded GM&O's fleet with IC's and infused a variety of new models into IC's roster. These included EMD F-units, GP30s, GP35s, and GP38s—many of which continued operating in GM&O paint and numbers for more than a decade.

▶ Notice the difference in Illinois Central's lettering on leading E7A No. 1007 as compared with the trailing E8A. This pair leads train No. 20 at St. Louis Union Station on July 22, 1958. IC No. 1007 was built in 1946. EMD's E7 was the most popular postwar passenger diesel. Illinois Central's came with 52:25 gearing for a maximum speed of 117 miles per hour. *Richard Jay Solomon*

FACTS

EMD E7A

Wheel arrangement: A1A-A1A

Transmission: DC electric

Engines: two 12-567As

Total horsepower: 2,000

Weight: 322,000 lbs.*

Tractive effort: 54,000 lbs.*

Intended service: long-distance passenger

Number operated: 14

Overall production: 429

Years built: 1945–1949

*Based on Illinois Central specifications.

▲ Some products of Illinois Central's Paducah, Kentucky, shops were among the most unusual EMD-derived diesels of their era. ICG SD20 No. 2005 leads a southward freight at Gilman, Illinois, on July 15, 1980; this was originally a Union Pacific SD24B 438B. In addition to internal changes, Paducah fabricated a cab for the one-time B-unit. *John Leopard*

◄ A quartet of IC's Paducah Geeps work a northbound Decatur Turn near Harvey City, Illinois, on August 13, 1990. IC No. 8465 is a GP10 rebuilt from a GP9. Among the changes are aftermarket air filters and a lowered short hood. Paducah rebuilt hundreds of EMD GP9s in a similar manner. *Scott Muskopf*

While it bought a few SD40-2s, during the 1970s and 1980s, ICG continued IC's tradition of rebuilding its own locomotives instead of buying new, which resulted in a variety of homegrown model designations. IC's Paducah, Kentucky, shops, which had modified and constructed hundreds of steam locomotives, went on to churn out a host of SW1300s, SW14s, GP8s, GP10s, GP11s, and SD20s, among other self-styled models. In the 1980s, ICG spun off many secondary routes, and with these lines it conveyed many of its Paducah-built diesels. Reflecting its paired-down route structure, IC dropped the G in 1988. In 1995 and 1996, it bought its last new locomotives: 40 EMD SD70s. These featured conventional cabs, unusual for the time, since by then most other lines had adopted the North American Safety Cab. Another late-era acquisition was four former Burlington Northern commuter service E9As for IC's company business train. In 1998, Canadian National bought the IC system.

39 INDIANA HI-RAIL

▶ On December 12, 1992, a southward Indiana Hi-Rail freight arrives at CSX's Howell Yard in Evansville, Indiana, with a mixed consist of Alco and EMD units, including both RDS-15s trailing. In the lead is C-420 No. 311 built in 1964 for Lehigh Valley. While Indiana Hi-Rail discontinued operations in the mid-1990s, some of its Alcos survive on other lines. *Scott Muskopf*

▶ Spokane, Portland & Seattle was largely an Alco road in its final years; most of its Alcos continued to work on Burlington Northern for another decade. On November 11, 1990, a former SP&S C-425 in BN paint leads an Indiana Hi-Rail freight southbound on CSX at Carmi, Illinois. Trailing is a former Santa Fe GP7u, and two more aged Alcos. *Scott Muskopf*

n the 1980s and 1990s, Indiana Hi-Rail was a short-line operator serving more than a dozen disconnected line segments in Kentucky, Illinois, Indiana, and Ohio. The most significant was a 100-mile former Illinois Central route between Newton, Illinois, and West Henderson, Kentucky. Its ragtag locomotive fleet was as diverse and eclectic as the lines it served. Many of its locomotives were Alcos, including a pair of former Santa Fe low-nose RSD-15s—known as Alligators because of their distinctive profile; several C-420s from Monon, Seaboard Air Line, and Lehigh Valley; a pair of former Spokane, Portland & Seattle C-425s (that worked in Burlington Northern paint for a few years); a lone former SAL RS-11; a pair of S-4 switchers; and a former Long Island Rail Road RS-1. The line had its fair share of antique EMDs as well, including a pair of former Great Northern GP20s, several GP35s from various former owners, and a collection of former Santa Fe GP7u rebuilds. Unusual combinations of diesels hauled grain trains over derelict track, much to the amusement of locomotive enthusiasts. However, derailments and other problems plagued the line, so in 1997 the railroad concluded its business. While portions of the operation were assumed by other railroads, much of the trackage was abandoned and its locomotives sold off or scrapped. A few of the Centuries were acquired by other Alco short-line operators, including Arkansas & Missouri and Genesee Valley Transportation. RSD-15 No. 442 was preserved on the Austin & Texas Central, where it has been repainted into Southern Pacific's black widow livery for tourist train service, while sister No. 443 is privately owned and stored at the Arkansas Railroad Museum in Pine Bluff.

▲ Santa Fe was among the largest buyers of Alco's 2,400-horsepower six-motor RSD-15. Two of these unusual locomotives operated on Indiana Hi-Rail as Nos. 442 and 443. On November 27, 1993, IHRC No. 443, former Santa Fe No. 843, catches the sun at Evansville, Indiana. This locomotive is preserved at Pine Bluff, Arkansas, and sister RSD-15 Santa Fe No. 842 (later Indiana Hi-Rail No. 442) has been preserved on the Texas & Austin Central, while another Santa Fe RSD-15, No. 841, that worked for Lake Superior & Ishpeming survives at the Illinois Railway Museum in Union, Illinois. *Scott Muskopf*

FACTS

ALCO RSD-15 (specification number DL-600B)

Wheel arrangement: C-C

Transmission: DC electric

Engine: 16-251B

Horsepower: 2,400

Weight: 382,400 lbs.

Tractive effort: 95,600 lbs.

Intended service: heavy freight

Overall production: 87

Years built: 1956–1960

By Chris Guss

▲ On the evening of June 13, 2009, Indiana Rail Road SD90MAC (SD9043MAC) No. 9006 leads a loaded unit coal destined for Indianapolis Power & Light in Indianapolis. Indiana Rail Road is one of a few American short lines that operates modern AC-traction diesels. *Chris Guss*

FACTS

EMD SD90MAC

Alternate designations: Upgradeable SD90MAC and SD9043MAC

Wheel arrangement: C-C

Transmission: three-phase AC electric

Engine: 16-710G3B (upgradeable to 16V265H)

Horsepower: 4,300 with 16-710G3B (6,000 with optional 16V265H)

Intended service: heavy

Overall production: 14

Years built: 1996–1999

A true Midwest regional, the Indiana Rail Road has grown from its inception in 1986 when it operated just 155 miles of railroad with 11 secondhand CF7 locomotives to a railroad with more than 550 miles of track (including trackage and haulage rights) and 33 locomotives in its fleet, including some modern AC-traction six axles. The railroad's first decade relied on former Santa Fe CF7s and six former Chesapeake & Ohio SD18s. As its traffic swelled, it acquired more locomotives. In the 1990s, Indiana Rail Road bought eight former Milwaukee Road SD10s, previously operated by Midwest regional Dakota, Minnesota & Eastern. It standardized its fleet in the early 2000s, acquiring EMD SD40-2s and GP38s (and similar units). The railroad eventually operated a dozen GP38s. In 2006, it acquired a dozen EMD SD60s. Indiana Rail Road was the latest short line to use AC traction in 2008 when it leased SD9043MACs. EMD originally designated this model as an upgradeable SD90MAC; they were powered by a 16-710G3 rated at 4,300 horsepower but were capable of being upgraded with installation of EMD's 6,000-horsepower 16V265H series engine. As a result, most operators have added the number 43 to the designation to distinguish the 4,300-horsepower upgradeable models from the as-built 6,000-horsepower SD90MAC-H locomotives. In 2011, Indiana Railroad had 14 of the big units that had replaced its SD60s in road service. Most recently, the railroad received its first GP40-3 mother-slug set, and second set was expected in early 2012.

On June 13, 2009, Indiana Rail Road SD40-2 No. 4001 and an SD90MAC work a southbound military train from the naval base at Crane, Indiana, to Louisville, Kentucky, on CSX's former Monon street trackage at Bedford, Indiana. *Chris Guss*

Indiana Rail Road had just opened this new coal spur at Bear Run when GP38-2 No. 3801 worked an inspection train. On May 7, 2010, it was the first train to use the new trackage. *Chris Guss*

KANSAS CITY SOUTHERN RAILWAY

▶ Kansas City Southern is one of the oldest names in Class 1 American railroading. In the nineteenth century, its fleet included the classic American Standard 4-4-0; today it operates with the latest high-horsepower AC-traction diesels. *Solomon collection*

▼ Kansas City Southern SD40-3 No. 619 works a northbound haulage train from Kansas City to Council Bluffs, Nebraska, on Union Pacific's Falls City Subdivision on July 9, 1995. In the mid-1990s, KCS bought a variety of 1970s-era EMD six-motor units redesignated SD40-3 to reflect substantially rebuilding with 16-645E3 diesels and equipped with solid-state electrical systems. KCS Nos. 619 and 620 feature SD45 bodies, locomotives that were originally powered by EMD's 3,600-horsepower 20-cylinder 645E3 engine. *Chris Guss*

I n 2012, Kansas City Southern survives as one of the last large railways in the United States operating under the same name since the steam era. Historically, in addition to locomotives assigned to its own routes, some have been assigned to Louisiana & Arkansas, a line that KCS has controlled since 1939. Among KCS' finest late-era steam power were 10 handsome Lima-built 2-10-4 freight haulers with 70-inch drivers. KCS began sampling diesels in the 1930s. In addition to switchers, it was an early EMC E-unit customer. Among its early Es was EMC E3A demonstrator No. 822, which became KCS No. 21. These debuted the railroad's classy red, yellow, and black livery for service on its streamlined *Southern Belle* passenger trains. After World War II, road operations were largely dieselized with EMD models: Es for passenger service, and F3s and F7s for freight. Perhaps its most unusual diesels were F-M's 2,000-horsepower Erie-built road units, initially assigned in four-unit A-B-B-A sets. KCS also bought a pair of F-M road switchers, one of which was later repowered with an EMD engine. These F-Ms and a few Baldwin switchers were an anomaly in what was otherwise an all–General Motors fleet. In the 1950s, KCS bought GP7s and GP9s; in the 1960s, GP30s and SD40s; and in the 1970s GP38-2s, GP40-2s, and SD40-2s. Also in the 1970s, it rebuilt some of its F-units to work as road slugs and road-slug control units, while investing in early radio-control remote technology. It was one of the first to sample EMD's Super Series with four SD40Xs in 1979, followed by EMD's SD50s in the early 1980s and SD60s in the early 1990s. KCS greatly expanded its operations in the mid-1990s and bought a variety of secondhand EMDs to augment its fleet, including remanufactured SD45s and former Southern Pacific Tunnel Motors, redesignated as SD40-3s. Since 2000, KCS has bought fleets of modern three-phase AC models from both EMD and GE.

▲ In recent years, KCS has reintroduced its 1930s-era "southern belle" livery to freight units. On August 16, 2011, KCS SD70ACe No. 4121 leads a pair of SD70MACs and another SD70ACe at Ginger Blue, Missouri. The second SD70MAC is lettered for KCS's Mexican affiliate, Transportación Ferroviaria Mexicana. *Brian Solomon*

FACTS

EMD SD70ACe

Wheel arrangement: C-C

Transmission: three-phase AC electric

Engine: 16-710G3C-T2

Horsepower: 4,300

Tractive effort: 191,000 lbs. (starting)

Intended service: heavy freight

Years built: 2003–present

◀ Kansas City Southern had been an all-EMD railroad for decades. This ended in 2000 when it began buying new GE six-motor AC-traction diesels. Among latest GEs in its fleet are ES44ACs, such as KCS No. 4713 seen working as a rear end of a unit coal train as a distributed power unit at Heavener, Oklahoma, on February 2, 2008. *Chris Guss*

42 LEHIGH & HUDSON RIVER RAILWAY

ehigh & Hudson River was a 97-mile bridge line connecting gateways at Easton, Pennsylvania; Port Morris, New Jersey; and Maybrook, New York. It largely forwarded coal from Pennsylvania connections to the New Haven Railroad for distribution across New England. It was among the last railroads to use anthracite burners; it operated a small fleet of remarkable well-proportioned camelback 4-6-0s and 2-8-0s as well as conventional-cab types with wide fireboxes. Between 1916 and 1918, it bought 2-8-2 Mikados, but a decade later it returned to the 2-8-0 wheel arrangement and ordered some exceptional examples of the type. These had enormous boilers and were capable of extraordinary output for a traditional eight-coupled locomotive. L&HR didn't embrace superpower designs, but during the World War II surge of traffic, it bought three modern Baldwin 4-8-2 Mountains—near copies of engines recently built for Boston & Maine.

While all of L&HR's late-era steam locomotives were Baldwin products, for diesels it turned exclusively to Alco. Between 1950 and 1951, it bought 13 RS-3 road switchers (Nos. 1–13) to replace steam. These were typical examples of Alco's most prolific postwar model; on L&HR they wore black with gold stripes that became cat whiskers on the long hood. Between 1963 and 1966, L&HR traded seven of its RS-3s back to Alco for a fleet of eight C-420s (Nos. 21–29). All were painted in a modern blue and gray livery. The railroad had very little on-line business, while the decline of anthracite followed by the merger movement of the 1960s denied L&HR most bridge traffic. It was teetering on oblivion when Penn Central's Poughkeepsie Bridge burned in 1974 sealing its fate; the line was among destitute carriers absorbed by Conrail in 1976. Today, Half of L&HR C-420s survive on Arkansas & Missouri, while New York's Battenkill Road still works L&HR RS-3 No. 10 as its No. 605.

▼ Lehigh & Hudson River's only modern steam locomotives were three Baldwin 4-8-2s delivered during World War II. Like many late-era steam locomotives, these had short lives. Notice the Boxpok drive wheels, smoke lifters on the sides of the boiler, and the centipede-style pedestal tender (featuring a ten-wheel rigid frame support at the back and four wheel truck at the front); all were features of late-era steam design. *Photographer unknown, Robert A. Buck collection*

◄ Lehigh & Hudson River didn't operate scheduled passenger services in the diesel era. However in June 1960, RS-3s Nos. 10 and 3 work a fan trip using Erie Lackawanna Stillwell cars. L&HR bought 14 Alco RS-3s in 1950 and 1951. While most of the more than 1,300 Alco RS-3s were scrapped year ago, No. 10 survives on the Battenkill Railroad, a New York state short line that operates on a section of former Delaware & Hudson, north from Eagle Bridge. *Richard Jay Solomon*

FACTS

ALCO RS-3
Wheel arrangement: B-B
Transmission: DC electric
Engine: 12-244
Horsepower: 1,600
Weight: 240,000 lbs.
Tractive effort: 52,500 lbs.
Intended service: general purpose
Overall production: 1,370
Years built: 1950–1956

▼ L & HR served as a bridge line between gateways at Maybrook, New York, and Easton, Pennsylvania. Three C-420s lead a southward freight at Maybrook Yard in October 1970. L&HR bought 10 C-420s between 1963 and 1966, trading back a few of its RS-3s to Alco as part of the deal. *George W. Kowanski*

▲ Built by Philadelphia manufacturer Richard Norris & Sons, Lehigh Valley's *Delaware* was a typical mid-nineteenth-century 4-4-0. Note narrow spacing of leading wheels, slightly off-level cylinders, narrow main rods, a highly polished boiler plate, and ornamentation on the tender. Although we see it in black and white, this was a very colorful locomotive. *Photographer unknown, Solomon collection*

▶ In late 1963, Alco introduced the C-628 and boasted that it was the most powerful single-engine diesel-electric in North America. It was a six-motor type powered by Alco's 16-cylinder 251C engine and rated at 2,750 horsepower. Lehigh Valley Nos. 639 and 627 lead a freight at Sayre, Pennsylvania, on June 27, 1971. *Doug Eisele*

Highlights of Lehigh Valley's steam era include the pioneer 2-8-0, designed in 1865 by Lehigh & Mahanoy's master mechanic, Alexander Mitchell. He did this during L&M's merger, i.e. consolidation, with Lehigh Valley, thus the name Consolidation was universally applied to the 2-8-0 arrangement. An anthracite hauler, LV embraced camelback types beginning in the late nineteenth century and operated many fine examples of these engines. In the mid-1920s, LV was early to sample Alco's three-cylinder simple engines and ordered a small, but significant fleet of three-cylinder 4-8-2s. During the darkest days of the Great Depression, when tumbleweeds were blowing through the halls of Eddystone and Schenectady, LV spread a little joy by dividing an order for 10 new 4-8-4s between Baldwin and Alco. These were known as Wyomings (in reference to Pennsylvania anthracite fields served by LV), rather than as Northerns. Later in the decade, LV contracted industrial designer Otto Kuhler to streamline five older Pacific types for its passenger services.

Lehigh Valley took an early interest in diesels, and in the mid-1920s it bought several boxcabs and other formative switchers. Later, LV procured a variety of mass-produced switchers from Alco, Baldwin, and EMD. It divided road diesel purchases between Alco and EMD, beginning with EMD's FT in 1945 and following up with F3s and F7s after the war. From Alco, it bought PAs for passenger service and FA/FBs for freight. It had a few Alco RS-2/RS-3/RS11s, but on LV EMD road switchers were scarce. It had a pair of Budd RDCs for its Lehighton to Hazelton, Pennsylvania, passenger services. In 1964, LV returned to Alco for 12 low short hood C-420s and then in 1965 and 1967 for several orders of C-628s (including nine traded back to Alco from Monon). During 1971 and 1972, EMD supplied GP38/GP38-2s, while LV's last locomotives were a fleet of GE U23Bs, delivered in 1974.

▲ In 1939 and 1940, Lehigh Valley applied Otto Kuhler–styled shrouds to three K-6B Pacifics built by Alco in 1924, including No. 2097 pictured. LV applied similar shrouds to a pair of K-5 Pacifics in 1938. Diesels arrived en masse after World War II. *Robert A. Buck collection*

FACTS

LV CLASS K-6B

Builders: Alco and Lehigh Valley (Sayre Shops)

Wheel arrangement: 4-6-2

Type: Pacific

Cylinders: 25x28 in.

Drivers: 77 in.

Engine weight: 291,000 lbs.

Tractive effort: 41,534 lbs. (51,534 lbs. with booster; 51,934 lbs. for streamlined engines)

Intended service: express passenger

Overall production: 12

Years built: 1924–1926 (three streamlined 1939–1940)

Long Island Rail Road is one of America's most unusual railroads. Its twentieth-century development as one of the nation's premier commuter railroads was shaped by its close association with Pennsylvania Railroad. Both LIRR's electrics and late-era steam were of PRR designs. Its third-rail DC electrification was part of PRR's massive Pennsylvania Station development in Manhattan. Among the electrics assigned to LIRR were Class B boxcabs and DD1 side rodders, along with a vast fleet of owl-eye electric multiple units (MUs), which provided the largest share of LIRR's suburban services. Although LIRR sampled early Alco-GE-I-R and Westinghouse boxcab-style "oil electrics," it didn't begin dieselization of steam operations until after World War II. It focused postwar dieselization on purchases from Alco and Fairbanks-Morse. From Alco, it bought switchers and road switchers; from F-M, it bought road switchers and C-liners with the nonstandard B-A1A wheel arrangement. High-output F-M diesels seemed well suited to rapid start-stop requirements of suburban services. However, by the mid-1960s the F-Ms and early Alcos were nearly worn out, and it reequipped with a fleet of Alco C-420s with high short hoods (one of the few passenger service Century fleets). In the 1970s, LIRR developed a new strategy for its diesel services: buying secondhand Alco FA diesels. It converted these to push-pull control cabs that also supplied head-end power, while powering trains with standard freight diesels (including GP38-2s and MP15ACs) at the opposite end of the consist. This obviated the necessity and complexity of ordering a specialized fleet of passenger diesels. In the meantime, it replaced all of its PRR-era electric MUs with modern Metropolitan series MU cars (M1 and M3). In the late 1990s, it ordered two fleets of specialized low-clearance locomotives from EMD: dual-mode (diesel-electric/third-rail electric) DM30ACs and similar-looking DE30ACs that have no third-rail capability. Also in the 1990s, New York & Atlantic assumed operation of some LIRR EMD switchers when it took over freight operations. In the early 2000s, a fleet of Bombardier-built M-7 MUs replaced the M1s and M3s.

▼ Long Island Rail Road No. 401 was the second stock-built Alco-GE–Ingersoll Rand boxcab diesel-electric locomotive, following CNJ No. 1000. Built in 1925, it was rated at 600 horsepower and powered by a pair of I-R six-cylinder 300-horsepower diesels. In its early days, it was used in switching service in Brooklyn, New York. A similar locomotive, No. 402, was delivered in 1928. Both were scrapped in the early 1950s. *Photographer unknown, Solomon collection*

FACTS

LIRR CLASS AA-2 BOXCABS
   (no model designation)
Builders: Alco-GE-I-R
Wheel arrangement: B-B
Transmission: DC electric
Engines: two I-R 6-cylinder diesels
Total horsepower: 600
Weight: 203,000 lbs. (based on LIRR 401)
Tractive effort: 60,000 lbs.
Intended service: switching
Number operated: 2
Years built: 1925 and 1928

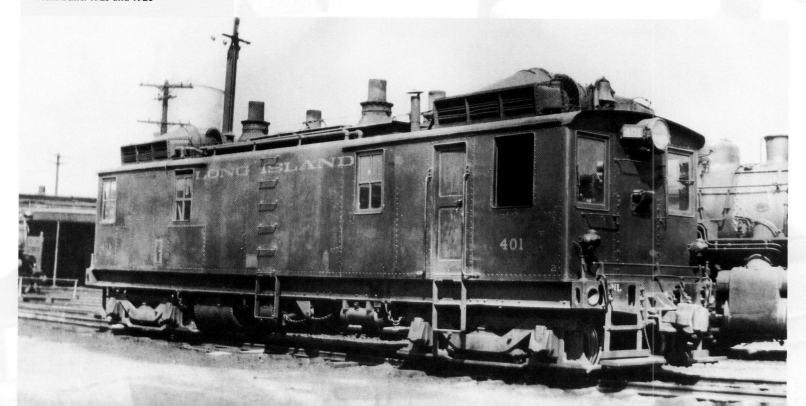

In 1951, LIRR bought five F-M CPA 24-5 C-liners for passenger work. F-M's CPA 24-5 was rated at 2,400 horsepower, compared with just 1,500 for EMD's F7A, sold at the same time; however, the powerful C-liner was bought by relatively few railroads. *Richard Jay Solomon*

Electro-Motive built 23 DE30AC-DMs for the LIRR in 1999. LIRR's dual-mode 500 series DE30AC-DMs are designed to work either from the onboard diesel or by drawing power from over-running 600 VDC third rail. They are rated at 3,000 horsepower, and the locomotives are specifically designed for service into New York's Penn Station with a low profiled body to accommodate the restrictive East River tunnel clearances. Similar looking are LIRR's 400 series DE30 locomotives, which are strictly diesel-electric units without third-rail capabilities. *Patrick Yough*

▲ The most modern passenger steam on Louisville & Nashville were 22 Baldwin-built L-1 Mountains delivered in two batches in 1926 and in 1930. These handsome machines were adequate, and L&N never bought 4-6-4 Hudsons or 4-8-4 Northerns, which were popular with other railroads. *Robert A. Buck collection*

Dating from the early 1850s, Louisville & Nashville had connected its namesake cites by the end of the decade and gradually grew to connect points in central Appalachia with markets in the Deep South. It eventually reached Gulf Coast ports, including New Orleans, in the 1880s. Key to its freight business was intensive development in eastern Kentucky coal fields. Among lines controlled by L&N was the Western & Atlantic, which during the Civil War was famous as the subject of the Andrews' Raid in 1862 (in it, Northern spies captured the Rogers, Ketchum & Grosvenor–built 4-4-0 *General*). Although not part of L&N at that time, W&A's *General* remains the most famous locomotive associated with the L&N system. It is preserved at the Southern Museum of Civil War and Locomotive History at Kennesaw, Georgia.

L&N's steam roster was straightforward; it avoided compounds and didn't own any articulateds. Among its most unusual engines was a pair of Alco three-cylinder experimentals. L&N adopted the 2-8-2 Mikado during the World War I period. This type remained its standard freight locomotive for the next 30 years, while the Pacific was its standard passenger hauler (although it bought 22 Baldwin 4-8-2 Mountains between 1926 and 1930 for heavy passenger work). L&N sampled diesel switchers in the late 1930s, and in 1940 it bought 16 EMD E6s for through passenger services. World War II brought its final new steam: a fleet of heavy 2-8-4s built for coal service. L&N began dieselizing road freight operations in 1949 with large numbers of new EMD Fs and GPs and Alco RS and FA/FBs. Although an important EMD customer, L&N continued to buy Alco products through the 1960s, while becoming a significant General Electric customer, beginning with purchasing U25Bs and U25Cs, in 1963. In the 1970s, its new diesels were dominated by EMD switchers, GP38-2s and SD40-2s for road service, but it also bought some GE Dash 7 models. It was a key part of the Family Lines network in the 1970s; it melded into CSX's Seaboard System in the early 1980s and finally CSX Transportation in 1986.

▲ Louisville & Nashville GP30 No. 1070 works a local freight at Belleville, Illinois, on October 14, 1978. In the 1950s, L&N bought large numbers of EMD road switchers, and in 1962 and 1963 it bought 58 GP30s, No. 1000–1057. GP35s and SD35s followed in 1964 and 1965, numbered in the 1100 and 1200 series, respectively. However, GP30 No. 1070 was not part of L&N's original GP30 fleet; acquired later, it was built new for the Seaboard Air Line in 1963. *Scott Muskopf*

FACTS

EMD GP30
Wheel arrangement: B-B
Transmission: DC electric
Engine: 16-567D3
Horsepower: 2,250
Weight: 256,000 lbs.
Tractive effort: 64,000 lbs.
Intended service: road freight
Overall production: 908
Years built: 1961–1963

▶ In addition to locomotives bought new, L&N's fleet expanded through secondhand acquisitions as well as locomotives acquired through merger. It absorbed the Monon in 1971, and U23B No. 2702 was originally Monon No. 603. L&N was among the most enthusiastic buyers of GE diesels, acquiring many different models beginning in 1963. *Scott Muskopf*

FACTS

MEC CLASS C-3
Builder: Alco
Wheel arrangement: 4-6-2
Type: Pacific
Cylinders: 24x28 in.
Drivers: 73 in.
Engine weight: 272,000 lbs.
Tractive effort: 36,500 lbs.
Intended service: passenger
Year built: 1924

Maine Central's (MEC) relatively light traffic levels and lightweight infrastructure was less demanding than on more heavily industrialized roads. In the nineteenth century, the 4-4-0 was perfectly adequate for its needs, and as the twentieth century dawned, MEC remained content ordering new 4-4-0s and 4-6-0s. In 1907, MEC adopted the Pacific for passenger service, acquiring 27 of this popular type by 1924. Last built and best known was No. 470; this engine was preserved and is now displayed adjacent to Waterville Shops.

In 1910, MEC acquired larger locomotives for freight service, buying some 2-8-0s for road freights. And a few years later, four former Boston & Maine 2-6-6-2 Mallets, made redundant by B&M's recent Hoosac Tunnel electrification, joined MEC's fleet. In 1914, MEC adopted the 2-8-2 Mikado, and in the 1930s and early 1940s it inherited a few 2-10-2s from B&M, but its last new steam power and its only modern steam was a pair of very light Baldwin-built 4-6-4s for express passenger services. In 1935, MEC and B&M jointly operated an EMC-powered Budd-built stainless-steel streamliner; this initially worked as the Boston–Bangor *Flying Yankee*. MEC sampled a pair of Alco high-hood 600-horsepower switchers in 1939 and continued to buy Alco switchers over the next 15 years. After World War II, MEC dieselized with EMD's E7As for passenger service and F3s for freight. Then in the early 1950s, it added two pairs of EMD switchers and some GP7s. Alco road switchers included RS-2s, RS-3s, and two RS-11s. In 1966, MEC traded F3s back to EMD for new GP38s. Ten General Electric U18Bs were delivered in 1975—each assigned a historic name. Roster additions included some secondhand units. A fleet of former Louisville & Nashville GP7s joined those units bought new, while in the early 1980s, shortly before Guilford Transportation acquired MEC, it picked up 14 surplus former Rock Island GE U25Bs.

▲ Maine Central's late-era diesel scheme was this classic bright yellow with green lettering. On August 29, 1986, MEC's MAPO (Mattawaumkeag to Portland) passes Pittsfield, Maine, at 1:53 p.m. In the lead is GP38 No. 254. By this time, Guilford Transportation Industries was operating the railroad and had begun to paint locomotives in its charcoal gray and orange livery. *Brian Solomon*

◄ In 1980, Maine Central picked up 14 U25Bs from Rock Island after liquidation of Rock's assets. This was among the last active fleets of General Electric's pioneering high-horsepower domestic road switcher. In the mid-1980s, Maine Central and Boston & Maine operations were joined under the banner of Guilford Transportation, and on September 30, 1984, a mix of Boston & Maine and Maine Central units were photographed at Cheapside west of B&M's sprawling East Deerfield, Massachusetts, yard. *Brian Solomon*

47 MAINE EASTERN RAILROAD

Maine Eastern operates from Rockland west over 57 miles of the former Maine Central Rockland Branch to a connection with Pan Am Railways at Brunswick, Maine, as well as former Maine Central trackage on the old Lower Road to Augusta. Established in 2003 and affiliated with New Jersey–based Morristown & Erie, Maine Eastern has provided freight service and a seasonal scheduled passenger service with classic diesels and 1940s- and 1950s-era streamlined passenger cars. The Dragon Cement plant at Thomaston—New England's only cement factory—is the line's largest freight shipper. Cement is largely moved in pressurized cement cars and transported just a few miles east from Thomaston to a Rockland pier—serviced by a short branch—for trans loading into coastal barges. Locomotives are serviced in traditional fashion at Rockland's roundhouse (complete with working turntable). Most locomotives come from Morristown & Erie's pool.

Freight locomotives serving in Maine have included several Montreal Locomotive Works units: a former Canadian Pacific C-424 and a pair of former Canadian National M-420s, as well also some interesting EMD models. Excursion service was initiated in 2004 using a pair of former Amtrak F40PH-2s that still featured their Amtrak numbers—265 and 291—but were painted in ME's attractive livery: pine-tree green and cream with red and gold stripes. Built in 1977, these 3,000-horsepower locomotives had run up countless millions of miles in two decades of Amtrak long-distance service. These have since been supplanted by a pair of FL9s, originally built for New Haven and later serving Penn Central and Amtrak, which had undergone significant internal modifications during their Amtrak years. Morristown & Erie acquired all six of Amtrak's active FL9s fleet; however, since neither M&E nor ME have electrification, these former dual-mode diesel-electric/electrics no longer carry third-rail shoes.

▼ New Jersey's Morristown & Erie is affiliated with Maine Eastern. In August 2004, an Morristown & Erie former Canadian Pacific C-424 running long hood first leads Maine Eastern's cement shuttle train. This short consist of former Burlington pressurized cement hoppers runs a circuit between the Dragon Cement plant at Thomaston and the Rockland Pier. *Brian Solomon*

▲ Maine Eastern No. 489 is one of six former New Haven Railroad FL9s rebuilt by Amtrak at Beech Grove between 1990 and 1993. New equipment included a 16-645E prime mover and a Dash 2–style engineer's controls. In the late 1990s, Amtrak replaced its FL9s with dual-mode GE Genesis units. *Brian Solomon*

FACTS

EMD FL9

Wheel arrangement: B-A1A

Transmission: DC electric

Engine: 16-567C/16-567D1 (as built); 16-645E (Amtrak's six rebuilt units)

Horsepower: 1,750 (16-567C); 1,800 (16-567D1)*

Intended service: passenger service to New York City terminals

Overall production: 60

Years built: 1956 and 1960

*2,000-horsepower after Amtrak rebuilding with 16-645E and modern electrical system.

▲ Maine Eastern assigned this former Amtrak F40PH No. 265 to its excursion train in 2004. In more recent years, Maine Eastern's former Amtrak FL9s have worked its seasonally scheduled roundtrips between Rockland and Brunswick. *Brian Solomon*

48 MASSACHUSETTS BAY TRANSPORTATION AUTHORITY

▼ In the 1980s, MBTA acquired several secondhand GPs to work sets of unpowered RDCs. Former South Eastern Michigan Transportation Authority No. 905 was seen at Lowell, Massachusetts, on August 20, 1987. While the other SEMTA units were of Grand Trunk Western heritage, No. 905 was formerly a New Haven Railroad locomotive; it had been rebuilt as a GP10 by ICG's Paducah Shops and later found its way back to New England after nearly a decade in Michigan. *Brian Solomon*

In the mid-1970s, Boston-based Massachusetts Bay Transportation Authority (MBTA)—operator of Boston's bus, streetcars, and rapid transit—became involved in Boston area suburban passenger operations. Routes radiated north and west from the old Boston & Maine North Station, and south and west from South Station on the former New York Central's Boston & Albany and former New Haven Railroad lines—both railroads having melded into the ill-fated Penn Central system in the late 1960s. Instead of running trains itself, MBTA contracted suburban operations with established companies. Initially, most trains consisted of 1950s-era Budd-built self-propelled rail diesel cars (RDCs) bought by Boston & Maine, New Haven, and New York Central to replace conventional locomotive-hauled passenger trains. The RDC's reliability had declined, and after 1978 MBTA towed its RDC fleet with locomotives. Adding to its fleet of inherited B&M RDCs, MBTA acquired a rainbow collection of RDCs from other operators. In its early years, MBTA also ran some southside services with tired-looking former Penn Central E8As hauling former New Haven Railroad streamlined cars.

Between 1978 and 1981, MBTA bought a fleet of 18 F40PHs (after Amtrak, it was the second operator to buy EMD's successful passenger adaptation of the GP40-2). In 1978 and 1979, MBTA contracted Illinois Central Gulf's Paducah, Kentucky, shops to rebuild 19 former Gulf, Mobile & Ohio EMD F-units (18 F3As and a one F7A). These were redesignated

▲ MBTA's F40PH No. 1002 shoves past Tower A in Somerville on its final lap to Boston's North Station. Among MBTA's unusual practices is painting large road numbers on the tops of locomotives and cars that makes it possible to identify specific equipment from the air. MBTA No. 1002 was part of its original order for F40PHs delivered in 1978. *Brian Solomon*

◄ The evening rush is about to begin on August 8, 2011. MBTA F40PH-2Cs idle at Boston's South Station. Locomotive No. 1052 on the right is dressed in a special livery to celebrate the reopening of the Greenbush Line— a former New Haven Railroad branch that had lost regular service in the 1950s. MBTA's later F40PH models, designated F40PH-2Cs, were 8 feet, 1 inch longer than the originals in order to accommodate auxiliary HEP equipment. *Brian Solomon*

▲ In August 1989, MBTA FP10 No. 1151 approaches North Station with the inbound Lowell train. This was one of a few locomotives treated to MBTA's short-lived maroon and silver livery. Originally Gulf, Mobile & Ohio F3A No. 884A, it was rebuilt by ICG's Paducah shops in 1978. It survives today as Adirondack Scenic Railroad No. 1502. *Brian Solomon*

as model FP10. Nos. 1100 to 1114 were equipped with auxiliary head-end power (HEP) generators, while unit Nos. 1150 to 1153 were initially fitted for steam heat, but later converted to HEP. In the mid-1980s, MBTA acquired a lone former BN GP9 and five GP10/GP18s from South Eastern Michigan Transportation Authority (after SEMTA discontinued Detroit-area suburban rail service). While these served in passenger services initially, in recent years surviving GPs have been retained primarily for maintenance trains.

In the 1990s, as MBTA expanded services and sold off its FP10 fleet, it bought additional F40 types. Where MBTA's original F40PHs were essentially built to Amtrak specifications and featured HEP working off the prime mover, later units, designated model F40PH-2C, provided HEP with an auxiliary generator powered by a small Cummins diesel. As a result the locomotives are 8 feet, 1 inch longer than the original F40PHs. Of these later units, 12 were built in 1992 and 1993 by Boise-based MK Rail using EMD primary components (Nos. 1025–1036) and have sometimes been described as F40PHM-2Cs. During 1996 and 1997, Alstom provided 25 GP40PH-2s (Nos. 1115–1139, sometimes described as GP40MCs) remanufactured from older freight-service types and equipped with North American Safety Cabs on road-switcher platforms. In 2010, MBTA announced an order for 20 new locomotives by MotivePower Industries, the Boise-based successor to MK Rail. Unlike earlier MotivePower diesels that used EMD primary components, the new engines will be built with primary components supplied by General Electric. As a stopgap to a motive power shortage, MBTA acquired a pair of Maryland Area Regional Commuter Rail (MARC) GP40WH-2s and a pair of surplus MP36PH-3Cs from Utah Transit. The latter streamlined locomotives carry Nos. 010 and 011. As with all MBTA locomotives, these display large roof-mounted road numbers—a peculiarity of the Boston fleet.

MBTA routes radiate out from Boston to suburban towns and cities. Looking like a vision from an apocalyptic futuristic Hollywood production, MBTA GP40PH-2, with "ghetto guard" grills over its windshields, charges into its station stop at Ayer, Massachusetts, on the old Boston & Maine. This consist is a far cry from B&M's 2-6-0s and splinter fleet that characterized suburban services of the early 1950s. *Brian Solomon*

FACTS

ALSTOM GP40PH-2
Wheel arrangement: B-B
Transmission: DC electric
Engine: 16-645E3
Horsepower: 3,000
Intended service: commuter
Number operated: 25
Years built: 1996–1997

▼ In 2010, to relieve a motive power shortage, MBTA acquired a pair of MP36-3Cs from Utah Transit. These 3,600-horsepower streamliners are the most powerful in MBTA's fleet and accelerate noticeably faster with heavy rush-hour trains than older models do. MBTA No. 010 basks under the sodium lights at the Worcester Layover Facility in October 2011. *Brian Solomon*

Massachusetts Central began in the 1970s as a homegrown effort to serve the vestiges of Boston & Maine's Central Massachusetts route in Ware. In 1979, the railroad assumed operations of the remaining 25 miles of the former Boston & Albany Ware River Branch between Palmer and South Barre. Mass Central initiated operations with a Whitcomb 44-tonner center cab. This was soon joined by former Southern Railway NW5 No. 2100, and this locomotive has remained on the roster ever since. However, unlike some small railroads that have used the same locomotives for decades, Mass Central has had a revolving fleet. In the mid-1980s, it benefited from Santa Fe's disposition of its CF7 fleet, acquiring Santa Fe No. 2443, which served the line for a decade. It also operated former Conrail GP No. 7015 for a few years, and in the early 1990s it acquired two former Milwaukee Road GP9s (Nos. 957 and 960). Milwaukee had a lowered short hood design and made other modifications as part of an upgrade program that resulted in an alteration to the model designation. Mass Central has retained No. 960 dressed in a retro livery inspired by the Delaware & Hudson's lightening stripe. In the 1990s, privately owned Alcos affiliated with the line included former Maryland & Delaware Alco RS-1 No. 21, primarily used for passenger excursions, and four former Burlington Northern Alco Centuries, two of which were painted for Mass Central—C-424 No. 4243 and C-425 No. 4264. Privately owned former Alaska Railroad F7A No. 1508 worked the line for a few years in the mid-1990s. Other locomotives have served the line, including GP9s of various lineages.

▼ EMD NW5 No. 2100 remains Mass Central's most iconic locomotive. Through the multitudes of Mass Central motive power changes, old No. 2100 has survived—although through years of rebuilding and modification very few of its factory-original components remain. In March 2009, it leads a short northward freight near Ware. *Brian Solomon*

FACTS

EMD NW5

Wheel arrangement: B-B

Transmission: DC electric

Engine: 12-567B

Horsepower: 1,000

Intended service: road switcher

Overall production: 13

Years built: 1946–1947

▲ Former Burlington Northern Alco C-424 No. 4243 served Mass Central for several years in the 1990s. It is seen working the Conrail interchange in Palmer, Massachusetts, on May 21, 1997. *Brian Solomon*

◄ In the late 1970s, Mass Central began switching operations on former Boston & Maine trackage at Ware, Massachusetts, using this Whitcomb 44-ton center-cab diesel. Whitcomb was a Rochelle, Illinois–based small locomotive builder, affiliated with Baldwin. *Brian Solomon*

50 METRA

▶ Metra operates one of the most intensive diesel-powered commuter services in North America. The latest model addition to its passenger fleet is the MP36PH-3S built by Boise's MotivePower Industries, which introduced a new look and paint livery to Chicago suburban services. The MP36PH-3S's 16-645F diesel produces a classic EMD engine roar. *Brian Solomon*

▲ Since the late 1980s, the F40PH has been the most common locomotive in Metra's fleet. This rooftop view offers a comparison between the standard F40PH-2 (left) and Metra's unusual variation designated F40PHM-2 (right), noted for a peculiar cab variation similar to that first applied to the pair of experimental F69PH-AC three-phase AC-traction test beds (built in 1989 and assigned to Amtrak). *Brian Solomon*

Metra is the trade name for the Northeast Illinois Regional Commuter Railroad, an organization that began as the Regional Transportation Authority in 1973 to assist and coordinate passenger rail transport in greater Chicago. In the 1980s, it moved into operations, and initially RTA-operated locomotives and equipment were inherited or leased from traditional Chicago-area railroads. Its locomotives included 10 EMD F7As from Chicago & North Western; dozens of EMD E-units from C&NW, Milwaukee Road, and Burlington Northern; and 15 EMD F40Cs acquired through a regional public agency for service on Milwaukee Road. The F40Cs, Nos. 600–614, were the last heritage units in regular passenger service. These had been primarily assigned to trains working northward from Union Station on former Milwaukee Road lines. In the mid-2000s, following arrival of new MotivePower Industries units (see facing page), most F40Cs were withdrawn from service; however, a couple were retained. Between 1977 and 1989, RTA/Metra bought 85 EMD F40PH-2s, Nos. 100–184; followed in 1991 and 1992 by 30 F40PHM-2s (a variation of the F40PH-2 with an unusual cab profile), Nos. 185–214. In 2003 and 2004, Metra bought a fleet of MotivePower Industries streamlined MPXpress model MP36PH-3Ss, Nos. 401–427. These employ a static inverter driven by the prime mover for head-end power (HEP) instead of an auxiliary diesel, as used by most MPXpress models. Metra has also operated a few secondhand EMD switchers for maintenance trains and yard work. Service on former Illinois Central electrified lines is provided by bi-level electric multiple units variously built by St. Louis Car Company, Bombardier, and Nippon-Sharyo.

◄ Unique to Chicago suburban services were 15 F40Cs bought in 1974 from EMD by regional agencies and assigned to Milwaukee Road. EMD's F40C was similar to the SDP40F bought by Amtrak for long-distance passenger work, except it was built with head-end electrical equipment instead of steam generators. Metra No. 614 roars passed Canal Street with a northward afternoon commuter train in June 2004. *Brian Solomon*

FACTS

EMD F40C

Wheel arrangement: C-C

Transmission: DC electric

Engine: 16-645E3

Horsepower: 3,200

Intended service: commuter service

Number operated: 15

Year built: 1974

161

51 METROLINK

os Angeles–area Southern California Regional Rail Authority was formed in 1991 as joint authority representing five participating counties. It negotiated arrangements for acquisition of railway lines and/or trackage rights from freight railroads. In 1992, it initiated Metrolink passenger services, most of which radiate from the historic Los Angeles Union Passenger Terminal (now called Los Angeles Union Station). One exception is the Inland Empire–Orange County Line that runs from San Bernardino/Riverside and then down the old Santa Fe Fourth District to Oceanside. Metrolink had an unusually short startup time, so to get its services up and running, it looked to simplify operations and aimed to emulate existing successful suburban services. It was modeled on Toronto's GO Transit—deemed among the most effective in North America—and so adopted General Motors Electro Motive Division's F59PHs (a road-switcher model featuring a wide-nose safety cab developed for GO in the 1980s) and Bombardier-built bi-level cars that offered high-capacity transport with low-level platforms. EMD supplied 23 F59PHs during 1992 and 1993 (Nos. 851–873). EMD's adaptation of the F59PH into the streamlined F59PHi for Amtrak California services encouraged Metrolink to acquire 14 of this type between 1995 and 2001 (Nos. 874–887). MotivePower Industries MP36PH-3Cs (Nos. 888–902) were acquired in 2008 and 2009. In addition, at least one secondhand F40PH-2 has appeared in Metrolink paint. As with most contemporary North American suburban passenger operations, Metrolink's trains operate in push-pull configuration with the locomotive at one end and a control cab at the other. Following the disastrous head-on Chatsworth accident in September 2008, Metrolink opted to redesign of its control cabs to insure better crashworthiness.

▼ On June 5, 2008, Metrolink F59PH No. 854 leads borrowed Sounder cars at Burbank, California, on the former Southern Pacific Coast Line. The 3,000-horsepower F59PH used most of the same equipment as a freight locomotive but tailored to commuter services. *Brian Solomon*

FACTS

EMD F59PH

Wheel arrangement: B-B

Transmission: DC electric

Engine: 12-710G

Horsepower: 3,000

Intended service: suburban passenger

Overall production: 83

Years built: 1988–1994

▲ The F59PH has been the backbone of Metrolink's diesel fleet for two decades. These work in push-pull fashion with Bombardier lentil-shaped bi-level cars on the sprawling Metrolink network, which includes service on the former Santa Fe Surf Line south from Los Angeles Union Station to Oceanside, California. Metrolink No. 860 shoves through San Clemente on a mild Saturday morning. *Brian Solomon*

◄ EMD's introduction of its streamlined F59PHI effectively ended production of the F59PH. Despite decidedly different appearances, the two models share the same essential equipment. The modern-looking F59PHI seems appropriate for Metrolink since EMD adapted the F59PH to meet California's strict emission requirements. *Brian Solomon*

Metro-North was established as a commuter rail subsidiary of New York's Metropolitan Transportation Authority in 1983 to assume operation of suburban services when Conrail exited its commuter rail business in New York and Connecticut. Primary routes operate north and east from Grand Central in Manhattan on historic New Haven Railroad and New York Central lines; in addition, Metro-North works with NJ Transit to provide service to Port Jervis, New York, from Hoboken, New Jersey. The Connecticut Department of Transportation works with Metro-North on Connecticut services and supplies some locomotives and equipment.

Principle routes are electrified, and most of MN's trains operate with electric multiple units. Services beyond the reach of electrification, including branch lines, are operated with push-pull equipment with locomotives on the north end. In addition, locomotives are required for switching and work train services. Metro-North began operations with a fleet of former New Haven Railroad FL9s as its primary passenger fleet. These dual-mode EMD F-units were equipped with third-rail shoes for operation to Grand Central. However, engineers report that the FL9s were underpowered when working as electrics. Furthermore, electric equipment didn't always function as intended, requiring use of diesel power to keep trains moving. The FL9s seemed to have nine lives. Many were rebuilt at least once, with a few lingering in service decades longer than most F-units. The first rebuilt were four units owned by the Connecticut Department of Transportation, sent to Chrome Crankshaft (operating at the former Rock Island shops at Silvis, Illinois), which modernized them while retaining most essential equipment. Later, locomotives received more substantial work; the American subsidiary of ASEA–Brown Boveri, ABB-Traction completely remanufactured 10 units with state-of-the-art three-phase traction

▼ On June 27, 1997, Metro-North FL9-AC No. 2042 shoves a Grand Central–bound train on the Hudson Line near Manitou, New York. This was one of seven FL9-ACs (Nos. 2040–2046) rebuilt by ABB Traction for Metro-North and known colloquially as Starships. Upgrading included a 710G engine and modern three-phase alternating-current traction system. *Brian Solomon*

◀ Both types of Metro-North's classic carbody units work back to back demonstrating the difference in length between an FP10 and an FL9. In the lead is Metro-North No. 413 (a former MBTA FP10 rebuilt from a Gulf, Mobile & Ohio F3A); trailing is MNR FL9 No. 2007, one of two FL9s painted similarly to MN's modern GE Genesis dual-mode units. *Brian Solomon*

◀ Among the locomotives used to haul Metro-North trains are those owned by the Connecticut Department of Transportation and painted in the classic McGinnis-style New Haven Railroad livery. CDOT owns four GE dual-mode Genesis (model P32AC-DM) units, Nos. 228 to 231. *Brian Solomon*

FACTS

GE P32AC-DM GENESIS

Wheel arrangement: B-A1A

Transmission: three-phase AC electric

Engine: 7FDL12

Horsepower: 3,200

Intended service: Grand Central–based suburban service

Number operated: 31

Years built: 1997–2001

technology and retained very little original F-unit machinery. In their last days, FL9s worked branch-line service—sans third-rail shoe—finishing up in February 2009.

In 1992, MN acquired four FP10s from Massachusetts Bay Transportation Authority, assigning these to branch services. These had been remanufactured in the 1970s by Illinois Central Gulf's Paducah shops from Gulf, Mobile & Ohio F-units. In its first decade, Metro-North operated seven former Conrail B23-7s; although primarily used in work train service, they also worked Croton–Harmon to Poughkeepsie, New York, shuttle trains. These left the roster in 1994, sent to work on Burlington Northern. These were replaced by six 2,000-horsepower GP35Rs rebuilt by Conrail. Metro-North assigned three former Niagara Junction E10B electrics to switching work in third-rail territory. A small fleet

of GP40FH-2s (remanufactured for passenger service by MK Rail from GP40s) and four former Amtrak F40PHs worked Port Jervis services operated by NJ Transit.

Between 1997 and 2001, Metro-North acquired a fleet of 31 P32AC-DMs—a specialized dual-mode variation of General Electric's Genesis line—to succeed the FL9s. Like the FL9, the P32AC-DM is both powered by a diesel engine and can draw power from trackside direct-current third rail using retractable third-rail shoes. The last four P32AC-DMs are owned by CDOT and painted in the 1950's New Haven livery. Beginning in 2008, Metro-North and CDOT bought Brookville BL20GH road-switcher diesels for branch-line and shuttle services beyond the third-rail territory. These are powered with a V-12 MTU–Detroit Diesel 12V4000 engine rated at 2,250 horsepower, while an auxiliary Caterpillar diesel generates head-end electrical power.

▼ Metropolitan series electric multiple units were the standard passenger vehicle on Metro-North electrified lines for more than three decades. In November 1999, Grand Central–bound multiple units pass Milford, Connecticut. M2, M4, and M6 series cars served the New Haven line. Modern M8 series cars were entering service in 2011 and 2012 to replace older cars. *Brian Solomon*

▲ Metro-North and CDOT have bought Brookville's model BL20GH, a modern passenger diesel in traditional road-switcher configuration and powered by a V12 MTU-Detroit Diesel rated at 2,250 horsepower. Head-end electrical power is generated from an auxiliary Caterpillar diesel. CDOT's units are painted in a New Haven Railroad–inspired scheme. *Patrick Yough*

FACTS

BROOKVILLE BL20GH

Wheel arrangement: B-B

Transmission: DC electric

Engine: V-12 MTU–Detroit Diesel
    12V4000

Horsepower: 2,250

Intended service: branch-line passenger

Year built: 2008

◀ A colorful lineup of dual-mode locomotives at Metro-North's former New York Central Harmon Shops finds CDOT New Haven–painted FL9M No. 2027 on the left, Metro-North GE Genesis P32AC-DM No. 212 in its as-delivered silver and blue at the center, and the latest Metro-North diesel scheme on P32AC-DM 203 on the right. *Patrick Yough*

MINNEAPOLIS, ST. PAUL & SAULT STE. MARIE RAILROAD

▼ Mountain type No. 4009 was one of 10 Class N-20s built by Alco for Soo Line in 1926. The first four were assigned to Minneapolis, St. Paul & Sault Ste. Marie; the remaining six, including No. 4009, were assigned to Wisconsin Central. It was seen at Minneapolis on June 26, 1953. Note the small "W.C." below the road number on the cab. An additional eight N-20s were built by Alco in 1928, followed by three more erected at Soo's Shoreham Shops in 1930. *John E. Pickett collection*

FACTS

SOO CLASS N-20*
Wheel arrangement: 4-8-2
Builders: Alco and Soo Line
   (Shoreham Shops)
Type: Mountain
Cylinders: 27x30 in.
Drivers: 69 in.
Engine weight: 342,000 lbs.
Tractive effort: 53,900 lbs.
Intended service: heavy freight
   and passenger
Overall production: 18 (Alco) and
   3 (Soo Line)
Years built: 1926–1930
*Specifications based on the later
   Alco-built engines (Nos. 4010–4017).

The Minneapolis, St. Paul & Sault Ste. Marie Railroad was formed in 1888 from lines that principally connected its namesake cities. Key to the line was the Canadian Pacific connection at Sault Ste. Marie, twin gateway communities of the same name on both sides of the border waterway between Ontario and Michigan's Upper Peninsula. CP acquired control of the railroad in the 1890s. Expansion over the next two decades included control of Wisconsin Central in 1909, providing a route to Chicago. The line was also closely affiliated with Duluth, South Shore & Atlantic. In 1961, MStP&SSM, WC, and DSS&A were merged into a company officially called the Soo Line Railroad.

Soo Line was largely a flatland railroad, and its steam locomotive fleet was pretty straightforward. Although it bought a large number of Alco cross compounds early in the twentieth century, these were soon converted to simple operation. Passenger trains were largely hauled by 4-6-0s and 4-6-2s, but the railroad also owned 15 4-4-2 Atlantics. Freights were primarily worked by eight coupled types, with Soo gradually accumulating a large number of 2-8-0s and 2-8-2s and some 4-8-2s between 1926 and 1930. Soo Line essentially ignored efforts by other lines to improve efficiency through innovations such Mallet articulateds, three-cylinder simples, and most of the Superpower types introduced in the 1920s. The exception was Soo's final steam power: four Lima 4-8-4s, Class O-20, that were assigned to fast freight on the competitive Chicago–Twin Cities route. Soo's steam exhibited a handsome utility. Later, as the railroad converted to diesel, it was generous in preserving examples of its steam power, and many locomotives were displayed in town parks along its lines.

Despite its comparatively old steam fleet, and having dabbled with a few switchers in the 1930s, Soo didn't begin serious dieselization until the late 1940s. Once it began the process, it completed the task quickly; by 1955, steam was done. Rather than standardize on a few common types, it approached diesel acquisition like a kid in candy shop. Soo and

▲ Soo's last and finest steam power units were its four Lima 4-8-4s built in 1938 for fast freight service. This was one of the smallest 4-8-4 fleets. Soo No. 5001 was a handsome engine. Here, it catches the sun in Minneapolis, Minnesota, on May 21, 1948. *John E. Picket collection*

◄ The thrill of the steam-to-diesel transition period was the incredible variety and combinations of motive power. On June 23, 1953, Soo No. 2380 (the lone Alco RSC-3 assigned to Wisconsin Central) and Class H-3 Pacific No. 730 team up to move freight at Neenah, Wisconsin. We can delight at the photographer's wisdom to chase the train on this well-oiled gravel road. *John E. Pickett collection*

FACTS

ALCO RSC-3*

Wheel arrangement: A1A-A1A

Transmission: DC electric

Engine: 12-244

Horsepower: 1,600

Weight: 251,100 lbs.

Tractive effort: 41,850 lbs.

Intended service: light-axle load road switcher

Overall production: 19

Years built: 1950–1952

*Specifications based on Soo No. 2380.

▲ Soo maintained the tradition of the mixed train into the diesel era. On June 1, 1961, F7A 2224-A leads mixed train No. 57 at Manistique, Michigan. Built in 1950, this was one of many F-units on Soo's roster. A few Fs served until the early 1980s, and some have been preserved. *Richard Jay Solomon*

its affiliates sampled small batches of many different models. Soo bought switchers from all major builders, including one GE 44-ton center cab. Its Duluth, South Shore & Atlantic was partial to Alco and Baldwin, taking a number of RS-1s and several Baldwin six-motor models. The most unusual were four massive DT6-6-2000 center-cab transfer units rated at 2,000 horsepower each.

Soo itself sampled a few Baldwin four motors, but preferred Alco and EMD products. From Alco, it bought RS-1s, lightweight RSC-2/RSC-3s that rode on A1A trucks, and a small fleet of FA/FB road units. EMD supplied F3/F7/FP7s, GP7/GP9s, and SD9s. In the 1960s, on trade from some RSC-2s, Alco supplied a pair of 2,400-horsepower RS-27s known as the Dolly Sisters, while EMD provided a succession of high-horsepower models: GP30s, GP35s, and GP40s. It also sampled GE's high-horsepower offering, buying 10 six-motor U30Cs. Having experienced the variety of early dieselization, in the 1970s Soo took a conservative approach and stuck with EMD standard models, buying SD40-2s and GP38-2s. Soo's fleet was melded with Milwaukee Road's as result of their 1985 merger, resulting in an influx of various types, mostly from EMD. In the late 1980s, Soo bought an SD60 fleet, including five SD60Ms that featured the early safety cab arrangement with a three-piece windshield. From the 1990s, Soo's fleet was gradually integrated with that of its parent, Canadian Pacific.

On January 13, 1994, a pair of former Milwaukee Road MP15ACs works cab-first toward Pigs Eye Yard, St. Paul, Minnesota. The second unit still wears Milwaukee paint. Soo's 1985 merger with Milwaukee resulted in adding several new locomotive types to its fleet. *Brian Solomon*

In the 1970s, Soo took a conservative approach toward diesel acquisition, ordering EMD's most common models, such as the SD40-2. Two are pictured here on November 26, 1993, in St. Paul, Minnesota, along with a former Milwaukee Road MP15AC. *Brian Solomon*

54 MISSOURI PACIFIC RAILROAD

Missouri Pacific's steam roster was made up largely of standard types, yet there were a variety of interesting and noteworthy engines. This included 4-6-2s built by Alco Brooks in 1902, deemed among the earliest examples of the Pacific type, and the first in the United States to use a radial trailing truck (which set an important precedent in the development of American passenger steam). In the 1920s, MP sampled a pair of Alco three-cylinder simple engines, but it didn't have much luck with them. In the early 1940s, MP's shops transformed its 25 Lima-built 2-8-4 Berkshires into impressive-looking 4-8-4s, while another 15 4-8-4s were built for MP by Baldwin in 1943. MP sampled diesels early. In addition to various switchers, in 1939 it bought a pair of EMD E3s, and during World War II it bought a small fleet of FTs. After the war, it bought more Es and Fs, along with Alco FA and PAs. Diesels were styled in a stunning blue and light gray livery for service on its streamlined *Eagles* styled by Raymond Loewy. Unique to MP was the 1,000-horsepower EMD passenger-type designated model AA (which used the unusual A1A-3 wheel arrangement). It bought numerous road switchers from Alco, Baldwin, and EMD, including a large fleet of GP18s delivered between 1960 and 1963, some of which rode on AAR trucks from Alco trades. MP's later diesel fleet was fairly typical for a Class I railroad, with large numbers of standard EMD four- and six-motor types, typified by GP38-2s and SD40-2s, along with the less-common GP15-1 and a moderate fleet of GP50s. It bought from GE as well, with U23Bs and U30Cs, and then in the late 1970s early 1980s, it added a sizable fleet of B23-7s. After merger with Union Pacific in 1982, some new locomotives, notably a fleet of GE C36-7s, were dressed in UP paint with MP lettering.

▼ Missouri Pacific's Lima-built 2-8-4 BK-63 Berkshires of 1930 were unusually handsome locomotives. MPs 25 Lima 2-8-4s (Nos. 1901–1925) spent their early days based in Texas, although later some regularly worked its Eastern Division between Kansas City and St. Louis. It also had five Alco-built 2-8-4s from 1928, originally assigned to its International–Great Northern affiliate. *Robert A. Buck collection*

▲ Missouri Pacific ordered Electro-Motive E4s distinctively styled with rows of porthole windows for service on its flashy *Eagles* passenger trains. The E3, as seen here, shared the same essential mechanical and electrical specifications as models E4, E5, and E6. In later years, MP bought similarly styled E7s, yet these featured the more standard bulldog nose typical of postwar E-units. *Robert A. Buck collection*

FACTS

EMC E3A

Wheel arrangement: A1A-A1A

Transmission: DC electric

Engines: two 12-567s

Total horsepower: 1,800

Weight: 321,000 lbs.

Tractive effort: 54,100 lbs.

Intended service: express passenger

Number operated: 2

Overall production: 16

Years built: 1939–1940

◄ A trio of Missouri Pacific SD40-2s lead a freight changing crew at Council Grove, Kansas. Setting an example as the epitome of modern freight railroading, MP standardized its diesel fleet in the mid-1970s, buying more than 300 SD40-2s, the most successful of EMD's Dash 2 line. *Scott Muskopf*

When Montana Rail Link was created in October 1987, it was Burlington Northern's largest and most significant regional spinoff. Operating 900 miles of former Northern Pacific lines in Montana and Idaho, MRL has handled local traffic while providing a corridor for overhead BN, and later BNSF, traffic. Typically, BNSF through traffic runs with BNSF locomotives, while MRL's fleet works on both its own local and through freights and provides helper service to BNSF through trains over Bozeman and Mullen Pass (and occasionally on Evaro Hill, east of Paradise, Montana). At startup, MRL acquired 52 locomotives from BN and then gradually assembled a fleet of secondhand EMDs acquired from a variety of sources. Switchers and GP9s are assigned to locals and yard work, while MRL's fleet of EMD six motors works in road freight service and helper duties, as well as in the railroad's lease fleet. While MRL's road fleet had consisted largely of older six-motor models, ranging from 1950s-era SD9s and early 1960s SD35s (powered by the turbocharged 16-cylinder 567), to more modern models such SD40-2s, its emphasis turned to models powered by EMD's 20-cylinder 645 engine (SD45s, SDP45s, SD45-2s), along with three former BN F45s. By the late 1980s, EMD's 645 engine had fallen out of favor on many railroads as a result of higher fuel consumption and greater maintenance cost. Yet for MRL, these locomotives offered 3,600 horsepower with relatively low investment. Toward the end of 2004, MRL announced an order for 16 new EMD SD70ACes to reduce its reliance on older models. Delivered in summer of 2005, these were MRL's first brand-new locomotives and have been typically assigned to road freights and helper services.

▼ Montana Rail Link crosses the Continental Divide via the former Northern Pacific line over Mullen Pass. Weather variances at high altitude may find it cloudy one minute and sunny the next. On July 9, 1994, MRL's daily westward freight from Missoula, Montana, to Sand Point, Idaho, has reached the skyline trestle led by SD40 No. 218, high-hood SD35 No. 701, and SD40 No. 200, with a four-unit manned midtrain helper assisting. *Brian Solomon*

FACTS

EMD SD35

Wheel arrangement: C-C

Transmission: DC electric

Engine: 16-567D3A

Horsepower: 2,500

Intended service: heavy freight

Number operated: 5

Overall production: 360

Years built: 1964–1966

◀ Manned midtrain helpers were common on heavy trains crossing Mullen Pass. On July 9, 1994, an eclectic combination of 20-cylinder EMDs catches a blast of sun as they roar westward. In addition to a pair of SD45-2s and an SD45 is one of three former BN F45s briefly owned by Wisconsin & Southern before coming to MRL. *Brian Solomon*

▼ In July 1991, a Montana Rail Link local works at Missoula with GP9 No. 108. MRL's EMD fleet included a variety of first-generation units, including the four-motor GP9 and its larger six-motor cousin, the SD9. Many of MRL's GPs came from Burlington Northern; this one was built for BN predecessor Great Northern. *Brian Solomon*

56 NAPA VALLEY WINE TRAIN

Since September 1989, Napa Valley Wine Train (NVWT) has provided a neo-retro culinary-based rail-excursion service over portions of the former Southern Pacific branch line through its namesake valley. The train serves as the venue for an experience aimed to capture the spirit of the golden age of railway travel without emulating any specific historic prototype. Most of the cars are Pullman heavy weights built for Northern Pacific and survived into the modern era in service on the Rio Grande Ski Train. NVWT's primary locomotives are four FPA-4s built by Montreal Locomotive Works for Canadian National during 1958 and 1959. Based on Alco's FA freight model, the FPA series was a passenger model and originally equipped with a steam generator to supply heat. Where the Alco FA/FB freight units were powered by the troubled 244 diesel, the FPA-4 featured Alco's more reliable 251 engine. Canada's VIA Rail inherited CN's FPA-4s in the late 1970s, assigning them to its long-distance services on eastern routes until the mid- to late 1980s, when they were retired in favor of new F40PH-2s. NVWT's four units are Nos. 70 to 73 and painted in burgundy and gold—wine-inspired hues that match the colors of the excursion train. Between 1999 and 2008, the locomotives were converted to burn-compressed natural gas instead of diesel oil as part of an experiment to reduce greenhouse emissions. NVWT also operates an Alco RS-11 road switcher, No. 62, and a GE 65-ton switcher, No. 52.

◀ A Napa Valley Wine Train engineer boards FPA-4 No. 72 at St. Helena, California, for the return run to Napa. Napa's four former VIA Rail FPA-4s are painted in a tasteful livery that incorporate wine-inspired shades intended to convey the elegance of classic railway travel, yet has no specific historic connotation. *Brian Solomon*

FACTS

Montreal Locomotive Works FPA-4

Wheel arrangement: B-B

Transmission: DC electric

Engine: 12-251B

Horsepower: 1,800

Intended service: passenger

Overall production: 36

Years built: 1958–1959

◀ A pair of FPA-4s chortles in low revs while leading the Napa Valley Wine Train afternoon excursion on March 30, 1990. Although similar to the once-common Alco FA, MLW's FPA-4 was strictly built for the Canadian market. Only in the 1980s, when VIA Rail sold off its fleet, did FPA-4s migrate to new owners south of the border. *Brian Solomon*

▼ For 23 years, these classic Montreal-built diesels have plied the rails in California's Napa Valley. In recent years, Napa Valley's FPA-4s have been adapted to burn compressed natural gas instead of traditional diesel oil to reduce greenhouse emissions. *Adam Pizante*

In February 1995, New England Central (reporting marks NECR) assumed 366 miles of operation from Canadian National's Central Vermont Railway. Initially, NECR largely relied on a dozen GP38s in an attractive yellow and blue livery with matched sets of GP38s standard on most NECR freights. However, these engines couldn't meet all of the railroad's needs, and in the mid-1990s, NECR acquired a few secondhand EMD GP40s and SD40s. NECR's original GP38 fleet was painted by Conrail at Altoona prior to delivery, but more recent locomotives added to NECR's roster have straggled in the paint of former owners. Adding to the mix of NECR locomotives have been those from sister operation, Connecticut Southern Railroad (reporting marks CSOR), formed in 1996 to assume Conrail's operations between Springfield, Massachusetts, and New Haven, Connecticut. Following the breakup of Conrail in 1999, CSOR locomotives have been common on NECR freights. RailTex operations, including those of NECR and CSOR, were acquired in February 2000 by short-line conglomerate Rail America, which resulted in locomotives from other Rail America properties frequenting NECR freights. In 2007, Fortress Investment Group, which also owns Florida East Coast, acquired Rail America, and since 2008 FEC GP40-2s and SD40-2s have also been regulars in NECR's operating pool. In recent years, a former Southern Railway SW1500, now CSOR No. 2340—known to crews as the black rat because of its all-black livery—has been a common sight working NECR's local freights based at Palmer, Massachusetts, and elsewhere on the line. While a few of the original NECR GP38s survive, they are less common on the railroad then a decade ago.

▼ In their first few years, GP38s were a New England Central mainstay. Originally, these were numbered in the 9500 series, but in the late 1990s they were renumbered in the 3800 series to reflect their model type. Now more than 42 years old, NECR's GP38s are as antique as were Central Vermont's Alco 2-8-0s in their final years.
Brian Solomon

FACTS

EMD GP38
Wheel arrangement: B-B
Transmission: DC electric
Engine: 16-645E
Horsepower: 2,000
Intended service: general purpose
Number operated: 12 (1995)
Years built: 1966–1971

New England Central GP38s are classics. With a conventional cab, Blomberg trucks, and a 16-645 diesel aspirated with a traditional Roots blower, these locomotives embody the looks and sounds of EMD's peak production. *Brian Solomon*

SD40-2 No. 722 has worked New England Central lines since 2008. Until late 2011, it carried Florida East Coast reporting marks, and it still wears Union Pacific armour yellow (that tells of its heritage), but it is now proudly lettered for New England Central. It sits quietly in the snow at Palmer, Massachusetts, on January 21, 2012. *Brian Solomon*

NJ Transit officially assumed operation of suburban passenger services in New Jersey on January 1, 1983, by which time some locomotives owned by New Jersey Department of Transportation had already been wearing NJT paint or NJDOT markings for a few years. Its heavy-rail services used six historic (pre-Conrail) railways and are focused on the New York City commuter market. While today NJT has a modern locomotive fleet, it began operations with the most eclectic collections of equipment operated by a North American commuter line.

Although the present locomotive fleet has been largely purchased new since 1987, NJT's specialized locomotive requirements means that it still has one of the most unusual and diverse fleets of any contemporary commuter railroad. Yet many trains on its core electrified routes are provided with a fleet of more than 425 electric multiple units, some more than 30 decades old. Its original ragtag fleet had diverse heritage; EMD E-units worked New York & Long Branch services, where they were exchanged at South Amboy for venerable former PRR GG1 electrics for the run to and from Penn Station. NJT's 13 GG1s made their final runs in October 1983. One locomotive, No. 4877, had been repainted into classic PRR Tuscan with gold stripes. No. 4876 was famous for its role in the January 15, 1953, Washington Terminal runaway, which had earned a front-page photo in most major newspapers. Trains on the former Central Railroad of New Jersey (including Newark–Long Branch runs) were operated with former CNJ passenger service GP40Ps and GP7s. Former Erie Lackawanna routes from Hoboken were served with 32 General Electric U34CHs, a six-motor U-boat type similar to the freight service U36C but equipped with an HEP generator to supply heat and lighting. A small fleet of Chicago & North Western F-units briefly augmented Hoboken services. A small fleet of Budd RDCs were assigned to some Port Jervis runs.

During the mid-1980s, NJT bought a variety of second-hand, remanufactured, and new locomotives to replace the

◀ NJ Transit began operations with an inherited fleet of worn-out locomotives, including more than two dozen E8As, such as No. 4328 pictured at South Amboy, New Jersey, in October 1982. E-units took over from GG1s at South Amboy for the non-electrified run to Bay Head Junction, much in the same manner as they had previously under Conrail, Penn Central, and the Pennsylvania Railroad. *Brian Solomon*

▲ Erie Lackawanna's 32 U34CH diesels were paid for by the New Jersey Department of Transportation and were assigned to commuter runs out of Hoboken Terminal, a practice that continued under NJ Transit. GE's U34CH was similar to the freight U36C, but with provision for passenger-car heating and lighting. NJT No. 4157 is pictured under the shed at Hoboken on October 10, 1992. *Brian Solomon*

FACTS

GE U34CH

Wheel arrangement: C-C

Transmission: DC electric

Engine: 7FDL-16

Horsepower: 3,430

Intended service: suburban passenger

Number operated: 32

Overall production: 32

Years built: 1970–1973

◀ NJ Transit's ALP44 is derived from the Swedish Rc6 and was built by ABB and its successor Adtranz. By comparison Amtrak's older AEM-7 was derived from the Rc4 model that predated the Rc6 by several years. *Brian Solomon*

FACTS

ADTRANZ–DAIMLER CHRYSLER RAIL SYSTEMS ALP-46

Wheel arrangement: B-B
Horsepower: 8,000*
Engine weight: 204,000 lbs.*
Tractive effort: 71,000 lbs.
Intended service: suburban passenger
Overall production: 29 (original order, plus 36 ALP46As)
Years built: 2001–2003 (original order only)

*Based on original order.

▲ NJ Transit F40PH No. 4120 meets Amtrak AEM-7 at speed on the North East Corridor near Hunter Tower in Newark, New Jersey, in 1986. *Brian Solomon*

majority of its inherited equipment. Ten Amtrak E60CPs were acquired to replace the GG1s, but operated for only a few years. New ALP-44 electrics built by ABB began arriving in 1990, and more were delivered in 1995 and 1997. The ALP-44 was a Swedish Rc6 electric derivative, similar to the AEM-7 (used by Amtrak). NJT's diesel acquisitions included a variety of EMD and EMD-derived 3,000-horsepower four-motor types, including 17 new EMD F40PHs (later rebuilt with auxiliary HEP supply in place of HEP powered by the prime mover) and GP40FH-2s (an unusual model remanufactured in 1987 and 1988 by MK Rail using retired freight service GP40s and cowls from BN F45s). In the early 1990s, it bought rebuilt former Conrail GP40s, redesignated as GP40PH-2Bs.

European design has influenced its most recent locomotives. Between 2001 and 2003, NJT took delivery of 29 extremely powerful ALP46 electrics, which were derived from contemporary European electric designs and built domestically by Bombardier. During 2005, Alstom supplied 33 4,200-horsepower diesel-electrics designated PL42-ACs that combined a European three-phase AC-traction system with a variation of the EMD-designed 710 diesel. In 2008, NJT approved the purchase of 26 dual-mode overhead electrics/diesel-electrics from Bombardier, designated ALP-45DP—the first modern overhead-electric dual-mode locomotives in the United States (similar engines have been also been ordered for Montreal's suburban services).

Alstom assembled New Jersey Transit's 33 PL42-ACs at the former Erie Railroad shops in Hornell, New York. The modern diesels are seen working push-pull bi-level sets on the former Central Railroad of New Jersey at Cranford. These locomotives are a far cry from CNJ's camelbacks that performed these same duties into the early 1950s.
Patrick Yough

59 NEW YORK CENTRAL SYSTEM

▲ Most famous of all New York Central engines was No. 999. As built in 1893, this locomotive was equipped with 86-inch drivers (among the tallest ever used by a North American steam locomotive) and lettered for the *Empire State Express*. Its staged speed run of May 10, 1893, made news all across the nation. In 1899, it was rebuilt with 70-inch driving wheels; since 1962, it has been an exhibit at the Chicago Museum of Science and Industry. *Solomon collection*

In the 1860s and 1870s, Cornelius Vanderbilt assembled a network of railroads that developed into the New York Central System, one of the busiest and most powerful lines in the eastern United States. It became known as the Water Level Route because its main line between New York City and Chicago had a low-grade profile following rivers and the Great Lakes. While the railroad benefited from easy grades, its early construction had produced a restrictive loading gauge that limited locomotive size. Exceptionally heavy traffic through America's industrial heartland required New York Central to expand the Water Level main line to four tracks, while it bought up parallel lines, such as the New York, West Shore & Buffalo, to quell competition and provide additional capacity. New York Central System operated one of America's largest locomotive fleets; its locomotives were exceptionally refined, and several classes have been deemed among the finest steam locomotives to work U.S. rails.

In 1893, New York Central & Hudson River Railroad staged a speed run under the direction of George H. Daniels, Central's general passenger agent (and unofficial chief publicity stunt coordinator), with a specially designed 4-4-0 No. 999, with uncommonly tall drivers. On May 10, with engineer Charles Hogan at the throttle, No. 999 sprinted west toward Buffalo with a special section of the *Empire State Express*. On a downgrade tangent near Corfu, New York, Hogan opened the throttle wide; to passengers on board telegraph poles along the line blurred by like a picket fence, and those timing the train claimed it hit 112.5 miles per hour. It was the fastest any locomotive anywhere had sped until that time. Without any verifiable evidence, newspapers around the nation reported the feat as fact, bringing fame to New York Central and its locomotives.

The 4-4-0 had been the staple of Central's passenger fleet since the mid-nineteenth century. But as Central's

FACTS

NYC CLASS J-1d

Builder: Alco

Wheel arrangement: 4-6-4

Type: Hudson

Cylinders: 25x28 in.

Drivers: 79 in.

Engine weight: 353,000 lbs.

Tractive effort: 42,300 lbs.

Intended service: express passenger

Years built: 1929–1930

trains grew longer and heavier, it moved to more capable types. The 4-4-2 Atlantic enjoyed a short reign, but it was soon usurped by the more powerful 4-6-2 Pacific, a type Central was early to embrace. Its first five 4-6-2s, Class KG, were built by Schenectady in 1903. Passenger traffic was growing, while the switch from wooden-bodied passenger cars to all steel during the early twentieth century necessitated substantially more power. Over the next 20 years, Central bought various classes of 4-6-2s to haul its Great Steel Fleet—as its long-distance service came to be known.

In the roaring twenties, Central was the penultimate American passenger road, and its burgeoning passenger traffic demanded even more powerful engines. To meet this need, New York Central worked with Alco in design of the Class J-1 4-6-4, the first of which emerged in February 1927. Central was the first to adopt this wheel arrangement, and the type was called the Hudson in honor of the river Central followed from New York to Albany. Compact, well proportioned, efficient, and extraordinarily

capable, New York Central's Hudson was one of the greatest of all American steam engines. In the 1930s, NYC's 4-6-4 was further refined, resulting in perfection of the type in the form of the J-3 class. Several of these were built with stylish shrouds designed by Henry Dreyfuss for service on the 1938 streamlined *Twentieth Century Limited*. Meanwhile, at the same time as Central's Hudsons were being built, the 4-8-4 Northern type was developed for Northern Pacific and other lines. Although New York Central initially refrained from this arrangement (except for an experimental three-cylinder locomotive built in 1930), at the end of the steam era it worked with Alco to refine the 4-8-4 and produced one of the finest examples of the type, known as its Class S Niagara. These were among the last steam locomotives built in the United States and set the standard in performance and availability for rival diesels in both freight and passenger service. Yet this was only one part of Central's steam story.

▶ On June 20, 1949, New York Central L-3a No. 3012
charges eastward through Warren, Massachusetts,
with a press run for the new Budd-streamlined *New
England States Limited* (Chicago to Boston). Orders for
65 L-3 4-8-2s were divided by Lima and Alco between
1940 and 1942. *Robert A. Buck*

Central's freight service had been largely the domain of eight-coupled types. In the late nineteenth century, the Class G 2-8-0 arrangement was standard. Then in 1912, Central adopted the 2-8-2 in large numbers, an arrangement that culminated in 1922 with the Lima-designed H-10 Super Mikado, a milestone locomotive that preceded development of Lima's Super Power in mid-1920s. By 1926, Central had acquired 300 H-10s, built by both Lima and Alco. In 1916, Central took delivery of another eight-coupled type, its first Class L-1 4-8-2, known not as a Mountain but as a Mohawk. Central continued to acquire 4-8-2s for the next two and half decades, and its later Mohawks, Class L-3s and L-4s, were dual-service engines. Central's Boston & Albany line made famous Lima's groundbreaking Super Power 2-8-4 Berkshires, a type built in three subclasses between 1926 and 1930 (see chapter 9). Unusual among Central's freight haulers were a few Pacifics, used for fast freight, especially perishable traffic.

Following a catastrophic wreck on the approach to Grand Central in 1902, Central was compelled to electrify its New York Terminal operations. Working with GE, it pioneered electric locomotive development and selected an under-running third rail for its New York lines. Its Class S motors were capable of 80 miles per hour. These were later supplemented by more powerful Class T motors for passenger work, and Class Q and R motors for freight service. In 1910, NYC electrified Michigan Central's Detroit River Tunnels with under-running third rail served by R-1 motors, and in the late 1920s, Central wired its Cleveland Union Terminal operation, acquiring General Electric–built Class P motors for

◄ New York Central called its 4-8-2s Mohawks rather than Mountains. Yet on September 28, 1947, NYC L-2A No. 2712 and Boston & Albany A-1a Berkshire No. 1400 pause for water at West Brookfield, Massachusetts, having crossed the rugged B&A Berkshire grade with an eastward freight. During World War II, NYC loaned some Mohawks to power-tight B&A; a few stayed until the end of steam. *Robert A. Buck*

FACTS

NYC CLASS L-2a

Builder: Alco

Wheel arrangement: 4-8-2

Type: Mohawk

Cylinders: 27x30 in.

Drivers: 69 in.

Engine weight: 364,000 lbs.

Tractive effort: 61,400 lbs.

Intended service: freight

Overall production: 100

Years built: 1925–1926

▲ New York Central T-2B No. 263 electric works a Grand Central–bound Harlem Division train passing Mott Haven Yard in the Bronx in the early 1960s. New York Central's third-rail electrification was necessary to comply with New York City's mandate to eliminate steam locomotives, a direct response to a disastrous fatal accident in the Park Avenue Tunnel in 1902 attributed to excessive locomotive smoke. *Richard Jay Solomon*

FACTS

NYC CLASS T-2B ELECTRIC

Builder: GE

Wheel arrangement: B-B+B-B

Horsepower: n/a

Engine weight: 267,500 lbs.

Tractive effort: 66,900 lbs.

Intended service: electric passenger

Overall production: 10

Year built: 1917

◄ General Electric remanufactured New York Central's P-2Bs in 1955 from Cleveland Union Terminal's P-1A overhead electrics. In July 1964, New York Central P-2B electric No. 237 works northward (timetable direction west) along the Hudson River near Riverdale, New York, with a passenger train bound from Grand Central toward Albany. In the distance is the famous George Washington Bridge. *Richard Jay Solomon*

▲ In the early 1950s, a pair of relatively new Alco PAs work the westward *New England States Limited* at West Brookfield, Massachusetts. Central had eight PA-1s, four PB-1s, seven PA-2s, and one PB-2. All in all, these Alco passenger units were relatively rare compared with Central's E-unit fleet, which totaled 110 units, with most out lasting the PAs by a decade. *Warren St. George, Robert A. Buck collection*

▲ *New England States* was inaugurated in with EMD passenger-geared F3 diesels, but later it operated with E7/E8s. On May 20, 1952, an E7A/E7B with train No. 27 lead the westward *New England States* past the Warren crossovers (east of the Warren, Massachusetts, passenger station). A pair of 12-cylinder 567A diesels, generating 2,000 horsepower per unit, powered EMD's E7; the E7 was the best-selling passenger diesel of the immediate postwar period. *Robert A. Buck*

the job. After CUT's electrification was discontinued, the P motors were converted to third-rail operation and transferred to the New York City operations.

New York Central was a diesel pioneer; its fleet of Alco-GE tri-power diesel-battery electrics were acquired in the late 1920s for switching work in New York City and Boston, and it also tested one of the first prototype road diesels. Although it purchased a few commercially developed switchers in the 1930s, and sampled EMD's FTs during World War II, NYC didn't begin serious dieselization until a few years after the war. Initially, it favored Alco, and it ultimately bought 770 Alco diesels—making it one Alco's most loyal diesel patrons. These diesels included large numbers of switchers, road switchers, FA/FB road diesels, and a few PA/PBs for passenger work. It also bought diesels from all the other major builders, with EMD another favorite. While Alcos were preferred on its eastern lines, EMDs dominated on its western lines. With the move toward higher-horsepower second-generation models in the 1960s, New York Central bought General Electric's U25Bs and subsequent models, along with EMD's GP20s, GP30s, GP35s, and GP40s. It sampled Alco's C-430 with a fleet of 10 units, representing the bulk of production. Significantly in the 1960s, NYC only bought four-motor types, shunning the trend toward six-motor models. This changed in 1968 when it merged with longtime rival, Pennsylvania Railroad.

New York Central sampled several varieties of Fairbanks-Morse cab units, including both freight and passenger service Erie-builts (assembled by GE at Erie, Pennsylvania), and 1,600-, 2,000-, and 2,400-horsepower C-liner models. In 1954, a pair of F-M's 2,400-horsepower CPA 24-5 C-liners leads an eastward passenger train east of the Warren station. This train has overtaken a pair of Budd RDCs seen in the distance and is about to cross back to the normal eastward main line at the Warren Crossovers. *Robert A. Buck*

FACTS

F-M CPA-24-5 C-LINER

Wheel arrangement: B-A1A

Transmission: DC electric

Engine: 12-cylinder opposed-piston diesel

Horsepower: 2,400

Weight: 303,000–313,000 lbs.*

Tractive effort: 62,600 lbs. (starting)

Intended service: passenger

Number operated: 8

Year built: 1952

*Varies depending on source.

FACTS

NKP CLASS S, S-1, S-2, AND S-3

Builders: Alco and Lima

Wheel arrangement: 2-8-4

Type: Berkshire

Cylinders: 25x34 in.

Drivers: 69 in.

Engine weight: 440,800 lbs.*

Tractive effort: 64,100 lbs.*

Intended service: fast freight

Years built: 1934–1949

*Based on the S-2.

Steam on the Nickel Plate Road (NKP) was characterized by its famous Class S Berkshires. However, NKP was late to adopt the type; it had been content to rely on 2-8-0s until 1917, when it adopted the 2-8-2 as its standard freight engine and then embraced derivatives of USRA 2-8-2 designs during the 1920s. In the mid-1910s, NKP had become the nucleus of a transport empire managed by Van Sweringen brothers, and in the 1930s, NKP availed of the Van Sweringens' central advisory committee, which provided it with an exemplary 2-8-4 design. NKP ordered its first Class S Berkshires from Alco in 1934. These were well proportioned, exceptionally capable, and well suited to fast freight work. In the 1940s, NKP turned to Lima for repeat orders for 2-8-4s, culminating with 10 built in 1949—the last new steam to emerge from the innovative locomotive builder. Despite this late order for road steam, NKP had already begun buying diesel switchers from EMD, Alco, and Baldwin, along with a fleet of 11 Alco's PAs for passenger service. In the 1950s, it bought myriad road-switcher models from all major builders with the largest number coming from EMD in the form of GP7s, GP9s, and SD9s. Among its more unusual models were a small fleet of Alco RSD-12s, Baldwin AS-16s, F-M H-12-44s, and some Lima-Hamilton 1,200-horsepower LS-12s. Steam survived in road service longer than most roads, with the Class S Berkshires working until summer 1958. In 1960, NKP returned to EMD for GP18s, and then in 1962 it bought GP30s from EMD and RS-36s from Alco. Its last new diesel was a lone GP35 bought in 1964, shortly before merger with Norfolk & Western.

◄ On a crisp autumn afternoon, EMD GP9 No. 494 and Baldwin AS-16 No. 320 lead an eastward Nickel Plate Road freight in northeastern Ohio. In 1959 (after this photo was exposed), Nickel Plate contracted Alco to repower AS-16 Nos. 320 and 321 with Alco 16-251B diesel engines. Another pair of AS-16s were similarly repowered by EMD using 567 engines. *J. William Vigrass*

▼ Less well known than Nickel Plate's famous Berkshires were its eight 4-6-4s. On most railroads, Hudsons were strictly passenger locomotives. While Nickel Plate's 4-6-4 began as passenger engines, in later years these were assigned to universal service after Alco PA diesels displaced them from premier passenger assignments. Where No. 174 was built by Lima in 1929, Nickel Plate's first four 4-6-4s were Alco-built, delivered in 1927 shortly after New York Central's famous pioneers. *J. William Vigrass*

61 | NEW YORK, NEW HAVEN & HARTFORD RAILROAD

▲ This Alco-built R-1b Mountain type was almost nine years old when photographed at East Hartford, Connecticut, on September 16, 1934. It was similar to USRA-designed 4-8-2s built for New Haven, classed R-1. Unlike some railroads that bought 4-8-2s for heavy passenger service, New Haven bought 4-8-2s for freight. *Donald Shaw, Robert A. Buck collection*

▶ In 1938, New Haven had no shortage of steam locomotives at Readville, Massachusetts. Those on the near track were stored serviceable with their stacks capped, while the engines beyond were live. Star of the show was a brand-new streamlined I-5 at center right. While some New Haven steam operated into the 1950s, ultimately all of it was sent to scrap; not one engine was saved for preservation. *Photographer unknown, Robert A. Buck collection*

Steam

Pieced together in the nineteenth century from dozens of smaller roads, New York, New Haven & Hartford gradually absorbed most of its competitors to dominate its territory across southern New England. At the turn of the century, 4-4-0s were predominant passenger type, while 2-6-0s were standard freight power. New Haven enjoyed exceptionally dense traffic, and unlike many roads passenger business was equally as important as freight. In the early twentieth century, New Haven moved to Ten-Wheelers and sampled 4-4-2 Atlantics, before settling on the 4-6-2 Pacific as its new standard passenger engine. Best remembered were the 50 Class I-4 Pacifics built by Alco in 1916 that featured a prominent Elesco feed-water heater at the top of the smokebox. It was this fast type that worked express trains between Boston and New Haven, characterized by operation on New Haven's flagship *Merchants Limited*. In the second decade of the twentieth century, New Haven's Central New England affiliate bought a few 2-8-0s and a sampling of 2-8-2s. Although New Haven also bought a few 2-8-2s, for heavy freight operations it preferred 2-10-2s and 4-8-2 Mountains. In the 1920s, New Haven ordered several peculiar locomotives featuring the McClellon boiler that incorporated a nonconventional water-tube firebox. In addition, it sampled Alco's 0-8-0 and 4-8-2 three-cylinder designs. Its final steam locomotives were 10 Baldwin streamlined 4-6-4s, Class I-5, built in 1937. These were a pleasant contrast to the rest of New Haven's fleet; where much of New Haven's twentieth-century steam was awkward looking and lacked the refined balanced appearance of other roads, the I-5s were handsome machines and New England's only as-built streamlined steam.

▲ New Haven I-5 No. 1408 is starting out of New London having just made its scheduled station stop. The 10 conservatively streamlined Baldwin 4-6-4s were New Haven's last new steam power. Known as Shoreliners, these worked New Haven's busy Shoreline route between Boston's South Station and New Haven, Connecticut, where they were exchanged for electrics. *Photographer unknown, Robert A. Buck collection*

FACTS

NEW HAVEN CLASS I-5

Builder: Baldwin

Wheel arrangement: 4-6-4

Type: Shoreliner

Cylinders: 22x30 in.

Drivers: 80 in.

Engine weight: 365,300 lbs.

Tractive effort: 44,000 lbs.

Intended service: express passenger

Overall production: 10

Year built: 1937

Electrics

New Haven helped pioneer mainline electrification, experimentally electrifying several short-line segments in the 1890s as a prelude to the intensive overhead wiring of its busiest routes in the early twentieth century. Although it was well versed with DC electrification, New Haven opted for an 11,000-volt, 25-cycle, single-phase AC system for its mainline electrification because it offered economical power transmission and lower electrical equipment cost for long extensions. AC service began between Stamford, Connecticut, and Woodlawn Junction, New York, in July 1907. (Woodlawn was the junction with New York Central's Harlem Line, and New Haven trains reached Grand Central on NYC using its under-running third rail). New Haven ultimately extended wires to its Connecticut namesake, branches to Danbury and New Canaan, on its parallel New York, Westchester & Boston affiliate, and via the Hell Gate Bridge to New York Penn Station, along with freight routes.

The majority of its early electrics were Baldwin-Westinghouse products, including 41 Class EP-1s built between 1906 and 1908; 36 freight locomotives, Class EF-1s built during 1912 and 1913; and 27 large passenger electrics with an 1-C-1+1-C-1 Class EP-2 built between 1919 and 1927. In the 1930s, General Electric supplied 10 70-mile-per-hour EP-3 articulated boxcabs and six technically similar but streamlined EP-4s. GE and Baldwin-Westinghouse split an order for 10 EF-3 freight streamliners in 1943. Its last new Electric locomotives were GE's Class EP-5 streamlined, double-ended ignitron rectifier passenger locomotives that featured a front end similar to Alco's FA diesel, but without the headlight nose grill. In the early 1960s, New Haven bought Norfolk & Western's (former Virginian) surplus EL-C ignitron rectifiers for freight service, and it classed these as its EF-4s.

◀ Built between 1919 and 1928, New Haven's EP-2 electrics had six powered axles. Each axle was powered by a dual set of traction motors that engaged a geared hollow quill, which surrounded the axle. The quill was connected to the wheel spokes by a flexible spring-cup system. This awkward arrangement was necessary because of the enormous size of traction motors and the desire to minimize unsprung weight on driving axles while distributing torque evenly. *Richard Jay Solomon*

FACTS

NHRR EP-2

Builder: Baldwin-Westinghouse

Electric supply: single-phase AC (11,000 volts and 25 cycle)

Wheel arrangement: 1-C-1+1-C-1

Horsepower: 2,000 (continuous)

Engine weight: 358,000 lbs.

Tractive effort: 47,500 lbs. (starting)

Intended service: passenger

Overall production: 27

Years built: 1919–1927

Diesels

New Haven adopted diesels early and followed a distinctly, but atypical path toward dieselization. In the 1930s, it bought diesel switchers both from General Electric–Ingersoll Rand and Alco. For passenger service, it bought a unique double-ended three-piece streamliner from Goodyear-Zeppelin, assigned as *The Comet* to fast Boston–Providence services. More significant was its fleet of 60 Alco DL109s delivered between 1941 and 1945. This represented the bulk of Alco's DL109 production and was one of the first American dual-service road-diesel fleets. After the war, New Haven returned to Alco for the bulk of its new diesels, buying switchers, road switchers, FA/FB road freight diesels, and PA passenger models. In the early 1950s, it bought Fairbanks-Morse H-16-44 road switchers and a fleet of streamlined 2,400-horsepower C-liners (that used the unusual B-A1A wheel arrangement).

▶ New Haven's 10 C-424s were among its last new locomotives and only served that line for five years before it was melded into the vast Penn Central system. Former New Haven C-424 was at PC's Dewitt Yard, near Syracuse, New York, on August 2, 1970. The locomotive survives as Livonia, Avon & Lakeville No. 425 and based at Lakeville, New York. *Doug Eisele*

▶ New Haven had a fleet of Alco switchers with an unusual low-profile cab, necessary for working in industrial areas and electrified territory with tight vertical clearance. Alco S-1 No. 0944 was inside New Haven's Van Nest Shops, in the Bronx, New York, on March 22, 1958. *Richard Jay Solomon*

◀ After World War II, New Haven bought 27 Alco PA diesels for through passenger services. Initially, these were painted in the same elegant Pullman green and gold striping that adorned New Haven's heavy electrics. In later years, some were adorned in the brash McGinnis-era livery introduced with the EP-5 electrics and popularized on the FL9s. New Haven PA No. 0778 and a DL109 are teamed up at Worcester, Massachusetts, in February 1950. *George C. Corey*

▲ New Haven's 60 DL109s represented most of Alco's production of its pioneer road diesel. While these primarily worked passenger services on the 157-mile run from Boston's South Station to New Haven, they also routinely worked north from New Haven to Springfield. Although often pictured in passenger service, they were intended for dual service. Bob Buck caught No. 0749 at Springfield, Massachusetts, on September 2, 1946. *Robert A. Buck*

FACTS

ALCO DL109

Wheel arrangement: A1A-A1A

Transmission: DC electric

Engines: two 6-539T diesels

Total horsepower: 2,000

Total weight: 357,500 lbs.

Tractive effort: 59,500 lbs.

Intended service: dual service

Number operated: 60

Overall production: 74 (DL109 and similar)

Years built: 1940–1945

Notably missing from New Haven's fleet were diesels from both Baldwin and America's dominant diesel producer, EMD. This changed in 1956, when New Haven took delivery of EMD's SW1200s, GP9s, and its first dual-mode FL9s. Unique to New Haven, the FL9 was the final development of EMD's successful F-unit, an adaptation of the F9 Series designed to work off New York–area third rail as well as its on-board 567 diesel. Like the F-M cabs, the FL9 used the B-A1A wheel arrangement. From Baldwin, it took a pair of diesel-hydraulic power cars. More FL9s were delivered in 1960, bringing the fleet to 60 units and concluding F-unit production. In 1964, New Haven returned to Alco one last time with an order for 10 C425s, and during 1964 and 1965 it took delivery of 26 GE U25Bs. In 1969, Penn Central absorbed New Haven.

▼ New York, Ontario & Western's difficult history, unusual motive power, illusive operations, and early demise have lent to an undeniable mystique. On June 10, 1947, slightly less than a decade before NYO&W concluded operations, 2-8-0 Mother Hubbard No. 213 leads a freight at Mayfield, Pennsylvania. *John E. Pickett collection*

FACTS

NYO&W CLASS P
Builder: Alco
Wheel arrangement: 2-8-0
Type: Mother Hubbard
Cylinders: 21x32 in.
Drivers: 55 in.
Engine weight: 200,000 lbs.
Tractive effort: 44,300 lbs.
Intended service: freight
Overall production: 20
Years built: 1900–1904

New York, Ontario & Western was formed in 1880 from the financial wreckage of New York & Oswego Midland. It connected Weehawken, New Jersey (opposite Manhattan), with Lake Ontario port, Oswego, New York, with several branches. The most significant reached to the Scranton, Pennsylvania, anthracite fields. NYO&W began operations with 4-4-0s, 2-6-0s, and 2-8-0s inherited from NY&OM. In the 1890s, NYO&W began buying twin-cab camelback locomotives with Wooten fireboxes to burn anthracite, commonly known on NYO&W as Mother Hubbards. Ultimately, it operated camelbacks in 0-6-0, 2-6-0, 2-8-0, and 4-4-0 arrangements, some surviving until the end of steam operations in the late 1940s. It continued to invest in bituminous-burning single cab types as well, and among its largest engines were 12 Class X 2-10-2s in 1915, known as Bull Moose, followed by 20 Class Y/Y-1/Y-2 4-8-2 Mountains built in several batches between 1922 and 1929, all Alco products. In the late 1930s, NYO&W's anthracite traffic collapsed, resulting in its bankruptcy. NYO&W was put in charge of a receiver who tried to save the line by cutting costs and improving operations; as a result, it dieselized early and installed centralized traffic control signaling. In 1941 and 1942, GE delivered five 44-ton center-cab switchers. In 1945, NYO&W acquired 18 EMD FT units based on Erie's positive experiences with this pioneering road type. Its last diesels were 21 EMD NW2 switchers and seven F3s, delivered in 1948. The valiant efforts to transform its operations into a bridge route failed, and in March 1957 NYO&W shut down. Its lines were salvaged for scrap, and most of its still relatively new diesels were sold to other lines.

NYO&W No. 245 was built as a Class U 2-6-0 in 1904; in 1924 it was rebuilt into a Class U-1 and survived until 1947 when it was sold for scrap. It's seen in happier days at Walton, New York, in 1938. NYO&W didn't follow up on the U-1, leaving the logical designation progression to be claimed by an American spy plane and later a famous Dublin rock band. *John E. Pickett collection*

On June 19, 1948, the paint was still fresh on F3A No. 503 when it led a short excursion at Carbondale, Pennsylvania. The Erie/Delaware & Hudson line can be seen below NYO&W's viaduct. After its anthracite traffic evaporated in the 1930s, NYO&W tried to redefine itself as a modern bridge line, but new diesels and centralized traffic control couldn't save the "Old and Weary." *John E. Pickett*

63 NEW YORK, SUSQUEHANNA & WESTERN RAILWAY

▲ In the early 1940s, New York, Susquehanna & Western's unusually antique steam fleet made the railroad an ideal candidate for dieselization. Two decades later, many of its original Alco switchers and RS-1 road switchers were still at work. NYS&W RS-1 No. 236 leads a one-car excursion in rural New Jersey on March 31, 1961. *Richard Jay Solomon*

New York, Susquehanna & Western was a northeastern maverick and bucked trends of eastern railroading, including avoiding inclusion in Conrail in 1976. In 1944, it was among the first railroads to achieve complete dieselization, largely with Alco S-2s and RS-1s and a handful of American Car & Foundry streamlined railcars. The RS-1s served in dual traffic, working both freights and Jersey City–Paterson-Butler (New Jersey) suburban runs. In 1962, NYS&W bought three new GP18s from EMD, and this fleet survived intact for 45 years. In 1980, Delaware Otsego, operator of several New York–based short lines, acquired the railroad. Under DO management, NYS&W expanded as Conrail retrenched from former Erie Lackawanna routes in the early 1980s. Among its new operations was the forwarding Delaware & Hudson double-stack container trains between Binghamton, New York, and Little Ferry, New Jersey, using haulage rights over Conrail. This required powerful road diesels, first with secondhand Alcos and later notably with former New York Central C-430s and former Burlington Northern 20-cylinder EMD SD45s and F45s. In 1988, it bought four new GE Dash 8-40Bs, temporarily augmented by another 20 units in 1989 when NYS&W served as designated operator of the bankrupt D&H (from 1988 to 1990). The second order of GEs was conveyed to CSX after D&H was acquired by Canadian Pacific. Over the next decade, NYS&W augmented its fleet with various secondhand EMD diesels, including a pair of former BN E9As for business and passenger train services. In the early 1990s, it acquired Chinese 2-8-2 No. 142 from Connecticut's Valley Railroad as an excursion engine. NYS&W's last new locomotives were a trio of EMD SD70Ms built in 1995.

▲ In 1962, New York, Susquehanna & Western received three new GP18s from General Motors' Electro-Motive Division. These were given even numbers—1800, 1802, and 1804—as had been NYS&W practice. NYS&W No. 1804 worked at North Hawthorn, New Jersey, in October 1963. Despite many changes to NYS&W and northeastern railroading, its GP18 fleet survived intact for more than four decades. *Richard Jay Solomon*

FACTS

EMD GP18

Wheel arrangement: B-B

Transmission: DC electric

Engine: 16-567D1

Horsepower: 1,800

Weight: 240,000 lbs.

Tractive effort: 73,200 lbs.

Intended service: general purpose

Years built: 1959–1963

◀ New York, Susquehanna & Western took delivery of four new Dash 8-40Bs built to Conrail specs for intermodal service in June 1988. That year, NYS&W was appointed designated operator of bankrupt Delaware & Hudson. With help from CSX, New York, Susquehanna & Western placed a second order for GE Dash 8-40Bs. These are seen at Buffalo, New York, in May 1989. *Brian Solomon*

203

◀ Just after 9 a.m. on July 31, 1958, one of N&W's famous Class A 2-6-6-4s crests the grade with a westward empty hopper train at Blue Ridge, Virginia; notice the extra water tender. With 43 engines, N&W was the largest user of the relatively obscure 2-6-6-4 arrangement. In the 1980s, N&W Class A No. 1218 was restored to service by Norfolk Southern as an excursion engine. *Richard Jay Solomon*

▶ Norfolk & Western continued to refine the Mallet compound decades after most railroads had given up on the concept. In the mid-1950s, N&W 2-8-8-2 Class Y-6 No. 2127 sails across a tall tower support-plate girder viaduct in Virginia's Shenandoah Valley. Although the railroad began dieselizing in 1954, the process wasn't completed until 1960, giving photographers ample time to capture big steam in action. *Jim Shaughnessy*

FACTS

N&W CLASS Y-6

Builder: N&W Roanoke Shops

Wheel arrangement: 2-8-8-2

Type: Mallet

Cylinders: 2 @ 25x39 in. ea.
or 2 @ 25x32 in. ea.

Drivers: 57 in.

Engine weight: 582,900 lbs.

Tractive effort: 152,200 lbs. (simple) or
126,838 lbs. (compound)

Intended service: drag freight

Overall production: 35 (Y-6), 16 (Y-6a),
and 30 (Y-6b)

Years built: 1936–1940 (Y-6), 1942 (Y-6a), and 1948–1952 (Y-6b)

Appalachian coal-hauler Norfolk & Western was famous for exceptional late-era steam locomotive refinement and its clinging to steam technology for a decade longer than most American railroads. Three classes of road locomotives defined N&W's final years of steam operations; most were built at the company's Roanoke, Virginia, shops. Its Class Y 2-8-8-2s for heavy drag service and road freight work were derived from the highly regarded USRA 2-8-8-2 design from the World War I era.

N&W's Class Y locomotives were anomalous in American practice because they perpetuated the Mallet compound (using a system of high-pressure and low-pressure cylinders to maximize efficiency) decades after most railroads had abandoned the concept. Its Y6s were enormously powerful at slow speeds. Working as a simple engine (high-pressure steam to all cylinders), these could deliver 152,200 pounds starting tractive effort; working as a compound, the figure was 126,838 pounds. The final development of this type was N&W's Y6b. Thirty were built at Roanoke between 1948 and 1952. For

FACTS

N&W CLASS J

Builder: N&W (Roanoke Shops)

Wheel arrangement: 4-8-4

Type: Northern

Cylinders: 27x32 in.

Drivers: 70 in.

Engine weight: 494,000 lbs.

Tractive effort: 73,000 lbs.

Intended service: express passenger

Overall production: 14

Years built: 1941–1950

fast freight, N&W developed its Class A 2-6-6-4s, a simple articulated type (all cylinders received high-pressure steam directly from the boiler). A total of 43 were built, giving N&W by far the largest number of the relatively unusual 2-6-6-4 arrangement. However, N&W's highest profile locomotives were its true thoroughbreds: the famous streamlined Class J 4-8-4s for passenger service. In addition to the Js, the railroad also applied similar streamlining to some older Class K 4-8-2s.

N&W's final new steam locomotives were Class S 0-8-0s for switching service. The last of these was completed in 1954, the year that N&W finally accepted the inevitability of dieselization. Its experiments with a single high-pressure coal-fired steam-electric turbine named *Jawn Henry*—after the legendary black laborer who raced against a steam hammer—couldn't match the overall cost efficiencies of modern diesels. Interestingly, prior to dieselization, N&W had discontinued its electric operations over Elkhorn mountain in favor of steam power.

N&W initially took a straightforward approach to dieselization and bought large numbers of standard EMD GP9s/GP18s and Alco RS-11s. It didn't buy new carbody units, although in the late 1950s it borrowed some E-units from Atlantic Coast Line and Richmond, Fredericksburg & Potomac to pinch-hit for Js. These diesels carried N&W

▼ Toward the end of the steam era, N&W borrowed E-units from Atlantic Coast Line and Richmond, Fredericksburg & Potomac to work passenger trains. These retained their owner's paint, but they were lettered for Norfolk & Western. Some of these Es are seen with one of N&W's Class S 0-8-0s at Bluefield in July 1958. *Richard Jay Solomon*

▲ In 1964, Alco built six C-424s for Wabash, delivered shortly before it was absorbed by Norfolk & Western (N&W Nos. 3900–3906). Wabash's followup order was delivered to N&W after the merger in the form of C-425s. N&W No. 1002 was among the Wabash-ordered C-425s delivered to N&W. Here it is seen at Buffalo, New York, on October 16, 1970. This was not the end to N&W's new Alcos. Alco built more C-425s, followed later by C-628s and C-630s. *Doug Eisele*

lettering. One element of N&W diesel operation ran contrary to American convention: it preferred locomotives with dual controls and so designated road switchers with long hoods as front and continued to order new locomotives with high short hoods for decades after the low short hood was the standard North American arrangement.

Mergers with Virginian, Nickel Plate Road, Wabash, and Pittsburgh & West Virginia resulted in an influx of model types to N&W's otherwise standardized fleet. Among the more unusual models to wear N&W paint were P&WV's, Virginian's, and Wabash's Fairbanks-Morse road switchers, including 2,400-horsepower Train Masters. N&W also briefly operated Virginian's electrics, but it discontinued overhead wire operations in favor of diesels, which better suited its operational patterns. Primarily, it used the Virginian route in one direction and its own line in the other. Virginian's relatively modern mercury-arc rectifiers were sold to New Haven Railroad. In its later years, N&W focused on standard models, ordering large numbers of EMD SD45s, GP38-2s, SD40-2s, and GE C30-7s.

In the diesel era, N&W was characterized for buying road switchers with dual controls and high short hoods. Although occasionally N&W dabbled with colors, most were painted black, the same as its freight steam. On May 6, 1980, N&W GP40 No. 1382 and GP9 No. 773 lead an eastward freight past semaphores at Farmdale Junction, Illinois. *George W. Kowanski*

Norfolk & Western was one of a few railroads to buy Alco's T-6 switcher, a type offered in the builder's final years. Only 57 units had been built by the time Alco ended domestic production in 1969. The 1,000-horsepower model was powered by a six-cylinder 251B diesel and shared styling introduced with the RSD-7 and RS-11 in the mid-1950s. N&W No. 14 wears fresh paint at Norfolk, Virginia, on September 5, 1982. *George W. Kowanski*

65 NORFOLK SOUTHERN RAILWAY

Norfolk Southern was the product of the 1982 merger between Norfolk & Western and Southern Railway. The line has operated many models inherited from its predecessors; it has also bought a variety of modern diesels, including several models unique to NS. It inherited Southern's interest in fuel-efficient, moderately powered, four-motor types, such as EMD's GP39X. NS was the sole buyer of EMD's GP59 (delivered in the late 1980s), which appears similar to the more common GP60. These were intended for high-horsepower applications, but instead of the 16-cylinder 710G rated at 3,800-horsepower (as on the GP60), the GP59 uses a conservatively rated 3,000-horsepower 12-cylinder 710G engine, making it roughly equivalent to the 1970s-era GP40-2. NS was the sole buyer of 45 Dash 8-32Bs, a 3,200-horsepower GE model delivered in late 1989 aimed at moderate power needs. In the 1980s, NS emphasized six-motor purchases by buying several types, including GE's C39-8s with the curved contoured cab—known to GE as Classics, as well as GE's more common C36-7 and EMD's SD50 and SD60 models.

Contrary to popular practice, in the 1990s NS continued to buy locomotives with conventional cabs; most other American railroads had adopted the modern safety cab as standard. Along these lines, NS was the *only* American railroad to order GE's freight service Dash 9s with the conventional cab style; all other lines bought Dash 9s with safety cab variations. Yet NS Dash 9-40C's cab is boxy and more crew-friendly than cabs found on the Classics. Also, while other Dash 9 buyers preferred high-output 4,400-horsepower models, NS Dash 9s were rated at just 4,000-horsepower—lowering maximum output saves fuel by curtailing locomotive performance in specific situations. In the late 1990s, NS finally bought GE's with safety cabs. Its Dash 9-40CWs are basically the same as General Electric's standard Dash 9-44CWs with the same frame, Hi-Ad trucks, a 16-cylinder 7-FDL engine, and 752AH-31 series traction motors; however, these are 4,000 horsepower rather than the standard figure of 4,400 horsepower.

▼ On July 31, 1987, a Norfolk Southern unit coal train led by C39-8 No. 8560 passes a variety of historic locomotives displayed at Roanoke, Virginia, for the annual National Railway Historical Society convention. General Electric's early Dash 8 models with contoured cabs and a transitional electrical system were known as Classics, and NS was the largest buyer of the C39-8 model. Initially, these were arranged with the long hood in the forward position. *George W. Kowanski*

◀ Norfolk Southern has continued to subletter locomotives for its component railroads, and GP38-2 No. 5172 has "SOU" for Southern Railway on its side. This is a high short hood unit, typical of Southern's late-era practice. In recent years, NS has been lowering the short hood when old locomotives like this are rebuilt. *Brian Solomon*

▼ High short hood diesels were trademarks of both Norfolk Southern predecessors, and numerous high-hood EMDs once worked NS rails. NS No. 3307, sublettered for Southern, works a local freight on the former Erie Railroad at Gang Mills, New York, in April 2004. Southern had 127 SD40-2s in its fleet in 1981; Norfolk & Western had 173. *Brian Solomon*

FACTS

GE DASH 9-40CW

Wheel arrangement: C-C

Transmission: DC electric

Engine: 7FDL-16

Horsepower: 4,000

Intended service: road freight

Years built: 1996–2005

Though GE's Dash 9 dominated NS purchases in the 1990s and early 2000s, since 2004 NS has focused on GE's Evolution series, initially taking preproduction units for road testing. Another peculiarity of GE's modern diesel fleet was its exclusive interest in traditional DC-traction models, ignoring the trend toward three-phase AC traction for heavy-haul applications that began at Burlington Northern in 1993. This changed in 2008, when NS sampled 24 GE ES44ACs. Not only are these AC-traction diesels, but also they feature additional ballast weight, allowing for exceptional tractive effort and dynamic braking power. Initially, NS assigned pairs of ES44ACs in helper assignments on its Pocahontas Division in Virginia and West Virginia that previously used three DC six-axle locomotives. No longer was NS wedded to DC traction, and in 2011 NS added EMD's SD70ACe model to its fleet.

In 1998 and 1999, NS and CSX divided Conrail's fleet and operations, adding many locomotives to their respective rosters. Conrail's last locomotives were actually ordered by CSX and Norfolk Southern and built to those railroads' specifications, but were delivered to Conrail; these included 2500 series SD70s built with the conventional cab and control stand favored by NS. Norfolk Southern has operated several variations of the SD70, both early- and late-era SD70Ms and the more modern SD70M-2 with its angular wide-cab designs. From Conrail, NS also inherited a few 5,000-horsepower SD80MACs, an AC-traction model only bought by Conrail, preceding NS's first new ACs by almost a decade. Former Conrail Dash 8-40CWs and SD60Ms/SD60Is added more North American wide cabs to the NS roster. One interesting application for the SD60Is has been on Pennsylvania Power & Light's Strawberry Ridge coal trains, where NS has assigned dedicated locomotive sets as result of the plant's rotary car dumper clearance restrictions. In addition to new locomotives, NS has rebuilt many former Conrail SD50s as SD40Es (The E infers "enhanced" and describes the modern electrical system that provides greater tractive effort than available from a conventional 1970s-era SD40-2.)

▲ Norfolk Southern SD40-2s, Nos. 3376 and 3374, are former Conrail units assigned to the Cresson, Pennsylvania, helper pool on the former Pennsylvania Railroad main line (operated by Conrail from 1976 to 1999). On a brisk November 2001 morning, the two units use their dynamic brakes to restrain a westward intermodal train passing Cassandra, Pennsylvania. *Brian Solomon*

◀ The foliage was near its autumnal peak on October 13, 2003, as Norfolk Southern SD50 No. 6522 passed the old searchlight signals at Nineveh, New York, on Canadian Pacific's Delaware & Hudson route. The SD50 was EMD's effort to extract 3,500 to 3,600 horsepower from the 16-645 block using the F series turbocharger. Although built in 1984 for NS, No. 6522 was one of seven SD50s assigned to Southern Railway subsidiary Central of Georgia. *Brian Solomon*

66 NORTHERN PACIFIC RAILWAY

▲ In the mid-1920s, Northern Pacific required a more powerful passenger locomotive and turned to Alco for a super Mountain type. Special requirements included the ability to burn low-grade Rosebud coal and to work very long runs. Alco's solution was the first 4-8-4. Among its unusual features were extended smokeboxes and very large ash pans. The first were built in late 1926 and delivered in early 1927. *Robert A. Buck collection*

Northern Pacific was the first northern transcontinental, connecting the Midwest with the Pacific Coast on August 22, 1883. Like the other western lines, its early operations were characterized by 4-4-0s, yet it soon adopted larger types. Notably, NP experimented with the 2-10-0 arrangement in helper service. By 1900, the 4-6-0 was among NP's standard engines. NP's choice of the new 2-8-2 Mikado for heavy freight service in 1904 set a national precedent. Its desire to burn low-yield Rosebud coal (procured from on-line mines) resulted in two significant types. In 1926, NP worked with Alco to build a better passenger engine; the result was the first 4-8-4 (named the Northern type in NP's honor, although many roads applied their own monikers). This was essentially an expansion of the 4-8-2; the additional trailing axle was necessary to support its abnormally large firebox and oversized ash pans. Then in 1928, NP worked with Alco to develop a massive simple articulated to work its Badlands grades east of Glendive, Montana. Alco produced the very first 2-8-8-4, named the Yellowstone type. Like the 4-8-4, it required a big firebox, but the Yellowstone's firebox was vast and large enough to host a banquet. Baldwin won the bid for NP's Yellowstone production, building 11 for NP. In the 1930s, NP ordered modern 4-8-4s and some impressive 4-6-6-4s.

NP didn't commit to total dieselization until 1954, although it began the process during World War II when it bought Alco and Baldwin switchers and EMD FTs. After the war, it ordered large numbers of EMD F-units while placing nominal orders for Alco and Baldwin road switchers. NP didn't order E-units or PAs, preferring Fs for passenger service. While it bought EMD GPs in the 1950s, it remained loyal to the F models longer than most lines. In the 1960s, NP bought high-horsepower six-motor diesels, including GE's U25C, U28C, and U33C, and EMD's SD45. NP merged with CB&Q and Great Northern to form Burlington Northern in 1970.

▲ Northern Pacific's later 4-8-4s were more gracefully proportioned than its pioneers. NP No. 2665 leads the first section of the *North Coast Limited*—NP's flagship passenger train (Chicago to Seattle). This was one of eight 4-8-4s, Class A-3, built by Baldwin in 1938. In 1944, NP locomotives consumed 1.4 billion gallons of water annually. *Robert A. Buck collection*

▲ Northern Pacific's 2-8-8-4 was designed to haul significantly heavier trains and simplify operations east of Glendive, Montana, an area famous for its rugged sawtooth profile. The locomotive required a phenomenally large firebox—the largest on any locomotive ever built—to burn NP's Rosebud coal. The prototype 2-8-8-4, No. 5000, was built by Alco, but NP's following order for 11 locomotives was awarded to Baldwin. *Robert A. Buck collection*

◄ In 1958, Northern Pacific train No. 26, the eastward *North Coast Limited* (Seattle to Chicago) led by an EMD F3A, waits at Pasco, Washington, as the Portland section of the train is switched into place. Northern Pacific preferred F-units for long-distance passenger trains. The four-axle F-unit was better suited to working NP's sinuous steeply graded lines than was EMD's E-unit with its six-axle A1A trucks. *Fred Matthews*

▲ On September 12, 1970, a pair of Penn Central E8s leads the westward *Duquesne* at MG Tower near Gallitzin, Pennsylvania. Passengers have just been treated to view of the magnificent Horseshoe Curve and continue to be serenaded by a quartet of 12-567 diesels laboring to bring them over the Eastern Continental Divide. *George W. Kowanski*

Penn Central was the unfortunate result of poorly planned merger of eastern giants Pennsylvania and New York Central Railroads in 1968 that included the financially destitute New Haven in 1969. While Penn Central is recalled as being one of the greatest financial debacles of its time—which contributed in the decision to create Amtrak in 1971 and Conrail in 1976, and the line is remembered for poor service, a badly maintained infrastructure, and a depressing paint scheme—one element of Penn Central that seems fascinating today was its motive power.

All three of its component railroads operated diverse and eclectic locomotive fleets, and combined they had by far the most interesting roster of locomotives in North America. For locomotive watchers, Penn Central offered an incredible variety of models. Not only did its fleet represent a virtual catalog selection of postwar models from Alco, EMD, and GE, but also PC's (and its predecessors') efforts at repowering locomotives produced some interesting blends of technology. Most numerous were repowered Alco RS-3s using EMD 567 engines from retired E-units. Work was largely performed at the former New York Central shops in DeWitt, New York, and the resulting locomotives were designated as RS-3Ms. To accommodate the larger engine, DeWitt built a crude boxy appendage atop the long hood. While necessary to protect the diesel within, this modification spoiled the well-balanced grace of Alco's road-switcher design. Similar re-powerings at Altoona shops lowered the engine mounts that produced a more tasteful result. PC also repowered a former Pennsylvania Railroad RSD-15 with an EMD engine, and this curious machine was semipermanently coupled with an RSD5 converted into a slug (with traction motors but no prime mover). The entire machine was numbered 6849 and assigned to hump service at DeWitt Yard.

▲ Penn Central inherited PRR's GG1 fleet and extended its territory to include the New Haven Railroad's electrified main line. GG1 No. 4870 wearing PC paint leads train No. 172, *Southern Crescent* (New Orleans to Boston), at Greenwich, Connecticut, in October 1972. The GG1s were steam-era machines and carried boilers to provide train heat. Evidence of this can be seen with the escaping steam from 4870's roof. *George W. Kowanski*

FACTS

PRR GG1 ELECTRIC

Builders: GE, Baldwin-Westinghouse, and PRR (Juniata Shops)

Wheel arrangement: 2-C+C-2

Horsepower: 4,620

Engine weight: 477,000

Tractive effort: n/a

Intended service: express passenger (some later geared for freight)

Overall production: 139 (including prototype)

Years built: 1934–1943

◀ Penn Central RS-3s Nos. 5329 and 5468 work a train of coal hoppers at Lackawanna, New York, on May 1, 1974. Alco's RS-3 was powered by the troubled 244 diesel. To extend the life of its RS-3s, PC opted to repower many of them using the more reliable 12-567 diesel taken from retired EMD E-units. Yet in this photo, both RS-3s remain as-built, with their 244s chortling loudly. *Bill Dechau, Doug Eisele collections*

FACTS

ALCO C-628

Wheel arrangement: C-C

Transmission: DC electric

Engine: 16-251C

Horsepower: 2,750

Intended service: road freight

Number operated: 15

Overall production: 135
(domestic units only)

Years built: 1963–1968

▲ Conrail's BA-2 passes Warren, Massachusetts, at 12:44 p.m. on February 6, 1977. Heavy snow at Buffalo had isolated New England routes, and the newly formed Conrail temporarily pressed older Alcos into road service. New Haven's 15 Alco RS-11s, Nos. 1400–1414, were renumbered as Penn Central Nos. 7660–7614. Alco's 1,800-horsepower RS-11 was built from 1956 to 1961. *Kenneth Buck*

Pennsylvania and New York Central had been America's first and second busiest passenger railroads, and after World War II both lines invested in large fleets of E7s and E8s. Combined, Penn Central had a vast sea of Es, many in relatively poor shape. With long-distance passenger services in sharp decline, PC assigned some Es to suburban services (as had its predecessors), while others were re-geared for fast freight work. Impressive consists of five or more Es could be found working priority mail trains on the former PRR main line, and these made for a really impressive show climbing around Horseshoe Curve west of Altoona.

When Amtrak was formed, it inherited a host of former PC E8s, many of which struggled along in PC black paint for more several years. PC also operated an impressive array of F-units. Most of the freight service Fs, including some former PRR FP7s built for passenger work, were concentrated on western lines, and they were maintained at the former New York Central shops at Collinwood, Ohio, near Cleveland. New Haven's 60-unit dual-mode FL9 fleet remained in the New York area to serve trains out of Grand Central, but the nature of their work changed under PC. Where New Haven had assigned FL9s largely to New York–Boston and New York–Springfield runs, PC gradually refocused the FL9s to suburban services and to some long-distance runs on the former New York Central Hudson Line. On the former New Haven route, it preferred to use E-units in non-electrified territory and electric locomotives under wire.

All three of PC's components had significant electrified territory and contributed electric locomotives (properly, but confusingly, described as "motors" by purists) to PC's fleet.

▲ In July 1970, Penn Central No. 4977, a former New Haven EP-5 electric, leads an eastbound train at Bridgeport, Connecticut. In the mid-1970s, PC assigned some of the EP-5s to freight service, by which time the 1950s-era rectifiers were nearly worn out. *George W. Kowanski*

◀ New York Central's first electrics were its General Electric–built S motors dating the early twentieth century. At 5:50 p.m. on September 7, 1969, Penn Central S-2 No. 4723 works train No. 72 (Delaware & Hudson train No. 34) running empty at Riverdale, New York, destined for Grand Central. By this late date, it was unusual to find a S motor out on the road; most of the surviving units were primarily used as switchers in third-rail territory. *George W. Kowanski*

From PRR, PC inherited the famous fleet of streamlined GG1s, plus relatively recent E44 freight motors and a handful of 1930s boxcabs. New York Central's third-rail fleet included a few ancient S motors, a few tired T motors, and former Cleveland Union Terminal P motors, some of which received fresh coats of PC black paint. From New Haven were the 10 GE-built streamlined EP-5s and a dozen former Virginian EL-C (EF-4 on New Haven, E33 on PC) freight motors. In addition, all three lines had substantial fleets of electric multiple units, including the recently debuted MP85 high-speed Metroliner cars.

▶ Eastward Penn Central freight MC-4-SU16 passes Sanborn, New York, on the former New York Central Falls Road (that connected Rochester and Niagara Falls) on June 13, 1970. In the lead is one of 10 former New York Central C-430s. Delivered by Alco in 1968, they were NYC's last new locomotives before the PC merger. *Doug Eisele*

▼ Pennsylvania Railroad's 20 General Electric U25Cs were built in 1965 and retained the same road numbers (Nos. 6500–6519) through both Penn Central and Conrail renumbering schemes. Penn Central No. 6510 is one of several U25Cs upgraded to U28C specifications. Still wearing PC paint, it was leading five GE units as it approached State Line Tunnel near Canaan, New York, with eastward Conrail freight NH-2 (Selkirk, New York, to New Haven, Connecticut) on August 18, 1977. *Kenneth Buck*

Among new locomotives added to PC's fleet were EMD's six-motor SD40s and SD45s and four-motor GP40s and GP38s. Its 35-unit order for SD38s was EMD's largest (only 50 were built in total), while numerous SW1500s were bought for yard work. PC was one of GE's best customers, and it bought the largest fleet of GE U33Bs (81 units, the majority of GE's production), as well as 24 U33Cs, 77 U23Bs, and 18 U23Cs (for yard service). When PC operations were conveyed to Conrail on April 1, 1976, its locomotives represented the lion's share of Conrail's fleet. And PC black diesels roamed the Conrail system well into the early 1980s.

▲ A black GE punctuates a pastoral winter scene at Warren, Massachusetts. Rolling westbound, PC-9 is led by a trio of U25Bs on January 17, 1976. Penn Central inherited GE U25Bs from all three of its predecessor roads, giving it the largest fleet of GE's pioneering high-horsepower road diesels. *Kenneth Buck*

Steam

▲ Refinement of PRR's E6s Atlantic was the topic of Frederick Westing's 1963 book, *Apex of the Atlantics.* Designed by PRR's Alfred W. Gibbs, the type was among PRR engines developed using the scientific method with the Altoona test plant. The E6s was capable of great speed and was believed to have exceeded 110 miles per hour on special runs. *Solomon collection*

The Pennsylvania Railroad embraced a scientific approach toward motive power development. It experimented with new technology, sampled new models, and made comparative tests of popular innovations, but it avoided wide-scale implementation of radical designs, shunned modern gadgetry, and opted for simple solutions in place of complexity. Key to this policy was its famed Juniata test plant at Altoona, Pennsylvania—considered America's first true locomotive laboratory. Once experimentation was concluded, PRR focused on mass production of successful standardized designs. PRR standardization avoided numerous subclasses and emphasized uniformity wherever practicable. It minimized differences between major types by using interchangeable parts whenever possible. Its twentieth-century steam was characterized by high-capacity boilers that used the boxy Belpaire firebox, which offered a greater heating surface than the more common radial-stayed designs. PRR was early to adopt superheated steam and was keen to identify superheated types with a small letter "s"—a well-intended policy that has caused a century of confusion.

While PRR's large-scale adoption of common types tended to lag years behind the national norm, its locomotives typically offered exemplary performance and were often among the finest of their types. As America's busiest railroad, PRR had greater locomotive demands than any other line. Of PRR's classic designs, its best regarded were the E6 Atlantics, H10 Consolidations, K4 Pacifics, L1 Mikados, I1 Decapods, G5 Ten-Wheelers, and M1 Mountains.

▲ Double-headed K4 Pacifics, Nos. 5493 and 5491, work an 11-car *Jeffersonian* on December 7, 1945. Intended for heavy passenger service, this type was developed at the same time as the E6 Atlantic. The prototype emerged in 1914, and the K4s was built en masse between 1916 and 1928, totaling 425 engines. A PRR classic, the K4s was a superheated type featuring a large body boiler and Belpaire firebox. *Photographer unknown, Solomon collection*

FACTS

PRR CLASS K4

Builders: PRR (Juniata Shops) and Baldwin

Wheel arrangement: 4-6-2

Type: Pacific

Cylinders: 27x28 in.

Drivers: 80 in.

Engine weight: 308,890 lbs.

Tractive effort: 44,460

Intended service: passenger

Overall production: 425

Years built: 1914–1928

▲ PRR's M1 Mountains were variously built by Baldwin, Lima, and PRR's own Juniata Shops in Altoona. Designed for fast freight, the M1 was highly refined but largely a straightforward design. They were constructed between 1923 and 1930 when other railroads were embracing novel types such as Alco's three-cylinder simples and Lima's superpower. The locomotives had 72-inch drivers and 27x30-inch cylinders supplied by a massive boiler. *Photographer unknown, Solomon collection*

In the 1920s and 1930s, PRR avoided trends toward superpower and simple articulated types, focusing instead on its own steam designs and electrification. Then from the later 1930s through World War II, PRR, spooked by the threat of diesel-electrics, embarked on a highly usual development path that pushed steam locomotive design to new limits. Its Juniata shops pushed Duplex designs (two sets of running gear on a nonarticulated frame) capable of enormous speed and power. Its massive Raymond Loewy–streamlined Class S-1 6-4-4-6 entertained tens of thousands at the 1939 New York world's fair. After the war, PRR ordered fleets of high-speed passenger 4-4-4-4 Class T1 and road-freight 4-4-6-4 Class Q2 types. Although these proved exceptionally capable, technical problems limited their reliability, and they couldn't come close to the cost efficiency offered by postwar diesel types. They didn't last long in service, and in fact the more traditionally designed K4s, L1s, and I1s types outlasted them. Another anomaly was its Class J 2-10-4, adapted during World War II from a C&O's Class T1 2-10-4. PRR concluded the steam era in 1957, but it set aside significant examples of its steam for preservation. Many of these are now displayed at the Railroad Museum of Pennsylvania at Strasburg.

◀ During the late 1930s and early 1940s, PRR reacted to the development of commercial high-output diesels by pushing steam locomotive development to new limits. The results were fantastic but unsuccessful. Class Q-1, No. 6131, pictured here, was a unique experimental using a 4-6-4-4 nonarticulated Duplex running-gear arrangement—especially unusual since its second set of drivers were powered by rear-facing cylinders. This was succeeded by PRR's Q2 type, with a 4-4-6-4 using both sets of cylinders in the forward position. Twenty-five Q2s were built in 1944 and 1945, but most were out of service by 1949. *Photographer unknown, Solomon collection*

▼ Perhaps PRR's most unusual locomotive was its lone Class S2 direct-drive steam turbine, No. 6200 built in 1944. Although it rode well, produced extraordinary power, and worked in both freight and passenger service—drawing such premier assignments as the *Broadway Limited*—it suffered from poor fuel consumption and high maintenance costs. It is best known because of the thousands of O-gauge models produced by Lionel after World War II. It was seen at Englewood, Illinois, on March 26, 1945. *Photographer unknown, Solomon collection*

Electrics

▲ For more than five decades, the owl-eyed MP54 multiple unit was Pennsylvania Railroad's most common electric vehicle. Over the years, hundreds of MP54s worked in New York and Philadelphia suburban service. A set of PRR MP54s makes a station stop at Media, Pennsylvania, in June 1962. *Richard Jay Solomon*

I n the 1890s, PRR was among the first American lines to recognize the advantages of electric operations and seriously experiment with electric design. For its large-scale electrification of Pennsylvania Station in New York City (opened in 1910), PRR adopted third-rail direct current, the standard used on its Long Island Rail Road affiliate. Passenger trains were whisked under the Hudson and East Rivers using enormously powerful DD1 jackshaft side-rod electrics (worked as semipermanently coupled pairs). In the mid-1920s, its DD1 fleet was augmented by central-cab Class L5, a bi-directional side-rod type. Despite success with third rail, PRR's later electrification was based on New Haven Railroad's high-voltage single-phase alternating current overhead system. PRR wired its Philadelphia suburban operations in 1913, providing service with self-propelled owl-eye MP54 electric multiple units. Its initial intent of electrifying its mountainous main line to Pittsburgh was refocused in the 1920s, and instead PRR ambitiously electrified its New York–Philadelphia–Washington routes. By 1939, this included lines from Harrisburg to Philadelphia and Baltimore and key freight cutoff routes.

Initially, PRR planned for fleets of boxcab electrics based on its most successful steam designs; it ordered O1 classes (two powered axles) for light passenger work, and P5 boxcabs (three powered axles) for heavy passenger service, with its L6 classes (four powered axles) intended for freight. The P5 boxcabs proved flawed in high-speed service, which forced a philosophical change that produced PRR's most famous electric: the articulated streamlined GG1. Styled by Raymond Loewy, the 138 GG1s—dressed in Brunswick Green with gold cat whiskers—became emblems of PRR's mainline electric service. In the 1950s, PRR experimented with modern electric designs, and in the early 1960s, it ordered a fleet of 4,400-horsepower E44s in road-switcher configuration from GE to replace the 1930s boxcabs in freight service. Its final electric development was using the Budd-built high-speed MP85 Metroliner multiple units in the late 1960s.

▶ The staple of PRR's electric fleet was its famous streamlined GG1. The GG1's 2-C+C-2 wheel arrangement was borrowed from New Haven's EP3 electric. In 1934, PRR built a lone GG1 prototype and tested it against a similarly styled R1 with a 2-D-2 arrangement; the GG1 prevailed, and PRR hired industrial designer Raymond Loewy to tidy up its appearance. Loewy's modifications included introduction of a welded body in place of the riveted skin used on prototypes. *Richard Jay Solomon*

FACTS

PRR GG1 ELECTRIC

Builders: GE, Baldwin-Westinghouse, and PRR (Juniata Shops)

Wheel arrangement: 2-C+C-2

Horsepower: 4,620

Engine weight: 468,400 lbs.*

Tractive effort: 70,700 (starting)*

Intended service: express passenger (some later geared for freight)

Overall production: 139

Years built: 1934–1943

*Weights varied. Figures based on locomotive No. 4876.

Diesels

Although PRR sampled diesel switchers in the 1930s, it resisted mainline dieselization until after World War II, partly as a result of its loyalty to steam and heavy investment in electrification. When PRR finally capitulated, it embarked on a frantic diesel acquisition that seemed to be the virtual antithesis of its careful scientific steam-era practices. In its rush to replace steam, PRR ignored earlier policies of standardization; it bought diesels in small lots from all the major builders. Along with common production models, it sampled many unusual types. By the early 1950s, PRR had America's most eclectic diesel-electric fleet. Unfortunately, it was the largest buyer of Baldwin diesels, acquiring just about every major type Baldwin had on offer. Baldwin diesels' low availability and lack of standardization between model types couldn't compete with EMD's highly engineered standard products, and in 1956 Baldwin exited the market. By the mid-1950s, PRR took a more conservative approach by focusing diesel acquisitions on Alco and EMD's standard road-switcher models. In the 1960s, it bought high-horsepower models from Alco, EMD, and GE. It embraced GE's entry into the American heavy diesel market, while buying EMD GP35, SD40, and SD45 models, and it was one of the last railroads to place major orders with Alco. PRR ordered some of Alco's last domestically constructed locomotives: the 3,600-horsepower six-motor model C-636s—ultimately delivered to PRR's successor, Penn Central.

▲ Perhaps the most unorthodox American diesel design was Baldwin's multiple-engine DR-12-8-3000, originally designated on PRR as Class BP60 and universally known a Centipede. PRR bought 12 semipermanently coupled pairs for passenger service but soon redeployed them for freight work. Most ran out their days working as helpers on Horseshoe Curve west of Altoona. *Photographer unknown, Solomon collection*

FACTS

BALDWIN DR-12-8-3000
Wheel arrangement: 2-D+D-2
Type: Centipede
Transmission: DC electric
Engines: two 8-cylinder 608SCs
Total horsepower: 3,000
Weight: 593,710 lbs.
Tractive effort: 102,250 lbs.
Intended service: high-speed
passenger (on PRR)
Number operated: 24
(12 semipermanent pairs)
Overall production: 54
Years built: 1945–1948

◄ PRR operated steam late on its north–south route to its Lake Erie port at Sandusky, Ohio. In the mid-1950s, a northward PRR freight waits to cross the Baltimore & Ohio main line at Attica Junction, Ohio. In the lead is Fairbanks-Morse H-20-44 No. 8935 (a 2,000-horsepower end-cab road switcher powered by F-M's 10-cylinder opposed-piston diesel) and a Class J 2-10-4 (derived from Chesapeake & Ohio's successful Class T-1 2-10-4 built by Lima in 1930). *J. William Vigrass*

69 PIONEER VALLEY RAILROAD

▲ Among Pioneer Valley's early locomotives was Alco S-2 switcher No. 106, which came to the line from sister Pinsly road Frankfort & Cincinnati. On October 12, 1984, it stands at the Westfield, Massachusetts, engine house ready for its trip to Holyoke and back. *Brian Solomon*

Pioneer Valley Railroad is one of the Pinsly lines—a company dedicated to short-line operation since 1938. PVRR was born in 1982 to assume operation of former New Haven Railroad routes radiating from Westfield, Massachusetts, spun off by Conrail. One of PVRR's key routes, the old Holyoke & Westfield line, connects its namesake endpoints. PVRR began operations with former Boston & Maine SW1s, Nos. 27 and 28. At the time, these were New England's oldest surviving diesels, built by Electro-Motive Corporation—before General Motors reorganized its locomotive-building subsidiary as the Electro-Motive Division in 1940. Dressed in Pinsly's classic fire engine red with black and yellow stripes, silver trucks, and featuring heavy steam-era bells, these were soon joined by another former B&M SW1, No. 1130, and Alco S-2 No. 106—from Pinsly sister line Frankfort & Cincinnati. In the early years, a pair of derelict RS-3s were also on the property. In spring 1985, Pioneer Valley acquired four former Santa Fe CF7s—road switchers remanufactured by Santa Fe's Cleburne, Texas, shops. Working from the railroad's F3A, F7A, and F9A fleet and recycling electrical components, trucks, and 16-567BC diesels engines, Santa Fe had produced 233 CF7s between 1969 and 1978. All CF7s are rated at 1,500 horsepower. Although delivered to PVRR in Santa Fe blue and yellow paint, these were soon repainted into Pinsly colors. While one CF7, No. 2565, was transferred to a sister line in Florida, the remaining three engines—Nos. 2558, 2597, and 2647—have served PVRR as their primary motive power for the last 25 years. PVRR's excellent maintenance policy has allowed continued reliable operation of these historic locomotives.

▲ In August 2007, PV CF7 No. 2647 leads the company's twenty-fifth anniversary special at Holyoke Heritage Park. While PV Nos. 2597 and 2558 featured the older cab style with a contour that reflects the locomotive's F-unit heritage, No. 2647 has the more spacious Topeka cab. *Brian Solomon*

FACTS

SANTA FE CF7
Builder: ATSF (Cleburne Shops)
Wheel arrangement: B-B
Transmission: DC electric
Engine: 16-567BC
Horsepower: 1,500
Intended service: road switcher
Number operated: 4
Overall production: 233
Years built: 1970–1978

◄ Pioneer Valley No. 2597 is one of three former Santa Fe CF7s that have worked the Massachusetts short line for the last 25 years. PV originally had four CF7s, but No. 2565 was conveyed to a sister road in Florida. Santa Fe No. 2597 was originally F7A No. 247C; its CF7 conversion was completed on October 25, 1972. *Brian Solomon*

Pittsburgh & West Virginia was an unusual road. Built by George Gould as the Wabash Pittsburgh Terminal Railway, P&WV is remembered for its late-era construction using extraordinary engineering, conducted at exceptional cost, to defy difficult geography. Where its competitors hugged river valleys, P&WV soared above them on gargantuan bridges and pierced mountainsides using a series of tunnels. It also had an unusual roster of locomotives. Initially, P&WV inherited WPT 2-8-0s as its primary freight power. In 1934, it took delivery of three distinctive Baldwin-built 2-6-6-4s with 63-inch drivers. Among the rarest of the simple articulated arrangements, P&WV's were especially unusual because they had Belpaire boilers and were intended for service in high-tractive effort applications at moderate speeds, rather than for sustained fast running. Another four followed in 1937. Its first diesel was a Baldwin VO1000 switcher, No. 30, built in 1943. When P&WV dieselized after World War II, it turned to Fairbanks-Morse as its primary supplier rather than General Motors, Alco, or Baldwin. Since it was strictly a freight hauler, F-M's relatively high-horsepower road switchers seemed ideal for its needs. F-M's locomotives were powered by its two-cycle opposed-piston diesel originally developed for marine applications. The staple of P&WV's fleet was F-M's 2,000-horsepower H-20-44—one of the most powerful diesels of its day. P&WV's last new diesels were four H-16-44s delivered in 1956 and 1957, shortly before F-M exited the domestic locomotive market. In 1964, P&WV was melded into the expanding Norfolk & Western system.

▼ Among Pittsburgh & West Virginia's freight engines were heavy 2-8-0s, such as No. 928. Despite the advent of the 2-8-2, some railroads continued to buy large 2-8-0s, a durable reliable type that placed relatively more adhesive weight on driving wheels. *Robert A. Buck collection*

▲ P&WV's three 2-6-6-4s were the first of their type. Although never common, Norfolk & Western and Seaboard Air Line also ordered noteworthy examples of the 2-6-6-4, and B&O later operated some of the SAL engines. *John E. Pickett*

FACTS

P&WV CLASS J-1 SIMPLE ARTICULATED
Builder: Baldwin
Wheel arrangement: 2-6-6-4
Cylinders: 4 @ 23x32 in. ea.
Drivers: 63 in.
Engine weight: 528,040 lbs.
Tractive effort: 97,500 lbs.
Intended service: road freight
Overall production: 7
Years built: 1934 and 1937

◄ Where most railroads dieselized with EMD and Alco models, P&WV opted for Fairbanks-Morse's unusual opposed-piston models, including the 2,000-horsepower H-20-44, which was the most powerful road switcher on the market when introduced in 1947. P&WV H-20-44s, Nos. 55 and 63, are shown at Rook, near Pittsburgh, Pennsylvania, in 1958. *Richard Jay Solomon*

71 PROVIDENCE & WORCESTER RAILROAD

▶ Providence & Worcester's one-unit order for GE's B23-7 in 1978 added to what was already the smallest fleet of modern GE diesels. P&W previously had bought a sole U18B from GE in 1976. Years later, P&W bought GEs secondhand from Conrail, CSX, and other lines. Note the full-lighting package on the nose of B23-7 No. 2201. *Brian Solomon*

Providence & Worcester regained independence in 1973, when it assumed operation of its historic namesake route from Penn Central. Over the next three decades, P&W gradually expanded its southern New England freight operations as Conrail retrenched services on former New Haven Railroad routes. P&W initiated operations with Alco RS-3s leased from Delaware & Hudson. In its first decade, it purchased new locomotives from all three major North American locomotive builders—an atypical acquisition pattern especially for a short line. (Today, most short lines acquire locomotives secondhand.) In 1974 and 1975, P&W bought five M-420Rs from Montreal Locomotive Works, a model its management had considered from the time of independence. The M-420R incorporated recycled components from Alco road switchers. This model variation was unique to P&W, which became the only American railroad to buy the M-420 new from MLW. In 1976, it bought a sole General Electric U18B, followed by a lone B23-7 a year later. Then in 1982, it bought four new GP38-2s from EMD.

Since that time, P&W has only acquired secondhand locomotives, and its roster has been a revolving door for various four-motor models. A pair of former Pennsylvania GP9s arrived in the early 1980s. One was sold to switching operator Quaboag Transfer in 1984; the other served until 1997 when it was conveyed to Bay Colony. While three former CSX GP40s and a pair of upgraded GP38-3s joined the railroad in the 1990s, most acquisitions over the last two decades have been for GE models, including a small fleet of Conrail and CSX U23B/B23-7s. During 2002 and 2003, these were largely replaced with newer and more powerful models: four former New York, Susquehanna & Western Dash 8-40Bs, five former Burlington Northern cab-less B30-7As, nine former GE LMX lease-fleet B39-8s, and a pair of remanufactured GE Super Sevens (originally U23Bs built for Western Pacific). Most recently in 2010, a trio of former Santa Fe 500 series Dash 8-40BWs joined the line.

▲ Freshly repainted former Santa Fe Dash 8-40BW No. 4005, with cab-less B30-7A No. 3007 and former LMX B39-8 No. 3903, leads P&W freight GRWO on its return from the Pan Am Railway interchange at Gardner, Massachusetts. It is seen passing Quinapoxet Reservoir in Princeton at 2:15 a.m. on June 9, 2011. P&W acquired three former Santa Fe Dash 8-40BWs in summer 2010. *Steve Carlson, Lumedyne lighting by Steve Carlson and Nick Palazini*

FACTS

GE DASH 8-40BW

Wheel arrangement: B-B

Transmission: DC electric

Engine: 7FDL-16

Horsepower: 4,000

Intended service: intermodal freight

Overall production: 83

Years built: 1990–1992

◀ P&W began operations with Alco RS-3s leased from Delaware & Hudson. Over the coming decades P&W expanded across southern New England. In the mid-1970s, it made the atypical move of acquiring small lots of new locomotives from three manufacturers. Since then, it has turned to the used locomotive market. *Jim Shaughnessy*

READING COMPANY

▲ Reading 2-8-0 No. 1575 was a powerful machine typical of the railroad's early twentieth-century road freight power. Riding astride the boiler was awkward for the engineer; space was cramped and he couldn't communicate directly with his fireman (who was confined to a scanty platform at the back). Yet for decades, locomotives like this were the mainstay of Reading's fleet. *Photographer unknown, Solomon collection*

One of America's earliest railroads, Philadelphia & Reading dated to 1833 and connected its namesake cities in December 1839. It gradually grew to dominate transport in the anthracite regions of southeastern Pennsylvania. In 1896, it became part of the Reading Company, and the railroad was known as such until its inclusion in Conrail in 1976. During the twentieth century, it was closely affiliated with Central Railroad of New Jersey, and locomotives on the two lines tended to share a family appearance. In addition to heavy coal traffic, intensive Philadelphia suburban services, and overhead freight traffic, Reading operated a few long-distance passenger trains. In later years, its lines in southern New Jersey were jointly run with Pennsylvania Railroad as Pennsylvania-Reading Seashore Lines.

In 1877, P&R general manager John E. Wootten developed a shallow, wide firebox designed with adequate grate area to allow complete combustion of slow-burning anthracite slack. This offered 2.5 times more grate area than typical locomotives but was too big to ride between the locomotive frames—the traditional firebox location. As a result, Wootten's wide firebox rode above the rear driving wheels; since this arrangement didn't provide ample room for the engineer's cab, a separate cab straddling the boiler was installed, while the fireman rode behind on a small platform. This peculiar configuration was called a camelback or Mother Hubbard. While P&R was a leading user of camelbacks, other railroads (many of them also anthracite coal haulers) also adopted it. Camelbacks were built in all sizes from 0-4-0 switchers to massive 0-8-8-0s built by Alco for the Erie Railroad. In the 1880s and 1890s, P&R experimented with single-driver locomotives, both in conventional cab and camelback arrangements. Some earned impressive speed records, but in general they were slippery and unable to haul more than a few lightweight passenger cars. During the twentieth century, Reading returned to the conventional single-cab arrangement, although many locomotives continued as anthracite burners.

▲ Philadelphia & Reading 4-4-0 No. 349, built 1886, was a classic example of an early locomotive with Wootten's broad grate firebox. Reading was first to develop the camelback design and many eastern railroads followed its example. The camelback type shouldn't be confused with Ross Winans' famous 0-8-0 Camels of an earlier generation that were an entirely different beast altogether. *Solomon collection*

▲ Philadelphia & Reading's John E. Wootten developed the camelback in order to take advantage of anthracite waste called culm. Among the smallest of this type were 0-4-0s, such as Reading Company No. 1175, seen at the Reading (Pennsylvania) car shop engine house on July 11, 1934. *Photographer unknown, Robert A. Buck collection*

FACTS

READING CLASS A

Builder: Baldwin

Wheel arrangement: 0-4-0

Type: Camelback

Cylinders: 16x24 in.

Drivers: 50 in.

Engine weight: 108,080 lbs.

Tractive effort: 20,890 lbs.

Intended service: switching

Years built: 1902–1913

▲ Several of Reading's Class T-1 4-8-4s worked into the diesel era as excursion locomotives. Locomotive fans flock to photograph Reading No. 2124 on October 25, 1959. This popular 4-8-4 has been preserved and today resides at Steamtown in Scranton, Pennsylvania. Also preserved is a pair of Reading's EMD FP7s (Nos. 902 and 903) that are displayed at the Railroad Museum of Pennsylvania at Strasburg. *Richard Jay Solomon*

FACTS

READING COMPANY CLASS T-1

Builder: Reading Shops

Wheel arrangement: 4-8-4

Cylinders: 27x32 in.

Drivers: 70 in.

Engine weight: 441,300 lbs.

Tractive effort: 68,000 lbs., + 11,100 lbs.
with booster

Intended service: road freight

Overall production: 30

Years built: 1945–1947

At the end of World War II, Reading bucked trends toward dieselization; using the boilers and fireboxes from its powerful I-10sa 2-8-0 Consolidations, it constructed modern 4-8-4s with 70-inch Boxpok disc drivers that were designated T-1 in accordance with Reading's long-standing alpha numeric classification system. In the late 1950s and early 1960s, a group of T-1s was used in the railroad's popular Reading Rambles passenger excursions.

Reading electrified its Philadelphia suburban lines, but its wires were strictly for commuter service operated with multiple units. Unlike on Pennsylvania Railroad, electrification was not expanded for multipurpose applications.

Reading was among the first to sample diesel switchers in the 1920s, buying more of various types in the 1930s. It was one of 25 railroads to buy EMD's Pioneering FT road diesels, a type oddly popular with anthracite railroads. Steam and diesels comingled for a few decades before diesels finally won out. After World War II, it bought more EMD Fs, including FP7s for passenger service, along with some GPs. From Alco, it bought RS-3s and FA/FBs; from Baldwin and Fairbanks-Morse, it bought road-switchers, including F-M's powerful 2,400-horsepower Train Masters. During the 1960s, it bought high-horsepower units from Alco, EMD, and General Electric. Among its last new diesels were EMD GP39-2s, delivered on the eve of Conrail, most of which went to Delaware & Hudson after the 1976 Conrail startup.

In later years, Reading applied Wootten broad fireboxes to locomotives with a conventional cab arrangement. Baldwin-built Pacific No. 178 is viewed at Central Railroad of New Jersey's Communipaw engine terminal at Jersey City. This style of anthracite-burning clean-lined locomotive was peculiar to Reading Company, a railroad noted for the distinctive appearance of its locomotives. *Robert A. Buck collection*

At Bayonne, New Jersey, in 1960, Reading Company FP7 No. 905 leads the railroad's pocket streamliner— a four-car Budd-built stainless-steel train with an observation car at each end that worked as *The Crusader* between Reading Terminal in Philadelphia and Jersey City, New Jersey. Originally, Reading operated ungainly stainless-steel streamlined Pacifics on the service. *Richard Jay Solomon*

In early 1976, a Reading GP30 rests alongside a Central Railroad of New Jersey SD35 at CNJ's Elizabethport, New Jersey, shops. Both lines were folded into Conrail on April 1 that year. Reading Company served the New York City area via rights over CNJ. *George W. Kowanski*

73 READING & NORTHERN RAILROAD

Reading & Northern began in 1983 as the Blue Mountain & Reading, operating on a short section of former Conrail trackage running north from Reading, Pennsylvania. Over the last three decades, it expanded by acquiring former Conrail lines in eastern Pennsylvania. Today, its network largely consists of former Reading Company, Lehigh Valley, and CNJ lines in anthracite coal mining country. During its early years, operations were handled with a collection of EMD switchers and former Santa Fe CF7s. Later, as Reading & Northern extended its reach, it acquired road units, many of them surplus Conrail models, including GE U23Bs and U33Bs. In addition, it operated two preserved steam locomotives: first, former Reading Company Class T-1 4-8-4 Northern No. 2102—one of the engines made popular during the Reading Rambles of the 1950s and 1960s—and second, former Gulf, Mobile & Northern Baldwin-built 4-6-2 Pacific No.425, dressed in an unusual blue livery. The GE's have left the roster, as have a few 20-cylinder EMDs; in 2011 R&N's contemporary freight diesel fleet consisted entirely of secondhand EMD units, dominated by former Union Pacific SD40-2s and SD50s for road service, but the fleet also includes four former Lehigh Valley SW8/SW8M 800-horsepower switchers, a pair of SW1500s, and a few SD38s (2,000-horsepower six-motor type) originally owned by Detroit, Toledo & Ironton. In addition, it has a pair of Budd-built self-propelled rail diesel cars (RDCs). Along with freight services, R&N provides excursion services via the Lehigh Gorge Scenic Railway running northward through its namesake from Jim Thorpe, Pennsylvania, typically using diesels positioned in push-pull fashion on both ends of a historic passenger consist.

▼ On a humid afternoon in August 2007, a lone Reading & Northern SD50 hauling a long freight has ascended the grade up to Penobscot, Pennsylvania. R&N No. 5049 is one of several former Union Pacific SD50s on the line. The railroad now relies entirely on secondhand EMD models for freight services. *Brian Solomon*

FACTS

EMD SD50

Wheel arrangement: C-C

Transmission: DC electric

Engine: 16-645F

Horsepower: 3,500–3,600

Intended service: heavy freight

Years built: 1981–1985

◄ Reading & Northern U23B No. 2399 leads a freight at Bear Creek Junction, Pennsylvania, on October 14, 1997. R&N painted this former Conrail GE in a livery similar to that used by the old Reading Company. *Brian Solomon*

▼ Reading & Northern SD40s lead a coal train at Port Clinton, Pennsylvania. Like other midsized railroads working former main lines, R&N's fleet of secondhand EMDs with classic paint gives it a retro look that appears more like a Class 1 carrier from the 1970s than a modern freight railroad. *Brian Solomon*

RICHMOND, FREDERICKSBURG & POTOMAC RAILROAD

► Smokebox-mounted air pumps combined with a high headlight and a multitude of external appliances and piping to give Richmond, Fredericksburg & Potomac 4-6-2 Pacific No. 305 (of the group 301 to 312) a rough-and-ready appearance. Although not the prettiest locomotive, this heavy machine had 75-inch drivers and was well suited to both freight and passenger work. Very similar to this class were four Baldwin Pacifics (Nos. 325–328) built in 1927 that were slightly heavier. *John E. Pickett*

FACTS

RF&P CLASS 325–328

Builders: Alco and Baldwin

Wheel arrangement: 4-6-2

Type: Pacific

Cylinders: 26x28 in.

Drivers: 75 in.

Engine weight: 332,600 lbs.

Tractive effort: 48,580 lbs.

Intended service: road service (freight and passenger)

Overall production: 12

Years built: 1918–1925

RF&P origin's dated to 1834, yet its twentieth-century form was a result of its six connecting railroads (Atlantic Coast Line, Baltimore & Ohio, Chesapeake & Ohio, Pennsylvania Railroad, Seaboard Air Line, and Southern Railway) agreeing in 1901 to transform it into an efficient double-track bridge route between Richmond, Virginia, and Washington D.C. Since it had large yards at both ends and no significant operating challenges on its 114-mile main line, RF&P was able to forward fast freight traffic and run numerous express passenger trains without requiring specialized fleets of freight and passenger steam locomotives. With a few exceptions, most of its engines were designed for dual traffic. RF&P's 4-6-0s from its early years were soon supplemented by various classes of 4-6-2 Pacifics; 4-8-2 Mountains came in 1924, and between 1937 and 1945 the railroad bought a fleet of 27 4-8-4s. The tide of World War II freight traffic demanded more power, and RF&P bought 10 Lima-built 2-8-4s for freight, essentially patterned after Lima's late-era Nickel Plate Road Berkshires.

The railroad began dieselizing yard operations with Alco S-2 switchers during the war. In the late 1940s and early 1950s, it dieselized road operations with EMD F-units and GP7s for freight and a tidy fleet of E-units and three FP7s for passenger work. In addition, ACL and SAL passenger diesels had been running through to Washington Union Station since the late 1930s. Steam finished in 1954. In the mid-1960s, RF&P completely re-dieselized, supplanting Alco switchers with the latest EMD SW1200s and SW1500s, and buying new high-horsepower GP35s and GP40s to replace freight Fs. Amtrak began in 1971, ending RF&P's need for passenger power. It capped off its roster with an order for seven GP40-2s in 1972. When RF&P was folded into CSX in 1991, its fleet totaled just 31 locomotives.

◄ RF&P E8A No. 1010 leads train No. 33, the *Silver Comet* (from New York's Penn Station to Birmingham, Alabama) at Alexandria, Virginia, on April 12, 1969. The locomotive wears the simplified blue and gray scheme that adorned RF&P diesels in its later years. RF&P's E8As were numbered 1001 to 1015; its E8Bs were numbered 1051 to 1055. *George W. Kowanski*

▼ On a baking hot August 1984 morning, RF&P GP40-2 No. 145 is getting up to speed south of Alexandria station with a Richmond-bound train. In its final years RF&P's entire fleet was made up of four-motor EMDs. In 1990, CSX absorbed RF&P, yet many of its locomotives remained in home territory because of RF&P's cab-signaling requirements. *Brian Solomon*

75 RUTLAND RAILROAD

▶ A classic New England scene. In March 1955, a pair of Rutland Railroad RS-3s leading northward freight CR-3 from Chatham, New York, toward Rutland passes Emerald Lake near North Dorset, Vermont. Rutland dieselized with just 16 locomotives, accounting for just 21,000 horsepower. *Jim Shaughnessy*

Rutland Railroad was synonymous with rural Vermont. Its roots dated to the mid-nineteenth century, but the railroad didn't reach its final form until the early twentieth century, by which time its lines reached connections at Ogdensburg and Chatham, New York. With rare exception, Rutland's motive power came from Alco. In the early twentieth century, 4-6-0s and 2-8-0s comprised the backbone of its freight locomotive fleet. During World War I, the U.S. Railroad Administration facilitated Rutland's acquisition of six light Mikados and a pair of 0-8-0s. Passenger services consisted of just a few trains daily, and most were covered by its high-driver 4-6-0s until the mid-1920s, when the railroad bought three light Pacifics. Another three Pacifics were delivered at the end of the decade, and these represented the railroad's last new motive power for more than 15 years. After World War II, the railroad's locomotive fleet was suffering; however, rather than invest in dieselization, Rutland made an atypical purchase of four modern 4-8-2 Mountain types. These featured lightweight Boxpok drivers and were delivered in handsome dark green paint. This move simply postponed the inevitable; in 1950, the railroad finally made the plunge. The greater availability and reliability offered by diesel locomotives combined with Rutland's declining traffic meant that six Alco's RS-1s, nine RS-3s, and a sole General

▲ In April 1954, Rutland's lease life had less than a decade left. Alco RS-3 No. 204 works interchange with Boston & Maine on a connecting track at North Walpole, New Hampshire. Today's Vermont Rail System component Green Mountain maintains a small yard that ends on the right, just shy of the road crossing. *Robert A. Buck*

▲ On July 21, 1951, Rutland No. 77, a nearly 40-year-old Class F-2j 4-6-0, and one of its modern Mountain types departs Burlington with train No. 65, the southward *Green Mountain*. While Rutland got its money's worth out of the old 4-6-0, the Mountain type was scrapped after less than a decade of service. Rutland itself only barely made it into the diesel era. *John E. Pickett*

FACTS

RUTLAND CLASS F-2k AND F-2j

Builder: Alco
Wheel arrangement: 4-6-0
Cylinders: 22.5x26 in.
Drivers: 69 in.
Engine weight: n/a
Tractive effort: 32,430 lbs.
Intended service: passenger
Overall production: 10
Years built: 1910–1912

Electric 44-ton switcher could handle all its motive power requirements. During the 1950s, Rutland retrenched; it abandoned the Corkscrew Line between Bennington, Vermont, and Chatham, and then discontinued all passenger services. Strikes doomed the line, and it ended operations in 1961. Its locomotives were sold off. Louisville & Nashville acquired its RS-3s, while RS-1 No. 405 survived on Green Mountain, a short line created in 1964 to operate the Rutland–Bellows Falls trackage.

St. Louis–San Francisco, known universally as the Frisco, was a Missouri-focused railroad connecting St. Louis and Kansas City with cities in Texas, Oklahoma, Alabama, and the Florida Panhandle. Until World War I, it relied on large numbers of 2-8-0s and 4-6-0s for most work. It began buying Pacifics in 1904. Its seven Alco 2-8-8-2 Mallets delivered in 1910 seemed out of character with the rest of its fleet. During World War I, Frisco was flooded with more modern types. In addition to USRA 2-8-2s and 2-10-2s, Frisco received 20 Russian Decapods—part of a large order of locomotives built in the United States for Russia but orphaned as result of the Bolshevik Revolution. In the mid-1920s, Frisco bought 30 4-8-2s that were middleweights and worked in both freight and passenger service. Between 1936 and 1942, Frisco's Springfield shops built more 4-8-2s using parts salvaged from older locomotives, while during World War II it bought 25 Baldwin 4-8-4s. In the late 1930s, Frisco's budget-tight desire for a streamliner was fulfilled by home shrouding three 1910-era Pacifics for service on its new Kansas City–Oklahoma City *Firefly*.

Steam concluded in 1952, but a number of Frisco engines were preserved. Best known is 4-8-2 No. 1522, which was restored in the late 1980s and was a prominent excursion engine for more than a decade. Frisco acquired diesel switchers during World War II, and after the war it sampled products from all major builders, except Lima-Hamilton. Models that dominated its road freight service included EMD Fs and GP7s, and Alco RS-2s and FA/FBs. A small fleet of EMD's E7s and E8s were bought for passenger work. In the 1960s, Frisco bought GE's U25Bs, including a few high-hood units, followed by U30Bs, as well as EMD high-horsepower GP35s and SD45s. In its final decade, EMD 1500-horsepower MP15s, 2,000-horsepower GP38-2s, and 3,000-horsepower GP40-2s and SD40-2s joined the fleet along with more GE U30Bs and B30-7s. Its last new locomotives were EMD GP50s, most of which were delivered after merger with BN in 1980.

▼ Originally a Baldwin Pacific built in 1917, Frisco No. 1063 was one of 10 4-6-2s later transformed into 4-6-4s by the company's Springfield, Missouri, shops. While stream-styled skirting and colorful paint caught the public eye, increased firebox capacity and slightly taller drivers combined with a feed-water heater made for a more capable locomotive. *Photographer unknown, Robert A. Buck collection*

▲ Frisco was late to adopt the 4-8-4. Where Northern Pacific pioneered the wheel arrangement in 1926, Frisco ordered them to accommodate demands of World War II traffic. Twenty-five were built by Baldwin during 1942 and 1943. Frisco No. 4513 is seen at Springfield, Missouri, on September 2, 1952. Springfield was the railroad's operational hub located at the heart of its network. *John E. Pickett collection*

FACTS

SLSF 4-8-4
Builder: Baldwin
Cylinders: 28x31 in.
Drivers: 74 in.
Engine weight: 462,500 lbs.
Tractive effort: 71,200 lbs.
Intended service: freight, some for
passenger service
Overall production: 25
Years built: 1942–1943

◄ St. Louis–San Francisco Railway was universally known as the Frisco, although the road never made it west of the Texas Panhandle. Frisco Nos. 770 and 769 were part of an order for 25 EMD GP40-2s delivered in 1979, seen at Chicago's Landers Yard in June of the that year. Frisco's final locomotives were 10 EMD GP50s. *Mike Abalos photo, courtesy of the Friends of Mike Abalos*

77 SEABOARD COAST LINE

▲ In the late 1960s, Seaboard Coast Line operated an intensive long-distance passenger service connecting Northeastern cities with points south. It was logical that it had one of the largest remaining E-unit fleets. On April 12, 1969, the *Florida Special* (Miami to New York City) arrives at Alexandria on the RF&P with a mix of former SAL and ACL E-units. In the lead is a rather tired-looking E7A. Next out is an E8A still wearing SAL's attractive white and orange livery. *George W. Kowanski*

▶ SCL was one of GE's best customers during the 1970s and 1980s. On May 4, 1984, B23-7 No. 5508 leads a quintet of four-motor GEs on an intermodal train on the former ACL route at Sanford, Florida. In its later years, SCL was part of the Family Lines, a marketing arrangement that included Louisville & Nashville and other affiliated railroads. *Terry Norton*

Seaboard Coast Line was created by the merger of the competing Seaboard Airline and Atlantic Coast Line systems. Seaboard's attractive green and yellow livery gave way to ACL's down-to-business black and yellow. The railroad began with an inherited diesel fleet, but it didn't hesitate to add new models while thinning out many of the older, more obscure types. In the 1970s, SCL, L&N, and other related lines were jointly marketed as the "Family Lines," a cosmetic simplification of a complex interrelationship among southern lines. SCL and L&N had many similar locomotive models. SCL was one of General Electric's best customers, and by the early 1980s, SCL's extensive GE fleet looked like a virtual catalog of Erie's U.S. production. Of the few models SCL was missing, most could be found on one of the other "Family Lines" railroads. In addition to stock models such as the U30C and B23-7, SCL also had a special order for 10 BQ23-7s—built in 1978 and 1979—which featured an oversized cab to allow for a full crew to ride the head end, obviating the need for a caboose. However, within a few years, reduction in crew sizes made extreme locomotive cabs unnecessary. SCL also bought the bulk of GE's 1,800-horsepower U18Bs, powered by an eight-cylinder FDL, that in higher throttle positions sounded like an oversized tractor. SCL paired some four-motor GEs with a variation of the cabless road slug known as a MATE (motors to assist tractive effort). EMD added to SCL's fleet as well with GP38/GP38-2s, GP40/GP40-2s, SD40-2s, a few SD45/SD45-2s on the main line, and MP15ACs for yard, local, and branch line work.

◄ On March 29, 1978, Seaboard Coast Line U18B No. 383 leads a weekday turn from Wildwood to Plymouth, Florida, on its return to Wildwood passing at Taveres, Florida. GE's U18B was marketed as a medium-output road switcher and sold between 1973 and 1976. The model was relatively unusual, and SCL was by far the largest domestic buyer. Many rode on EMD Blomberg trucks from locomotives traded back to GE. *Terry Norton*

FACTS

GE U18B

Wheel arrangement: B-B

Transmission: DC electric

Engine: 7FDL-8

Horsepower: 1,800

Intended service: light-duty
     road switching

Number operated: 105

Overall production: 118*

Years built: 1973–1976*

*Domestic production only.

▲ Unlike many suburban rail operations, such as Boston's MBTA, New York's Metro-North, or Philadelphia-based SEPTA, which have historic ties to traditional railroad-run commuter services, *Sounder* suburban services are an entirely new creation designed to provide commuter services on heavy-rail lines where none had existed in modern times. A *Sounder* F59PHI approaches the station at Tukwila, Washington. *Adam Pizante*

▶ *Sounder* provides suburban services on BNSF routes in the greater Seattle area. *Sounder* commuter trains share tracks with BNSF freights and Amtrak long-distance trains. At Tukwila, Washington, on September 30, 2009, *Sounder* F59PHI No. 905 meets an Amtrak train led by a former F40PH converted into a "cabbage," a combined control-cab and baggage car. *Adam Pizante*

Sound Transit is a multimodal Seattle-centered transit provider serving Washington's Puget Sound region. Among its services are two heavy-rail routes radiating from Seattle, which are operated as the *Sounder*. South Line service to Tacoma via Auburn began in September 2000, while North Line services to Everett began in December 2003. The daily schedule offers four roundtrips north and nine south, with additional trains operated during special events. As of December 2011, Sounder operated 11 EMD F59PHI diesel-electrics (Nos. 901 to 911), purchased new between 1999 and 2001. These streamlined passenger locomotives were developed by General Motors' Electro-Motive Division as a contemporary equivalent to the successful F40PH locomotive for Amtrak's West Coast operations. Rated at 3,000 horsepower, F59PHI is powered by a 12-cylinder 710G3B diesel. It uses an auxiliary diesel engine/alternator combination to generate head-end power. This arrangement allows the prime mover to idle at a lower throttle notch, thus saving fuel, reducing wear and tear and producing less noise. As designed, the F59PHI is intended for a maximum speed of 108 to 110 miles per hour, although in practice they are rarely operated faster than 79 miles per hour in order to comply with railroad imposed speed limits. Equipment is shrouded in a cowl while the F59PHI's aerodynamic design also reduces wind resistance with a bulbous nose constructed from fiberglass composite. *Sounder* plans to expand service in 2013, and in September 2011, it ordered three locomotives from MotivePower Inc. It is expected these will be a 4,000-horsepower design intended to meet federal Tier III emissions standards.

▲ *Sounder* adopted EMD F59PHI, a short-range passenger model designed to meet the needs of Amtrak California in the 1990s. This attractive, modern streamlined diesel is a contrast from the boxy utilitarian designs of the 1970s and 1980s. *Sounder* F59PHI No. 901 is seen at Seattle with a three-piece bi-level push-pull set. *Adam Pizante*

FACTS

EMD F59PHI

Wheel arrangement: B-B

Transmission: DC electric

Engine: 12-710G3B

Horsepower: 3,000

Weight: 265,000 lbs.

Tractive effort: 65,000 lbs. (starting based on 25 percent adhesion)

Intended service: passenger

Number operated: 11

79 SOUTHERN PACIFIC RAILROAD

▲ SP's cab-forward types were among the most distinctive mainline locomotives in America. One of their final haunts was the lonely Modoc Line, which spanned hundreds of miles of desolate high desert between Fernley, Nevada, and Klamath Falls, Oregon. SP's AC-10 No. 4213 leads an extra freight near Pyramid Lake in 1955. *John E. Pickett*

In the late nineteenth century, SP's freight service was handled by 2-6-0s, 2-8-0s, and an abnormally large fleet of the relatively unusual 4-8-0s. Passenger trains were typically assigned 4-4-0s and 4-6-0s. The Harriman era, beginning in 1901, resulted in a period of standardization for freight services, dominated by hundreds of 2-8-0s built to specifications common with Union Pacific and its affiliates.

In 1911, SP adopted the 2-8-2 for general freight, and later it used the 2-10-2 (known to SP as Decks rather than the more common Santa Fe). During the 1920s, Alco promoted its three-cylinder simple types, building 49 4-10-2s for SP. However, SP's most distinctive steam locomotives were its cab-forward (or cab-ahead) articulateds. In 1909, Baldwin delivered a pair of 2-8-8-2s Mallet compounds in the conventional configuration. SP had difficulties using them in the high-altitude snowsheds and in long tunnels on Donner Pass where bad ventilation threatened to asphyxiate crews. The solution was to reverse the engine's operating arrangement by putting the cab at the front and the smokebox facing the tender. Such an unorthodox arrangement was possible because SP engines were oil burners, and the fuel was easily piped to the front. Over the next three decades, SP adopted several classes of cab-forward articulateds, all built by Baldwin. In 1928, SP opted for new, simple articulated cab forwards (where all cylinders received high-pressure steam) and similarly began converting its older Mallets to simple operation. The last cab forward was AC-12 No. 4294 built in 1944. This engine was preserved and is displayed at the California State Railroad Museum in Sacramento.

SP Steam Locomotive Classification

Every railroad had its own classification system. From 1913 onward, Southern Pacific assigned a letter code for each wheel arrangement followed by a numerical suffix to indicate the subclass. Its most common classes were as follows:

CLASS	WHEEL ARRANGEMENT	TYPE	CLASS	WHEEL ARRANGEMENT	TYPE
A	4-4-2	Atlantic	F	2-10-2	Deck (SP shunned the term Santa Fe)
AC	4-8-8-2/2-8-8-4	Articulated Consolidation	GS	4-8-4	General Service or Golden State
AM	4-6-6-2	Articulated Mogul			
B	2-8-4	Berkshire	M	2-6-0	Mogul
C	2-8-0	Consolidation	MC	2-8-8-2	Mallet Consolidation
D	2-10-0	Decapod	P	4-6-2	Pacific
E	4-4-0	Eight-Wheeler (American)	S	0-6-0	Switcher
			T	4-6-0	Ten-Wheeler

▲ In their heyday, SP's *Daylights* were among the most famous (and most profitable) passenger trains in America. On August 24, 1952, SP GS-4 No. 4455 charges passed Bayshore with train No. 98, the *Morning Daylight* on the first leg of its run from San Francisco to Los Angeles. SP's Lima 4-8-4s have been considered some of the most handsome steam locomotives ever built, and the GS-4 was deemed the zenith of the type. *John E. Pickett*

FACTS

SP GS-4

Builder: Lima

Wheel arrangement: 4-8-4

Type: General Service or Golden State

Cylinders: 25.5x32 in.

Drivers: 80 in.

Engine weight: 475,000 lbs.

Tractive effort: 64,760 lbs. (plus 13,000 lbs. with booster)

Intended service: passenger and freight

Overall production: 28

Years built: 1941–1942

SP's twentieth-century passenger steam progressed from 4-4-2s to 4-6-2s, to 4-8-2s and finally 4-8-4s. Its first 4-8-4s, Class GS-1s, were built by Baldwin in 1930; but its best-remembered 4-8-4s were successive classes of Lima-built, semi-streamlined engines styled for service on its *Daylight* streamliners.

SP's first experience with diesels came from operating UP's EMC-powered *City of San Francisco* streamliners in the mid-1930s. While SP remained loyal to steam through

FACTS

Krauss-Maffei ML-4000

Wheel arrangement: C-C

Transmission: Voith torque converter

Engines: twin Maybach
  MD-870 V-16 diesels

Total horsepower: 3,540 (4,000 at
  engine shaft)

Intended service: heavy freight

Number operated: 6 carbody units; 15
  road-switcher units

Years built: 1961 and 1963

▲ Poor ventilation in the high-altitude tunnels and snow sheds on Donner Pass presented operational difficulties resulting in development of cab-forward articulated steam locomotives before World War I. Then in the 1970s, Electro-Motive's Tunnel Motor–style second-generation diesel with low level air intakes. Where the 3,600-horsepower SD45T-2 was built exclusively for SP, the 3,000-horsepower SD40T-2 was built for both SP and Rio Grande. SP's SD45T-2 is easily identified by the row of three panels above air intakes at the back of locomotive; the SD40T-2 has only two panels. *Brian Solomon*

FACTS

EMD SD45T-2 TUNNEL MOTOR

Wheel arrangement: B-B

Transmission: electric

Engine: 20-645E

Horsepower: 3,600

Intended service: road freight in
  mountains

Number operated: 247

Years built: 1972–1975

World War II, it began dieselization of road trains after the war, purchasing a potpourri of models from all the major builders. Large numbers of Alco PA/PBs were bought for passenger services, along with EMD E-units and FP7s. EMD's F3 and F7s were its standard road freight power, while EMD's GP7s and GP9s worked secondary services, along with various models of Alco, Baldwin, and Fairbanks-Morse road switchers. SP was an early proponent of six-motor models. In addition to Alco and Baldwin models, it bought large numbers of EMD SD7s and SD9s. Noteworthy was its fleet of F-M 2,400-horsepower Train Masters assigned to San Francisco–San Jose Commute services. These also worked freights on weekends.

In the 1960s, SP's desire for high-horsepower single-unit diesels led it to buy two batches of German-built Krauss-Maffei diesel hydraulics while sampling a hydraulic type from Alco. Meanwhile, SP encouraged General Electric's entry into the heavy road locomotive market, buying a large pioneer fleet of its U25Bs. It sampled EMD and GE's double diesels. Then in the mid-1960s, SP began trading in its legions of F-units for new high-horsepower models, including EMD's 3,600-horsepower SD45. Difficulties with operation of high-horsepower models on Donner Pass led SP to work with EMD in design of its SD45T-2 and SD40T-2 Tunnel Motor variations with low-level air intakes. For intermodal services, SP bought various high-horsepower four-motor four-axle models, and it continued to prefer this type of motive power into the 1990s, longer than most American lines. The EMD GP60s built for its final order were the last new high-horsepower four-axle road-freight units built in the United States. Shortly before SP was absorbed into UP, it acquired fleets of both DC- and AC-traction GE 4,400-horsepower six-motor models and 25 EMD SD70Ms.

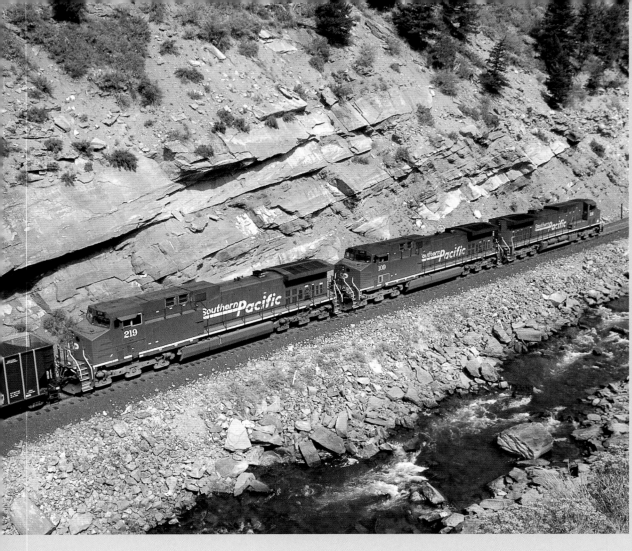

In SP's final years, it bought several fleets of modern safety cab diesels. Most significant were GE AC4400CWs. Three of these new engines lead a unit coal train on the former Rio Grande near Minturn on the ascent of Tennessee Pass. Another four units worked midtrain with two more at the back. These all were controlled using Harris-Locotrol radio-remote technology. *Brian Solomon*

Southern Pacific faced stiff grades across its Pacific lines and operated more manned helper districts than any other western road. In February 1990, SD40T-2 No. 8284 and a SD45 (still wearing the Kodachrome scheme from the ill-fated merger attempts with Santa Fe in the mid-1980s) work the back of a westward train descending California's Donner Pass. Careful use of dynamic brakes helped control heavy trains on this steep downgrade. *Brian Solomon*

Among SP's trademark locomotive features was its full-house lighting. On most diesels, this included a twin sealed-beam headlight, twin oscillating headlight, red oscillating warning light, and classification lamps (necessary under the old timetable and train order rules.) By May 1990, SP SD9E No. 4372 was a rare example of a locomotive retaining all of its lights. By that time, SP had begun to remove extraneous lights from locomotives; typically class lamps were the first covered over. *Brian Solomon*

Southern's steam may best be remembered for its laudable late-era steam practice of dressing passenger locomotives in a handsome shade of green with gold trimming. This began with an order for Ps-4 Pacifics in 1926 and was ultimately implemented across its fleet. The Southern Ps-4 was a magnificent example of the Pacific type; it had been refined from USRA's heavy Pacific type. Southern Ps-4 No. 1401 is preserved and on public display at the Smithsonian in Washington D.C. Except for a few 2-8-8-2 simple articulateds, Southern shied from the later phases of steam development; it neither bought superpower, nor invested in new steam locomotives after 1928. It phased out steam operations as quickly as practicable after World War II, but reintroduced steam power in the 1960s for its popular steam excursion program. Among the engines drafted for this burst of corporate nostalgia was 2-8-2 Mikado No. 4501—one of the few engines deserving of an entire book in its honor, authored by esteemed *TRAINS* magazine editor David P. Morgan.

Southern allocated many diesels, as it did its steam, to its various subsidiaries, and these were lettered and numbered according to how they tended to operate across the Southern system. Southern preferred EMD models, ordering switchers, Es, and vast fleets of F-units (including World War II–era FTs), and later large fleets of EMD road switchers. Yet in the early years of dieselization, it also invested in a few Baldwin switchers, some Fairbanks-Morse road switchers, and a fair sampling of Alco diesels, including some rarely pictured DL109s and PAs. Southern was keen to embrace high-horsepower models, buying F-M Train Masters in 1955 and EMD's SD24s in 1959, followed by a succession by various higher horsepower models. These efforts culminated with acquiring EMD's GP40X in the late 1970s and GP50s in the early 1980s. Southern remained loyal to high short hood designs and continued to buy diesels with high hoods. First, even its GE U-boats and Dash 7s were delivered with high short hoods, and it maintained this practice through its 1982 merger with Norfolk & Western.

▼ Southern's most recognized locomotive was its famed Ps-4 Pacific, such as No. 1379 pictured at Washington D.C. on April 23, 1950. Sister engine No. 1401 is now a popular display at Washington D.C.'s Smithsonian Institution. For three decades, these proud Pacifics led Southern's named passenger trains between Washington Union Station and points south. *John E. Pickett collection*

FACTS

SOUTHERN CLASS Ps-4*

Builders: Alco and Baldwin

Wheel arrangement: 4-6-2

Cylinders: 27x28 in.

Drivers: 73 in.

Engine weight: 304,000 lbs.

Tractive effort: 47,500 lbs.

Intended service: express passenger

Overall production: 54 (includes those built for affiliated lines)

Years built: 1923–1928

*Specifications based on Southern Railway No. 1401 displayed at the Smithsonian Museum.

▲ Mountains in Florida? In this classic view, Southern 4-8-2 No. 1456 leads a passenger train near Pensacola. Southern No. 1456 was a Class Ts 4-8-2 built by Baldwin in 1917. As on the Pennsylvania Railroad, Southern used the small "s" to indicate that a class of locomotive was superheated, not to infer the plural. *Robert A. Buck collection*

◄ EMD's GP30 used a transitional body style unique to that model. While most GP30s feature a low short hood, the exceptions were those ordered by Norfolk & Western and Southern Railway. On November 30, 1980, a rare westward unit coal train finds Southern GP30 No. 2599 in the lead east of Belleville, Illinois. Under traditional timetable and train order rules, white flags indicated an extra train, which distinguished it from a scheduled service. *Scott Muskopf*

81 UNION PACIFIC

▲ Unique to Union Pacific were its famous 9000 series three-cylinder 4-12-2s. On July 2, 1955, the first of these monsters was still working, 29 years after its introduction. It is seen marching westward at Lexington, Nebraska. Unlike other railroads, which later converted three-cylinder locomotives to two-cylinder operation, UP's retained the 4-12-2s as built. *John E. Pickett*

FACTS

UP CLASS UP-1 TO UP-5
Builder: Alco
Wheel arrangement: 4-12-2
Type: Union Pacific
Cylinders: 1 @ 27x31 in. and
    2 @ 27x32 in. ea.
Drivers: 67 in.
Engine weight: 495,000–515,000 lbs.
Tractive effort: 96,650 lbs. (typical)
Intended service: mainline freight service
Overall production: 88
Years built: 1926–1930

During the first decade of the twentieth century, E. H. Harriman controlled both UP and SP (and affiliated properties). Among his improvements was standardization across many elements of railroad operations, equipment, and infrastructure. Under his administration, Union Pacific's standard locomotive types included 2-8-0s for freight service and 4-4-2s and 4-6-2s in passenger service. UP and SP were separated after Harriman's death in 1909. During the period of USRA control, UP moved to larger standard types for freight work, focusing its acquisitions on 2-8-2 Mikados and 2-10-2s.

Although standardization had its benefits, UP's insatiable desire to move ever heavier freight trains over very long distances resulted in its acquisition of varieties of nonstandard, but massive and extremely powerful locomotives that set new records for size, weight, and power output. It began by acquiring Mallet articulateds in 1909, and by the 1920s it was operating fleets of 2-8-8-2s and 2-8-8-0s. In the mid-1920s, it embraced Alco's three-cylinder concept, first taking 11 4-10-2s—similar to those ordered by SP, but lighter. Impressed with this novel design, UP worked with Alco to expand it into the 4-12-2. Unique to UP, this new arrangement was appropriately named the Union Pacific type. In total, 88 were built, and these were among the most successful American-built three-cylinder locomotives, enjoying nearly three decades of service. However, their long wheelbase made them impractical for widespread application, so in 1936 UP worked with Alco in the design of the articulated 4-6-6-4 Challenger that offered greater flexibility yet had six driving axles with ample boiler capacity for sustained speed and power. Key to its design was an improved bearing service for the forward engine that allowed it to operate much faster than previous articulated designs. The Challenger's success not only resulted in UP placing repeat orders for type, but also many other railroads as well.

In 1941, UP urged Alco to expand the Challenger into the 4-8-8-4 Big Boy. Twenty-five of this famous type were built. These were among the largest steam locomotives ever built and conceived, primarily to avoid double heading on heavy freights working east over the Wasatch. UP's final steam passenger power consisted of its iconic Alco-built 800-Class 4-8-4s, considered among the best examples of the type. The last of these, UP 844—built in 1944—survived the end of steam, and it remains on the modern roster for excursion work.

UP was open to other means of propulsion, and it tried some of the most unusual locomotives of the mid-twentieth century. Among these were experiments with General Electric steam turbine electrics in the late 1930s

▲ Union Pacific's 4-6-6-4 Challengers were built for power and speed, and they were more flexible than either the 4-12-2s or 4-8-8-4s. On July 1, 1955, UP No. 3967 works westbound with a freight in eastern Wyoming. In the 1980s, UP restored Challenger 4-6-6-4 No. 3985, which remains in excursion service and is the world's largest operating locomotive, as none of the eight surviving UP 4-8-8-4 Big Boys are in operable condition. *John E. Pickett*

◄ UP worked with General Electric in development of very powerful gas turbine locomotives. Since these unusual machines only achieved maximum efficiency working at full power, they were limited to mainline road service. They were also extraordinarily loud, which further restricted their operation to the unpopulated expanses of the West. *John E. Pickett*

In the mid-1930s, Union Pacific bought a fleet of pioneering diesel streamliners. These were powered by Electro-Motive's Winton 201-A diesel and assembled by Pullman. A pair of its articulated trains featuring the later styling treatment (M10003–M10006) is seen at Chicago & North Western's servicing facilities in Chicago. *Robert A. Buck collection*

▲ During the 1980s, General Electric surpassed EMD as America's leading locomotive builder. Beginning in 1987, UP purchased large numbers of GE's successful Dash 8-40C model. UP No. 9180, typical of these 4,000-horsepower microprocessor-controlled diesels, leads an eastward freight descending Sherman Hill on September 27, 1989. *Brian Solomon*

▼ Among the most innovative locomotives in Union Pacific's modern fleet are Railpower's RP20CDs, a three-genset six-motor model powered by Deutz diesels. Genset locomotives use groups of low-emissions diesel gensets in place of a conventional single, large diesel engine; individual gensets are switched on only as required to meet power demands. In May 2008, UP displayed one of its brand-new genset locomotives in Sacramento at the California State Railroad Museum. *Brian Solomon*

and early 1940s. While unsuccessful, in the 1950s UP returned to GE for America's only fleet of freight-service gas-turbine electrics. All were exceptionally powerful, a trait in keeping with UP's intent to move freight as efficiently as possible; the last and most powerful were rated at 8,500 horsepower.

During the mid-1930s, UP pioneered experiments with Electro-Motive's high-speed diesel streamliners (UP's *Streamliner* of 1934 was actually powered by a spark-ignition engine rather than a diesel, but its later streamliners used General Motors Winton diesel engines). The early streamliners were successful, and while UP followed up with more diesel-powered passenger trains (including some of Electro-Motive's earliest E-units), the railroad refrained from widespread dieselization until 1948.

When it finally began the conversion to diesel, UP sampled locomotives from all commercial manufacturers, but ultimately it was Electro-Motive's standard models (E, F, GPs, and switchers) that formed the bulk of its postwar diesel power. In the late 1950s, UP's continued desire for great power resulted in turbocharging EMD GP9s to raise their output from 1,750 to 2,000 horsepower (a move that encouraged EMD to develop its own turbocharged models). UP responded by buying a significant fleet of EMD's powerful SD24 (rated at 2,400 horsepower). Then in the 1960s, UP encouraged all the manufacturers to build massive double diesels, and it remained the primary market for these enormous curiosities (the only other railroad to buy them was SP, and then only in small numbers). The last and most powerful double diesel was EMD's DDA40X, built in 1969 and rated at 6,600-horsepower per unit—effectively a pair of GP40s on one frame with a D-D wheel arrangement.

During the 1970s, UP standardized its fleet by purchasing large numbers of EMD SD40-2s and GE C30-7s. EMD's SD60s and GE's six-motor Dash 8 models were standard in the late 1980s and early 1990s. During the mid-1990s, it again pushed the envelope with 6,000-horsepower SD90MAC-Hs from EMD and AC6000CWs from GE. It has since returned to ordering standard, more conservatively rated models, such as EMD's SD70M and, more recently, GE's ES44AC.

▲ General Electric's Dash 8 line introduced the era of microprocessor controls. GE's system used three computers: one to oversee locomotive control functions, one to manage the main alternator, and one to control fan and blower motors. Union Pacific bought hundreds of GE Dash 8-40Cs in the late 1980s, followed by Dash 8-40CWs in the 1990s. *Brian Solomon*

◀ Union Pacific bought hundreds of EMD's popular SD40-2s in the 1970s and early 1980s. More were added to the roster as result of mergers in the 1980s and 1990s. A quartet of SD40-2s led a coal train on the Los Angeles & Salt Lake route in March 1997. The lead locomotive was among those with an elongated nose section designed to house equipment for radio-control helper operations. *Brian Solomon*

◀ Union Pacific was one of two railroads that bought EMD's 6,000-horsepower SD90MAC-H. In addition, it acquired large numbers of convertible locomotives that came equipped with the more conventional 4,000-horsepower 16-710G engine, but these could be upgraded with the 6,000-horsepower H engine, as these locomotives seen at O'Fallon, Nebraska, on August 28, 1998, have been. *Brian Solomon*

FACTS

EMD SD90MAC-H
Wheel arrangement: C-C
Transmission: three-phase AC electric
Engine: 16V265H
Horsepower: 6,000
Intended service: heavy freight
Years built: 1996–1999

82 VERMONT RAIL SYSTEM

Vermont Railway (VTR) and Green Mountain Railroad (GMRR) were created in 1963 and 1964 to operate portions of the defunct Rutland Railroad. VTR began operations in autumn 1963 with a secondhand General Electric 44-ton switcher. This was soon augmented by another 44 tonner and a handful of secondhand Alco road switchers. In 1966, one of the Alcos was traded to EMD for a SW1500, and then between 1972 and 1974 VTR bought a pair of new GP38s from EMD. All of its subsequent locomotive acquisitions have been secondhand, with an emphasis on GP38s and GP40 types. Its 2,000-horsepower GP38s are numbered in the 200 series and the 3,000-horsepower GP40s are in the 300 series. In 1972, VTR acquired the Clarendon & Pittsford and continued to operate it as an affiliate.

In its first two decades, Green Mountain Railroad relied upon first-generation Alco switchers and road switchers for all of its freight work, while hosting operations of Steamtown until 1983. During the 1980s, it largely replaced its Alcos with secondhand EMD GP9s, although former Rutland RS-1 No. 405 was retained for excursion services that began after Steamtown was relocated to Scranton, Pennsylvania.

In 1997, Vermont Rail System grouped the VTR, GMRC, and Clarendon & Pittsford under one banner; Washington County Railroad was added in 1999. Also part of its system is the New York & Ogdensburg, another former Rutland line. While VRS has sampled modern types, including trials with leased 4,300-horsepower SD90MACs and brief acquisition of former Texas-Mexican GP60s, it has primarily relied upon its fleet of EMD four-motor units, giving the railroad a decidedly 1970s appearance. Locomotives carry reporting marks from the various VRS railroads without respect to their actual assignment.

The toughest job on the system is the climb over Mount Holly between Rutland and Bellows Falls, where steep grades and tight curvature brings heavy freight to a crawl. Here, VRS typically assigns multiple locomotives to its daily freights and occasionally requires pushers.

◀ On November 2, 1993, Green Mountain's daily freight XR-1 running from Bellows Falls to Rutland and return passes the former Rutland Railroad station at Ludlow. In the lead is a GP9 built for Chesapeake & Ohio and one of several EMD units acquired by Green Mountain in the 1990s. By 1990, the versatile and once-common GP9 had vanished from many Class 1 rosters, yet it remained popular with short lines. *Brian Solomon*

▶ Vermont Rail System routinely mixes locomotives lettered for its various component lines. Working south from Rutland on October 21, 2005, through freight No. 261 is led by Green Mountain GP40 No. 302, Vermont Railway GP40 No. 307, former Canadian National GP40-2L No. 310, and GP40-2 No. 303—originally Boston & Maine No. 314. VRS's logo mimics the appearance of the Green Mountains. *Brian Solomon*

◄ For Steamtown's final run in Vermont in October 1983, all three of Green Mountain's RS-1s teamed up with Canadian Pacific 4-6-2 No. 1246 for the trip from Bellows Falls to Rutland and back. Although a rainy day, photographers were out in force. On the left, overseeing activities with Hasselblad in hand, is Steamtown director Don Ball Jr. *Brian Solomon*

FACTS

ALCO RS-1*

Wheel arrangement: B-B
Transmission: DC electric
Engine: 6-cylinder 539T
Horsepower: 1,000
Weight: 72,000 lbs.
Tractive effort: 242,400 lbs.
Intended service: general purpose
Overall production: 400+
Years built: 1940–1951 (1960 for export)

*Specifications based on Green Mountain No. 405.

83 VIA RAIL

► Montreal Locomotive Works built 31 M429LRC locomotives for service on VIA's new light, rapid comfortable tilting trains. These worked corridor services in Ontario and Quebec. The unusually low-profile locomotives with a wedge-shaped front end were powered by an Alco-designed 251 diesel. An eastward LRC glides through Bayview Junction, Ontario, on July 24, 1987. *Brian Solomon*

FACTS

BOMBARDIER M429LRC

Wheel arrangement: B-B

Transmission: DC electric

Engine: 251 diesel

Horsepower: 3,725

Intended service: light, rapid, and comfortable power car

Number operated: 31

Overall production: 34 (includes 1973-built 2,900-horsepower demo)

Years built: 1973–1984

VIA Rail began in 1977 as Canadian National's passenger operating subsidiary. A year later, it became a separate company and assumed operation of both CN and Canadian Pacific's intercity passenger services. Since that time, it has served as Canada's primary intercity passenger train operator, similar to Amtrak's role in the United States. VIA inherited a mix of 1950s-era passenger locomotives from CN and CP, including a pair of rebuilt CN Montreal Locomotive Works–built FPA-2s and FPB-2s, and a sizeable fleet of more modern MLW FPA-4/FPB-4s. Also included were a significant number of FP7s, FP9s, and cabless B-units built by General Motors Diesel, Electro-Motive Division's Canadian subsidiary. Among the rarest locomotives in VIA's original fleet was a pair of former CP EMD-built E8As (the surviving members of an three-unit order, and the only E's built for a railroad outside the United States). VIA also inherited self-propelled trains, including a fleet of Budd-built RDCs and three United Aircraft TurboTrains built for CN. Between 1981 and 1984, MLW built 31 M429LRC locomotives (with distinctive wedge-shaped front ends) to serve as power cars for its LRC (light rapid comfortable) tilting trains. In mid-1980s, VIA began buying EMD F40PH-2s to replace its aged cab unit fleet. The F40PH-2's angular lines and turbocharged roar offered a stark contrast with the gentle contours and mellower sounds of the 1950s cabs. After two decades of service, the M429LRCs were replaced with a fleet of modern General Electric 4,230-horsepower model P42DC Genesis series diesels, which began arriving in 2001.

▲ VIA replaced most of its 1950s-era carbody units with F40PH-2s in the 1980s. Ultimately it bought 58 for long-distance services. Most were painted in VIA's standard gray and yellow, but a few have been dressed in special advertising liveries. No. 6404 celebrates CBC-Radio Canada. *Brian Solomon*

◀ GE designed its Genesis series in the 1990s to meet Amtrak specifications. Unusual-looking locomotives, these use a structural integral monocoque body typical of European designs. VIA's units were delivered in 2001 with a flashy new paint scheme that some observers have deemed the most attractive to adorn the Genesis series. VIA P42 No. 913 pauses at Coteau, Quebec, on October 23, 2004. *Brian Solomon*

▶ Not only was Virginian's late dieselization atypical, but its choice of Fairbanks-Morse as its primary supplier was unusual. On July 29, 1958, four-year-old F-M H-16-44 No. 15 was caught on film at Princeton, West Virginia. *Richard Jay Solomon*

▲ Although a relatively new machine, Virginian 0-8-0 No. 251 was stored out of service in 1958, having been recently displaced by Fairbanks-Morse diesels. This was one of 15 0-8-0s built by Lima in 1942 and 1943. In its early years, Virginian relied upon Alco and Baldwin for its steam, but its last new acquisitions were all with Lima. *Richard Jay Solomon*

Virginian was essentially an early-twentieth century creation; built to very high modern standards, its 443-mile line connected the Appalachian mountain town of Deepwater, West Virginia, with its purpose-built Hampton Roads coal port at Sewells Point, Virginia, in 1909. It primary served as a high-volume bituminous conduit. Although highly engineered, its main lines featured some difficult grades (more than 2 percent in places); these grades, combined with operation of some the heaviest freights in the United States, required the largest and most powerful locomotives of the day. Although it initially settled on heavy 2-8-2 Mikados for universal freight service, its heavy coal drags required more specialized types. In 1909, it adopted the 2-6-6-0 Mallet, and Virginian became one of the most enthusiastic users of both the 2-6-6-0 wheel arrangement and the Mallet compound; a year later, it ordered 2-8-8-2s from Baldwin. Then, in 1912, Alco built a half-dozen massive examples of this type that were briefly deemed the world's largest locomotives. In 1916, Virginian took title to a unique 2-8-8-8-4 Baldwin triplex (Erie owned three with a 2-8-8-8-2 wheel arrangement). This was classed XA and given road No. 700; although huge and very powerful, it was famously unsuccessful. Nearly as outlandish, but far more practical, were 10 Alco-built 2-10-10-2s delivered in 1918. Equipped with enormous boilers, these were capable of supplying sustained steam at maximum throttle for prolonged periods. They featured front low-pressure cylinders four feet in diameter—the largest on any North American locomotive—and when starting as a simple engine (high-pressure steam to all cylinders) delivered 176,600 pounds, the greatest of any conventional reciprocating engine. In the 1920s, Virginian bought more 2-8-8-2s, and then in the 1940s, it took an order for six 2-6-6-6 Alleghenies and five 2-8-4 Berkshires, both near copies of successful Chesapeake & Ohio types built by Lima. After the war, it held off dieselizing for a few years.

FACTS

VIRGINIAN CLASS AE

Builder: Alco

Wheel arrangement: 2-10-10-2

Cylinders: 2 @ 30x32 in. ea. (low
pressure), 2 @ 48x32 in ea.
(high pressure)

Drivers: 56 in.

Engine weight: 684,000 lbs.

Tractive effort: 176,600 lbs. (starting,
as a simple engine)

Intended service: heavy freight

Overall production: 10

Year built: 1918

In the 1920s, Virginian adopted a high-voltage single-phase AC electrification—similar to that recently employed by Norfolk & Western—for its mountain route between Roanoke, Virginia, and Elmore, West Virginia. It bought state-of-the-art boxcab locomotives, designated Class EL-3A, that used phase splitters to convert single-phase current to three-phase for use by enormous synchronous induction motors. Power was transmitted from motors to drive wheels using jackshafts and side rods. The three-phase AC motors delivered enormous power but were limited to just two running speeds. To augment the 1920s side rodders, in 1948, GE supplied two pairs of semipermanently coupled streamlined AC-DC motor-generator electrics, Nos. 125 to 128. Finally, to replace its original electrics, Virginian ordered a dozen Ignitron rectifiers, Class EL-Cs, from GE in 1955.

The coal-hauling Virginian was initially reluctant to consider diesels. However, when it finally dieselized in the mid-1950s, it did so in an unusual way: where most railroads embraced EMD or Alco, buying cab units and later road switchers, Fairbanks-Morse was Virginian's choice supplier. Virginian bought 19 2,400-horsepower H-24-66 Train Masters and 33 1,600-horsepower H-16-44s. The era of Virginian's brightly painted opposed-piston F-Ms was short; in 1959, the road merged with its competitor, Norfolk & Western.

FACTS

VIRGINIAN CLASS EL-2B ELECTRIC

Builder: GE

Wheel arrangement: B-B+B-B (per unit)

Horsepower: 6,800 (based on a pair)

Engine weight: 1,032,832 lbs.
(based on a pair)

Tractive effort: 260,000 lbs.
(based on a pair)

Intended service: heavy coal service

Overall production: two semipermanently coupled pairs
(four units)

Year built: 1948

▼ As one of America's premier gateways served by more than a dozen railroads, St. Louis was a popular place to take locomotive photos. Wabash 4-6-4 No. 700 catches the sun at St. Louis Union Station in the mid-1940s. Wabash, Chesapeake & Ohio and Illinois Central were among railroads that rebuilt older types into powerful 4-6-4s. *Robert A. Buck collection*

FACTS

WABASH CLASS P-1

Builder: Wabash (Decatur Shops)

Wheel arrangement: 4-6-4

Type: Hudson

Cylinders: 26x28 in.

Drivers: 80 in.

Engine weight: 374,690 lbs.

Tractive effort: 44,200 lbs.

Intended service: fast passenger

Overall production: 7

Years built: 1943–1947

Wabash was a Midwestern trunk route connecting principle gateways, including Buffalo, Detroit, Chicago, St. Louis, Omaha, Des Moines, and Kansas City. In the late 1890s, it bought some 4-4-0 Baldwin Vauclain compounds with an unusual clerestory style cab roof favored by a few Midwestern railroads. More typical of its road power was the 2-6-0, a type it bought in large numbers into the early twentieth century. It progressed to the 2-6-2 and then to 2-8-2 by World War I, yet it retained a few 2-6-0s to work lightly built lines until the end of steam in 1955. In 1930, Wabash invested in dual-service 4-8-2s, and in 1931, it purchased freight service 4-8-4s, both from Baldwin. During the 1940s, it transformed five Alco three-cylinder 2-8-2 Mikados into handsome high-drivered 4-6-4 Hudsons for passenger service; a pair of two-cylinder 2-8-2s were similarly rebuilt. Dieselization began in 1939, when Wabash bought a sampling of switchers from Alco, EMC, and GE. More followed during World War II, and after the war Wabash bought diesels liberally from all builders. Noteworthy were a fleet of Canadian-built F-units, built by General Motors Diesel at London, Ontario, for Canadian service on Wabash's route between Buffalo and Detroit that crossed Ontario. In addition to Alco FA/FBs and PAs and EMD Es, Fs, and GPs, Wabash bought a significant fleet of Fairbanks-Morse 2,400-horsepower Train Master road switchers. These were originally operated in semipermanently coupled pairs designated as 4,800-horsepower diesels. Among its more unusual diesels were a dozen Lima-Hamilton 1,200-horsepower switchers. In the early 1960s, it bought GE U25Bs, EMD GP35s, and Alco C-424s. Wabash was merged with Norfolk & Western in 1964.

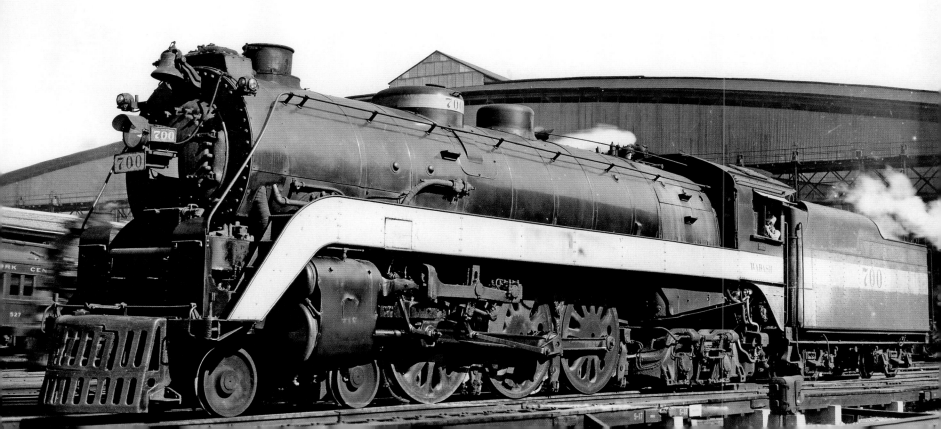

▲ Like many railroads, Wabash sampled diesel switchers in the late 1930s and early 1940s. Then after World War II, it invested in road diesels. Wabash Alco S-1 No. 151 was pictured in Chicago on September 1, 1951. Alco's S-1 may be distinguished from similar switcher models by its combination of a small exhaust stack, narrow radiator (at the front of the hood), and Blunt-style trucks. Alco's more common S2 also used the Blunt truck but had a wider radiator, while later switchers (built after 1950) used AAR-type A-style drop-bolster trucks. *John E. Pickett*

◄ On July 22, 1958, Wabash E8A No. 1007 departs St. Louis Union Station with train No. 9, the *City of St. Louis*, destined for Kansas City. Wabash was unusual in that its passenger trains served St. Louis from both east and west. Wabash bought 14 E8As from EMD between 1949 and 1953, which augmented its E7s and Alco PAs in passenger service. *Richard Jay Solomon*

estern Maryland operated a Y-shaped network reaching west from Baltimore across its namesake to Cumberland, where one arm reached southwest into the West Virginia coal fields and the other went northwest to the interchange gateway at Connellsville, Pennsylvania. In steam days, WM was partial to the 2-8-0 as its staple freight locomotive, continuing to order this traditional arrangement many years after the 2-8-2 and 2-10-2 were adopted for similar service by most other lines. WM bought two batches of 2-10-0s, including some Russian Decapods delivered during World War I. It was keen on articulated types, beginning with some 2-6-6-2 Mallets in 1909 for helper service and culminating with one of the few Eastern fleets of 4-6-6-4 Challengers, the latter built by Baldwin in the early 1940s. Despite national tends toward dieselization after the war and having already bought diesel switchers, WM invested in a small fleet of 4-8-4s for fast freights. Yet it also sampled road switchers, buying three DRS-4-4-1500s from Baldwin, an RS-2 from Alco, and a pair of BL-2s from EMD. In 1950, it bought diesels en masse: GPs and Fs from EMD, RS-2/RS-3s and FA/FBs from Alco, and a few more Baldwins in the form of AS-16s. Its relatively new 4-8-4s didn't have a chance and were off the roster by 1954. In 1963, it bought EMD's high-horsepower GP35s, six-motor SD35s in 1964, and SD40s in the mid-1960s. WM was absorbed into the Chesapeake & Ohio–Baltimore & Ohio's Chessie System with its locomotive fleet largely integrated into Chessie's, although locomotives retained WM sublettering.

▼ Western Maryland 2-10-0 Decapod No. 1125 was all cleaned up for public display in Hagerstown, Maryland, on September 13, 1937. No freight locomotive normally looked this good, especially one 10 years on the job. Hagerstown was location of a key WM classification yard. *Robert A. Buck collection*

W.M.R.R. 1125.

HAGERSTOWN, M.D.   SEPT-13-1937.

▲ Constructed in 1945, Western Maryland No. 6 was the last and largest Lima Shay built. Designed for high-tractive effort on poor track, the three-truck Shay type was capable of working exceptionally steep grades. Most were sold to timber and industrial lines, and they were relatively rare on major carriers. Western Maryland and Kansas City Southern were among the exceptions. *John E. Pickett collection*

FACTS

LIMA THREE-TRUCK SHAY

Wheel arrangement: B+B+B

Cylinders: 3 vertical @ 17x18 in. ea.

Drivers: 48 in.

Engine weight: 324,000 lbs.

Tractive effort: 96,000 lbs.

Intended service: slow-speed steeply graded freight

Overall production: 2

Years built: 1918 and 1945

◄ In 1970, Western Maryland hosted Nickel Plate 2-8-4 No. 759 on a series of special trips. On the climb west of Cumberland, WM assigned a set of EMD Fs to assist the Berkshire over the mountains. Look carefully in this image at Corriganville, Maryland, on October 18, 1970. Buried behind the bulldog-nose F-units is the Lima 2-8-4 under steam. Western Maryland No. 51 is a late-build F3A, which looks near identical to early F7As. *George W. Kowanski*

87 WESTERN PACIFIC RAILROAD

Western Pacific was a twentieth-century creation built to fulfill George Gould's vision of a transcontinental rail empire. Its main line was complete in 1909, and it began services with 2-8-0s for freight service and 4-6-0s for passenger service. During World War I, it began acquiring 2-8-2s and ordered oil-fired 2-6-6-2 Mallets from Alco—initially for road freights in Feather River Canyon. In 1931, Baldwin 2-8-8-2 simple articulateds took over most Feather River Canyon road freights. WP was unusual because never owned a Pacific, especially odd for a Western railroad. Instead, it remained content with 4-6-0s until the mid-1930s, when it bought 10 surplus 4-8-2s from Florida East Coast. In 1938, WP took delivery of seven handsome 4-6-6-4 Challengers, largely assigning them to road freight work in the high desert east of Portola, where they toiled in relative obscurity for a dozen years. Its last new steam engines were 10 near copies of SP's austerity Class Gs-6 4-8-4. Built during World War II, these 4-8-4s enjoyed less than a decade of service.

Dieselization was straightforward. In 1939, WP sampled Electro-Motive's SW1 and NW2 switchers. Then during World War II, it made successive orders for A-B-B-A FTs. After the war, it ordered F3s and F7s for freight. Of its Fs, its small fleet of FP7s enjoyed the most exposure as power for WP's high-profile *California Zephyr* streamliner. In 1953, WP began buying EMD road switchers, and over the next three decades it added GP7s, GP9s, GP20s (with high short hoods), GP35s, GP40s, and, finally, in 1979, some GP40-2s. Except for some Alco and Baldwin switchers, WP relied on EMD products exclusively until the late 1960s. In 1967, it began augmenting its road fleet with General Electric U30Bs, acquiring 20 between 1967 and 1971, followed by 14 U23Bs in 1972. Union Pacific absorbed WP at the end of 1981. A representative selection of WP diesels and 0-6-0 switcher No. 165 have been preserved at the Western Pacific Railroad Museum in Portola, California.

▼ The 4-6-6-4 Challenger was developed for Union Pacific, but many western railroads adopted the type for fast freight services. WP No. 402 was only a year old when pictured at Wendover, Utah, in 1938. Like most Challengers, it had a short service life. WP replaced it with diesels a few years after World War II. *John E. Pickett collection*

FACTS

WP CLASS M-100

Builder: Baldwin

Wheel arrangement: 4-6-6-4

Type: Challenger

Cylinders: 4 @ 22x32 in. ea.

Drivers: 70 in.

Engine weight: 590,000 lbs.

Tractive effort: 99,600 lbs.

Intended service: road freight

Overall production: 7

Year built: 1938

◄ Among Western Pacific's peculiarities was that it exclusively bought four-axle diesels, unusual for a western road. WP GP40-2 No. 3546 was part of an order for 15 units built between 1979 and 1980, shortly before the railroad was absorbed by Union Pacific. Unlike WP, UP didn't hesitate to assign six-axle (and in some instances eight-axle) DDA40Xs to freights working the WP route. *Mike Abalos photo, courtesy of the Friends of Mike Abalos*

◄ On August 23, 1976, Western Pacific U30B No. 3067 and U23B No. 2259 lead two Union Pacific SD40-2s westbound at the famed Keddie Wye in California's Feather River Canyon. Although EMD units dominated WP's road fleet, between 1967 and 1971 it bought 20 GE U30Bs, followed by 14 U23Bs in 1972. GE later used a few former WP U23Bs for conversion into Super-7 road switchers. *Brian Jennison*

FACTS

EMD GP40-2

Wheel arrangement: B-B

Transmission: DC electric

Engine: 16-645E3

Horsepower: 3,000

Intended service: road freight

Number operated: 15

Overall production: 1,131

Years built: 1972–1986

88 WHEELING & LAKE ERIE RAILWAY

▲ Wheeling & Lake Erie acquired a fleet of unusual GP35s built for the Southern Railway using AAR-style trucks from Alco trades. These featured high short hoods. By comparison, the majority of EMD's GP35 production featured low short hoods and came with standard Blomberg B trucks. W&LE was still operating a few of its oddball GP35s in 2011. *Brian Solomon*

FACTS

EMD GP35

Wheel arrangement: B-B

Transmission: DC electric

Engine: 16-567D3A

Horsepower: 2,500

Weight: 260,000 lbs.*

Tractive effort: 65,000 lbs.*

Intended service: road switcher and fast freight

Overall production: 1,333

Years built: 1963–1966

*Varied depending on options. Locomotives with AAR trucks had slightly different specifications.

▼ The most unusual locomotive in W&LE's fleet is No. 3046, a prototype SD40 model built on the short frame designed for the SD35 and sometimes designated as an SD40X. It was part of a group of eight EMD SD40 demonstrators built in 1966 that were later sold to UP as Nos. 3040–3047. W&LE has upgraded No. 3046 with modern electrical controls, designating it an SD40-3. *Brian Solomon*

The modern Wheeling & Lake Erie was carved out of the Norfolk Southern system in 1990 and consists largely of former Akron, Canton & Youngstown; Pittsburgh & West Virginia; and historic Wheeling & Lake Erie routes. Originally a 578-mile network, the breakup of Conrail in the late 1990s enabled significant expansion of W&LE's route structure, largely through trackage rights, and the system now reaches approximately 850 miles. W&LE's locomotive fleet exclusively consists of secondhand EMD units. The railroad's early fleet included former NS locomotives acquired with the trackage, notably former Southern Railway high-hood GP35s riding on AAR-style trucks recycled from Alco trade-ins. W&LE has rebuilt many of these at its Brewster, Ohio, shops, redesignating them as GP35-3s to reflect modifications, especially third-party micro-processor electrical control. Likewise, W&LE has acquired SD40/SD40-2 models, including former Union Pacific/Missouri Pacific, Milwaukee Road, and Algoma Central units that Brewster Shops have rebuilt and redesignated as SD40-3s. Among its six-axle locomotives is No. 3046, an SD40 prototype (sometimes designated as an SD40X) that was built on an SD35 frame. Also rebuilt are a half-dozen GP40-3s and a few un-rebuilt GP40s from various owners. Now off the roster are several former N&W SD45s. In addition to road units, the W&LE roster included former Grand Trunk Western modified GP9s and a pair of SW1500s assigned to its Akron Barberton Cluster. Many W&LE locomotives have been painted in a scheme inspired by Rio Grande's late-era livery, yet some units still wear paint from former owners.

▲ On August 11, 2011, a westward Wheeling & Lake Erie extra freight sails across one of the many tall steel tower—supported plate-girder viaducts that characterize the style of late-era construction on its former Pittsburgh & West Virginia route in southwestern Pennsylvania. In the lead is SD40-3 No. 3034 (originally a Union Pacific SD40) and SD40X No. 3046, demonstrating the difference in length between a production model SD40 and the short frame prototype. *Brian Solomon*

89 WISCONSIN & SOUTHERN RAILROAD

Wisconsin & Southern (reporting marks: WSOR) was born as result of Milwaukee Road's 1980 reorganization; over the subsequent three decades, it assembled a 700-mile regional rail network serving southern Wisconsin and northern Illinois. Its locomotive fleet has been entirely comprised of secondhand EMD models. While the newest units date to the mid-1970s, many have been substantially rebuilt and modified since leaving LaGrange. In the 1990s, WSOR's roster was dominated by GP7s, GP9s, GP18s, and former Southern Pacific GP20s and GP35s, plus a few switchers, a pair of E9As, and an FP7As assigned to its business and passenger trains. WSOR also briefly operated some former Burlington Northern F45s. During the 2000s, most of the older GPs were replaced by newer and more reliable EMD models. Various models have come and gone, including a small fleet of SD18s and some former Illinois Central SD20s—remanufactured from SD24s. The contemporary fleet largely consists of GP38 types—some are GP38-2s that originally served National Railway of Mexico, others were remanufactured from GP40s—as well as SD40-2s and a half-dozen former Milwaukee Road MP15ACs. Most WSOR road locomotives are numbered to reflect their model type—GP20s were numbered in the 2000 series, GP38s in the 3800 series, and SD40-2s in the 4000 series. Although some locomotives have worked for years wearing liveries of previous owners, most of today's fleet are dressed in WSOR's corporate red and silver. Typically, SD40-2s work road freights to Chicago, while four-motor models are assigned to branch lines and secondary runs to collect freight. At the end of 2011, short-line operator WATCO Transportation Services acquired control of WSOR.

◀ In the 1980s and 1990s, WSOR operated with a variety of older secondhand diesels, including this former Rock Island GP18. As built, this had a high short hood, but it was later rebuilt and modified with a low short hood (and redesignated a GP9). It led WSOR's daily freight west of Waukesha, Wisconsin, in May 1996. *Brian Solomon*

▶ Wisconsin & Southern GP38 No. 3805, in resplendent red and gray paint, catches the morning light at the Janesville, Wisconsin, roundhouse in July 2005. Behind is one of the former Illinois Central SD20s that served the line for a few years. WSOR's collection of vintage EMDs gives it a look more akin to a mainline railroad of the 1970s than of today. *Brian Solomon*

▲ On the afternoon of June 25, 2010, Wisconsin & Southern MP15AC No. 1506 works the former Chicago & North Western yard in Madison, Wisconsin. This is one of six former Milwaukee Road MP15ACs acquired by the line in recent years. EMD's MP15 line was the final phase of its end-cab switcher types. They were designed in the 1970s as a moderately powerful (1,500 horsepower) multipurpose diesel with all the benefits of a traditional switcher, but carried on Blomberg road trucks. *Brian Solomon*

FACTS

EMD MP15AC

Wheel arrangement: B-B

Transmission: DC electric

Engine: 12-645E

Horsepower: 1,500

Intended service: multipurpose switcher

Number operated: 6

Overall production: 255

Years built: 1975–1984

90 WISCONSIN CENTRAL RAILROAD

Wisconsin Central Limited began operations in 1987 on a network carved out of the old Soo Line; over the next dozen years, it expanded its reach through line acquisition, mergers, and reciprocal arrangements. WC never bought new locomotives, and part of its success as a dynamic regional line was acquiring large numbers of secondhand EMD diesels and rehabilitating them at its North Fond du Lac, Wisconsin, shops. By 1998, the backbone of its road fleet consisted of about 120 20-cylinder six-motor EMDs, mostly SD45s and F45s, many former Santa Fes and Burlington Northerns. Many were equipped with aftermarket electronics to improve performance and fuel economy, while taking advantage of upgraded heavy electrical components such as newer traction motors. Pairs of SD45s were standard on most road freights, while three SD45s worked heavy runs, such as unit coal trains and ore moves. WC also inherited a handful of SD40-2s from Algoma Central. While locals worked with a variety of EMD four-motor types—including GP9s, GP30s, GP35s, GP40s, and GP40-2s—some of these also worked high-priority intermodal runs. WC acquired 22 SW1500s, and more than a half-dozen SW200 switchers, largely for yard work, along with a sole SW1 that was used as shop switcher in North Fond du Lac. In addition to more common models, the railroad also inherited or acquired cheaply a variety of oddities, including light-axle load SDL39s built for Milwaukee Road branch-line service, a few high-hood SD24s, and an SD35 that came with purchase of the Fox River Valley Railroad in 1993. Although Canadian National acquired the property in 2001, Wisconsin Central–painted locomotives continued to operate in home territory for several more years.

While most of WC's network featured relatively gentle grades, one exception was the climb over Byron Hill south of Fond du Lac on the Chicago Subdivision. This prolonged 1 percent climb slowed most trains to a crawl. To keep the heaviest trains from stalling and to avoid assigning unnecessary locomotives on more level stretches, WC would assign helpers to southward trains out of Fond du Lac. Typically, a pair of six-motor units would tie on to the back of a train at North Fond du Lac and shove to the top of the grade near Byron, cut off, and return to the yard. During the mid-1990s, when WC was handling a steady volume of iron ore traffic, loaded ore trains would be held at North Fond du Lac and dispatched in succession to maximize the use of a single helper crew.

▲ Rated at 2,250 horsepower, EMD's GP30 was only produced from 1961 to 1963, when it was supplanted by the 2,500-horsepower GP35. WC operated a small fleet of secondhand GP30s. Those in the 700 series, such as No. 711 pictured at Waukesha, were former Soo Line units, while those in the 2250 series had Chicago & Northwestern heritage. *Brian Solomon*

◄ In 1995, WC took control of Ontario's Algoma Central and inherited AC's fleet of SD40-2s, which were largely reassigned to WC's Wisconsin lines. Where the SD40/SD40-2 was the most common six-motor type on North American railroads in the 1970s and 1980s, WC's handful of SD40-2s were anomalous in a fleet dominated by the more powerful SD45. *Brian Solomon*

▲ A pair of Wisconsin Central SD45s leads a southward freight holding on the main line at Byron, Wisconsin, for a northward train on April 6, 1996. In the late 1980s and early 1990s, WC took advantage of SD45s made surplus by the larger railroads, and these remained its most numerous locomotive. *Brian Solomon*

FACTS

EMD SD45

Wheel arrangement: C-C

Transmission: DC

Engine: 20-645E3

Horsepower: 3,600

Intended service: road freight

Years built: 1966–1972

SOURCES

Books

Alexander, Edwin P. *American Locomotives*. New York: Bonza Books, 1950.

———. *Iron Horses*. New York: Bonza Books, 1941.

Anderon, Elaine. *The Central Railroad of New Jersey's First 100 Years*. Easton, PA: Center for Canal History and Technology, 1984.

Archer, Robert F. *A History of the Lehigh Valley Railroad: Route of the Black Diamond*. Berkeley, CA: Howell-North Books, 1977.

Armitage, Merle. *The Railroads of America*. Boston: Duell, Sloan and Pearce–Little, Brown, 1952.

Armstrong, John H. *The Railroad: What It Is, What It Does*. Omaha, NE: Simmons-Boardman Publishing Corp., 1982.

Asay, Jeff S. *Track and Time: An Operational History of the Western Pacific Railroad through Timetables and Maps*. Portola, CA: Feather River Rail Society, 2006.

Austin, Ed, and Tom Dill. *The Southern Pacific in Oregon*. Edmonds, WA: Pacific Fast Mail, 1987.

Bean, W. L. *Twenty Years of Electrical Operation on the New York, New Haven and Hartford Railroad*. Pittsburgh, PA: American Railway Association, 1927.

Beaver, Roy C. *The Bessemer & Lake Erie Railroad 1869–1969*. San Marino, CA: Golden West Books, 1969.

Bell, J. Snowdon. *The Early Motive Power of the Baltimore and Ohio Railroad*. New York: Angus Sinclair, 1912.

Bezilla, Michael. *Electric Traction on the Pennsylvania Railroad 1895–1968*. State College, PA: Pennsylvania State University Press, 1981.

Brown, John K. *The Baldwin Locomotive Works 1831–1915: A Study in American Industrial Practice*. Baltimore: The Johns Hopkins University Press, 1995.

Bruce, Alfred W. *The Steam Locomotive in America: Its Development in the Twentieth Century*. New York: Norton, 1952.

Bryant, Keith L. *History of the Atchison, Topeka, and Santa Fe Railway*. New York: Macmillan, 1974.

Burgess, George H., and Miles C. Kennedy. *Centennial History of the Pennsylvania Railroad*. Philadelphia: The Pennsylvania Railroad Company, 1949.

Burke, Davis. *The Southern Railway: Road of the Innovators*. Chapel Hill, NC: The University of North Carolina Press, 1985.

Bush, Donald J. *The Streamlined Decade*. New York: George Braziller, 1975.

Byron, Carl R. *A Pinprick of Light: The Troy and Greenfield Railroad and Its Hoosac Tunnel*. Shelburne, VT: New England Press, 1995.

Casey, Robert J., and W. A. S. Douglas. *The Lackawanna Story*. New York: McGraw-Hill, 1951.

Castner, Charles B., Ronald Flanary, and Patrick Dorin. *Louisville & Nashville Railroad: The Old Reliable*. Lynchburg, VA: TLC Publishing, 1996.

Churella, Albert J. *From Steam to Diesel*. Princeton, NJ: Princeton University Press, 1998.

Collias, Joe G. *Mopac Power: Missouri Pacific Lines, Locomotives, and Trains 1905–1955*. Howell-North Books, San Diego, CA: 1980.

Condit, Carl. *Port of New York*. 2 vols. Chicago: University of Chicago Press, 1980, 1981.

Conrad, J. David. *The Steam Locomotive Directory of North America*. 2 vols. Polo, IL: Transportation Trails, 1988.

Corbin Bernard G., and William F. Kerka. *Steam Locomotives of the Burlington Route*. Red Oak, IA: Random House Value Publishing, 1960.

Daughen, Joseph R., and Peter Binzen. *The Wreck of the Penn Central*. Boston: Beard Books, 1971.

Del Grosso, Robert C. *Burlington Northern 1980–1991 Annual*. Denver: Hyrail Productions, 1991.

Delaware & Hudson Company. *A Century of Progress: History of the Delaware and Hudson Company 1823–1923*. J. B. Lyon: Albany, NY, 1925.

DeNevi, Don. *The Western Pacific: Railroading Yesterday, Today, and Tomorrow*. Seattle: Superior Publishing, 1978.

Dixon, Thomas W. Jr. *Chesapeake & Ohio: Superpower to Diesels*. Newton, NJ: Carstens Publications, 1984.

Doherty, Timothy Scott, and Brian Solomon. *Conrail*. St. Paul, MN: MBI Publishing, 2004.

Dolzall, Gary W., and Stephen F. Dolzall. *Diesels from Eddystone: The Story of Baldwin Diesel Locomotives*. Milwaukee: Kalmbach Publishing, 1984.

———. *Monon: The Hoosier Line*. Glendale, CA: Interurban Press, 1987.

Dorsey, Edward Bates. *English and American Railroads Compared*. New York: John Wiley, 1887.

Droege, John A. *Freight Terminals and Trains*. New York: McGraw-Hill, 1912.

———. *Passenger Terminals and Trains*. New York: McGraw-Hill, 1916.

Drury, George H. *Guide to North American Steam Locomotives*. Waukesha, WI: Kalmbach Publishing, 1993.

———. *The Historical Guide to North American Railroads*. Waukesha, WI: Kalmbach Publishing, 1985.

———. *The Train Watcher's Guide to North American Railroads*. Waukesha, WI: Kalmbach Publishing, 1992.

Dubin, Arthur D. *Some Classic Trains*. Milwaukee: Kalmbach, 1964.

———. *More Classic Trains*. Milwaukee: Kalmbach, 1974.

Dunscomb, Guy, L. *A Century of Southern Pacific Steam Locomotives*. Modesto, CA: Guy L. Dunscomb & Son, 1963.

Farrington, S. Kip Jr. *Railroading from the Head End*. New York: Doubleday, Doran & Co., 1943.

———. *Railroads at War*. New York: Doubleday, Doran & Co., 1944.

———. *Railroading from the Rear End*. New York: Doubleday, Doran & Co., 1946.

———. *Railroads of the Hour*. New York: Doubleday, Doran & Co., 1958.

———. *Railroads of Today*. New York: Doubleday, Doran & Co., 1949.

———. *Railroading the Modern Way*. New York: Doubleday, Doran & Co., 1951.

Fay, Robert L. Jr., ed. *Encyclopedia of American Business History and Biography: Railroads in the Nineteenth Century*. New York: Bruccoli Clark Layman and Facts on File, 1988.

Fitzsimons, Bernard. *150 Years of Canadian Railroads*. Toronto: Royce Publications, 1984.

Forney, M. N. *Catechism of the Locomotive*. New York: The Railroad Gazette, 1876.

Frailey, Fred W. *Twilight of the Great Trains*. Waukesha, WI: Kalmbach, 1998.

———. *Zephyrs, Chiefs & Other Orphans: The First Five Years of Amtrak*. Godfrey, IL: RPC Publications, 1977.

Frey, Robert L. *Railroads in the Nineteenth Century*. New York: Facts on File, 1988.

Garmany, John B. *Southern Pacific Dieselization*. Edmonds, WA: Pacific Fast Mail, 1985.

Glischinski, Steve. *Burlington Northern and Its Heritage*. Osceola, WI: Motorbooks, 1996.

———. *Santa Fe Railway*. Osceola, WI: Motorbooks, 1997.

Grant, H. Roger. *Erie Lackawanna: Death of an American Railroad, 1938–1992*. Stanford, CA: Stanford University Press, 1994.

Greenberg, William T. Jr., and Robert F. Fischer. *The Lehigh Valley Railroad East of Mauch Chunk*. Martinsville, NJ: The Gingerbread Stop, 1997.

Gruber, John. *Railroad History in a Nutshell*. Madison, WI: Center for Railroad Photography and Art, 2009.

———. *Railroad Preservation in a Nutshell*. Madison, WI: Center for Railroad Photography and Art, 2011.

Gruber, John, and Brian Solomon. *The Milwaukee Road's Hiawathas*. St. Paul, MN: Voyageur Press, 2006.

Hampton, Taylor. *The Nickel Plate Road*. Cleveland, OH: World Publishing, 1947.

Harding, J. W., and Frank Williams. *Locomotive Valve Gears*. Scranton, PA: International Textbook, 1928.

Hare, Jay V. *History of the Reading*. Philadelphia: John Henry Strock, 1966.

Harlow, Alvin F. *Steelways of New England*. New York: Creative Age Press, 1946.

———. *The Road of the Century*. New York: Creative Age Press, 1947.

Haut, F. J. G. *The History of the Electric Locomotive*. London: Allen and Unwin, 1969.

———. *The Pictorial History of Electric Locomotives*. Cranbury, NJ: Oak Tree Publications, 1970.

Hayes, William Edward. *Iron Road to Empire: The History of the Rock Island Lines*. New York: Simmons-Boardman, 1953.

Heath, Erle. *Seventy-Five Years of Progress: Historical Sketch of the Southern Pacific*. San Francisco: Southern Pacific Bureau of News, 1945.

Hedges, James Blaine. *Henry Villard and the Railways of the Northwest*. New Haven, CT: Yale University Press, 1930.

Heimburger, Donald J. *Wabash*. River Forest, IL: Heimburger House Publishing, 1984.

Helmer, William F. *O&W: The Long Life and Slow Death of the New York, Ontario & Western Rwy*. 2nd ed revised. San Diego: Howell-North, 1959.

Hidy, Ralph W., and Muriel E. Hidy, Roy V. Scott, and Don L. Hofsommer. *The Great Northern Railway: A History*. Boston, MA: Harvard Business School, 1988.

Hilton, George W. *American Narrow Gauge Railroads*. Stanford, CA: Stanford University Press, 1990.

Holbrook, Stewart H. *The Story of American Railroads*. New York: Crown Publishers, 1947.

———. *James J. Hill*. New York: Random House, 1955.

Holland, Rupert Sargent. *Historic Railroads*. New York: Grosset & Dunlap, 1927.

Holton, James L. *The Reading Railroad: History of a Coal Age Empire*. 2 vols. Laurys Station, PA: Garrigues House, 1992.

Hofsommer, Don. L. *Southern Pacific 1900–1985*. College Station, TX: Texas A&M University Press, 1986.

Hoyt, Edwin P. *The Vanderbilts and Their Fortunes*. New York: F. Muller, 1962.

Hungerford, Edward. *Daniel Willard Rides the Line*. New York: G. P. Putman's Sons, 1938.

———. *Men of Erie: A Story of Human Effort*. New York: Random House, 1946.

Ivey, Paul Wesley. *The Pere Marquette Railroad Company*. Lansing, MI: Lansing Historical Commission, 1919.

Jones, Robert C. *The Central Vermont Railway*. 3 vols. Shelburne, VT: Sundance Publications, 1995.

Jones, Robert W. *Boston & Albany: The New York Central in New England*. 2 vols. Los Angeles: Pine Tree Press, 1997.

Karr, Ronald Dale. *The Rail Lines of Southern New England*. Pepperell, MA: Branch Line Press, 1995.

Keilty, Edmund. *Interurbans without Wires*. Glendale, CA: Interurban Press, 1979.

Kiefer, P. W. *A Practical Evaluation of Railroad Motive Power*. New York: Simmons-Boardman, 1948.

Kirkland, John F. *Dawn of the Diesel Age*. Pasadena, CA: Interurban Press, 1994.

———. *The Diesel Builders*. 3 vols. Glendale, CA: Interurban Press, 1983.

Kirkman, Marshall M. *The Compound Locomotive*. New York and Chicago: World Railway Publishing, 1899.

Klein, Maury. *History of the Louisville & Nashville Railroad*. New York: Macmillan, 1972.

———. *Union Pacific*. 2 vols. New York: Doubleday, 1989.

———. *Union Pacific: The Reconfiguration—America's Greatest Railroad from 1969 to the Present*. Oxford and New York: Oxford University Press, 2011.

Kratville, William, and Harold E. Ranks. *Motive Power of the Union Pacific*. Omaha, NE: Kratville Publishing, 1958.

Lamb, W. Kaye. *History of the Canadian Pacific Railway*. New York: Macmillan, 1977.

Leachman, Rob. *Northwest Passage*. Mukilteo, WA: Hundman Publishing, 1998.

LeMassena, Robert A. *Colorado's Mountain Railroads*. Golden, CO: Sundance Publications, 1963.

———. *Rio Grande to the Pacific*. Denver: Sundance Publications, 1974.

Lemly, James H. *The Gulf, Mobile & Ohio*. Homewood, IL: Richard D. Irwin, 1953.

Leopard, John. *Wisconsin Central Heritage*. Vol. 2. La Mirada, CA: Four Ways West Publications, 2008.

Lewis, Oscar. *The Big Four*. New York: A. A. Knopf, 1938.

Malone, Michael P. *James J. Hill: Empire Builder of the Northwest*. Norman, OK: University of Oklahoma Press, 1996.

Marre, Louis A., and Jerry A. Pinkepank. *The Contemporary Diesel Spotter's Guide*. Milwaukee: Kalmbach Publishing, 1985.

Marre, Louis, A. *Diesel Locomotives: The First 50 Years*. Waukesha, WI: Kalmbach Publishing, 1995.

Marre, Louis A., and Paul K. Withers. *The Contemporary Diesel Spotter's Guide, Year 2000 Edition*. Halifax, PA: Withers Publishing, 2000.

Marshall, James. *Santa Fe: The Railroad That Built an Empire*. New York: Random House, 1945.

McDonald, Charles W. *Diesel Locomotive Rosters*. Milwaukee: Kalmbach Publishing, 1982.

McDonnell, Greg. *U-Boats: General Electric Diesel Locomotives*. Toronto: Boston Mills Press, 1994.

McMillan, Joe. *Santa Fe's Diesel Fleet*. Burlingame, CA: Chatham Publishing, 1975.

McLean, Harold H. *Pittsburgh & Lake Erie Railroad*. San Marino, CA: Golden West Books, 1980.

Middleton, William D. *When the Steam Railroads Electrified*. Milwaukee: Kalmbach Publishing, 1974.

———. *Landmarks on the Iron Road*. Bloomington, IN: Indiana University Press, 1999.

Middleton, William D., George M. Smerk, and Roberta L. Diehl, eds. *Encyclopedia of North American Railroads.* Bloomington and Indianapolis: Indiana University Press, 2007.

Mika, Nick, and Helma Mika. *Railways of Canada.* Toronto and Montreal: McGraw-Hill Ryerson, 1972.

Miner, Craig H. *The St. Louis–San Francisco Transcontinental Railroad.* Lawrence, KS: University of Kansas Press, 1972.

Mohowski, Robert E. *New York, Ontario & Western in the Diesel Age.* Andover, NJ: Andover Junction Publications, 1994.

Morgan, David P. *Steam's Finest Hour.* Milwaukee: Kalmbach Publishing, 1959.

————. *Canadian Steam!* Milwaukee: Kalmbach Publishing, 1961.

Mott, Edward Harold. *Between the Ocean and the Lakes: The Story of Erie.* New York: John S. Collins, 1900.

Murray, Tom. *Canadian National Railway.* St. Paul, MN: MBI Publishing, 2004.

Myrick, David F. *Life and Times of the Central Pacific Railroad.* San Francisco: Book Club of California, 1969.

————. *Western Pacific: The Last Transcontinental Railroad.* Golden CO: Colorado Railroad Museum, 2006.

Overton, Richard C. *Burlington West.* Cambridge, MA: Harvard University Press, 1941.

————. *Burlington Route.* New York: Knopf, 1965.

Pennsylvania Railroad. *1846–1896 Fiftieth Anniversary of the Incorporation of the Pennsylvania Railroad Company.* Pennsylvania Railroad: Philadelphia, 1896.

Potter, Janet Greenstein. *Great American Railroad Stations.* New York: John Wiley, 1996.

Ransome-Wallis, P. *The Concise Encyclopedia of World Railway Locomotives.* New York: Hawthorn Books, 1959.

Reck, Franklin M. *On Time.* LaGrange, IL: Electro-Motive Division of General Motors, 1948.

————. *The Dilworth Story.* New York: McGraw-Hill, 1954.

Reed, S. G. *A History of the Texas Railroads.* Houston, TX: St. Clair Publishing, 1941.

Riegel, Robert Edgar. *The Story of the Western Railroads.* Lincoln, NE: Macmillan, 1926.

Rosenberger, Homer Tope. *The Philadelphia and Erie Railroad.* Potomac, MD: Fox Hills Press, 1975.

Salisbury, Stephen. *No Way to Run a Railroad.* New York: McGraw-Hill, 1982.

Saunders, Richard Jr. *Main Lines: American Railroads 1970–2002.* DeKalb, IL: Northern Illinois University Press, 2003.

————. *Merging Lines: American Railroads 1900–1970.* DeKalb, IL: Northern Illinois University Press, 2001.

————. *The Railroad Mergers and the Coming of Conrail.* Westport, CT: Greenwood Publishing, 1978.

Saylor, Roger B. *The Railroads of Pennsylvania.* State College, PA: Pennsylvania State University, 1964.

Schafer, Mike, and Brian Solomon. *Pennsylvania Railroad.* Minneapolis: Voyageur Press, 2009.

Schrenk, Lorenz P., and Robert L. Frey. *Northern Pacific Diesel Era 1945–1970.* San Marino, CA: Golden West Books, 1988.

Shaughnessy, Jim. *Delaware & Hudson.* Berkeley, CA: Howell North Books, 1967.

————. *The Rutland Road.* 2nd ed. Syracuse, NY: Howell-North, 1997.

Signor, John R. *Beaumont Hill.* San Marino, CA: Golden West Books, 1990.

————. *Donner Pass: Southern Pacific's Sierra Crossing.* San Marino, CA: Golden West Books, 1985.

————. *Rails in the Shadow of Mount Shasta.* San Diego: Howell-North Books, 1982.

————. *Southern Pacific's Coast Line.* Wilton, CA: Signature Press, 1994.

————. Southern Pacific's *Western Division.* Wilton, CA: Signature Press, 2003.

————. *Tehachapi.* San Marino, CA: Golden West Books, 1983.

Sinclair, Angus. *Development of the Locomotive Engine.* New York: A. Sinclair Publishing, 1907.

Smalley, Eugene V. *History of the Northern Pacific Railroad.* New York: G. P. Putnam's Sons, 1883.

Smith, Warren L. *Berkshire Days on the Boston & Albany.* New York: Quadrant Press, 1982.

Solomon, Brian. *Alco Locomotives.* Minneapolis: Voyageur Press, 2009.

————. *Amtrak.* St. Paul, MN: MBI Publishing, 2004.

————. *Baldwin Locomotives.* Minneapolis: Voyageur Press, 2010.

————. *Burlington Northern Santa Fe Railway.* St. Paul, MN: Voyageur Press, 2005.

————. *CSX.* St. Paul, MN: Voyageur Press, 2005.

————. *EMD Locomotives.* St. Paul, MN: Voyageur Press, 2006.

————. *GE Locomotives.* St. Paul, MN: MBI Publishing, 2003.

————. *Locomotive.* Osceola, WI: MBI Publishing, 2001.

————. *Railroad Signaling.* St. Paul, MN: MBI Publishing, 2003.

————. *Railroads of Pennsylvania.* Minneapolis: Voyageur Press, 2008.

————. *Railway Masterpieces: Celebrating the World's Greatest Trains, Stations and Feats of Engineering.* Iola, WI: David & Charles, 2002.

————. *Southern Pacific Passenger Trains.* St. Paul, MN: Voyageur Press, 2005.

————. *Super Steam Locomotives.* Osceola, WI: MBI Publishing, 2000.

————. *The American Diesel Locomotive.* Osceola, WI: MBI Publishing, 2000.

————. *The American Steam Locomotive.* Osceola, WI: MBI Publishing, 1998.

————. *Trains of the Old West.* New York: MetroBooks, 1998.

Solomon, Brian, and Mike Schafer. *New York Central Railroad.* Osceola, WI: Motorbooks, 1999.

Staff, Virgil. *D-Day on the Western Pacific.* Glendale, CA: Interurban Press, 1982

Starr, John W. *One Hundred Years of American Railroading.* Millersburg, PA: Dodd, Mead & Co., 1927.

Staufer, Alvin F. *C&O Power.* Carrollton, OH: A. F. Staufer, 1965.

————. *Pennsy Power III.* Medina, OH: A. F. Staufer, 1993.

————. *Steam Power of the New York Central System.* Vol. 1. Medina, OH: A. F. Staufer, 1961.

Staufer, Alvin F., and Edward L. May. *New York Central's Later Power.* Medina, OH: A. F. Staufer, 1981.

Steinbrenner, Richard T. *The American Locomotive Company: A Centennial Remembrance.* Warren, NJ: On Track Publishers, 2003.

Stevens, Frank W. *The Beginnings of the New York Central Railroad.* New York: G. P. Putnam, 1926.

Stover, John F. *History of the New York Central Railroad.* New York: Macmillan, 1975.

————. *The Life and Decline of the American Railroad.* New York: Oxford University Press, 1970.

————. *The Routledge Historical Atlas of the American Railroads.* New York: Routledge, 1999.

Strapac, Joseph A. *Southern Pacific Motive Power Annual 1971.* Burlingame, CA: Chatham Publishing, 1971.

————. *Southern Pacific Review 1953–1985.* Huntington Beach, CA: Pacific Coast Chapter of the Railway and Locomotive Historical Society, 1986.

————. *Southern Pacific Review 1981.* Huntington Beach, CA: Pacific Coast Chapter of the Railway and Locomotive Historical Society, 1982.

Stretton, Clement E. *The Development of the Locomotive: A Popular History 1803–1896.* London: Bracken Books, 1896.

Swengel, Frank M. *The American Steam Locomotive: Volume 1, Evolution.* Davenport, IA: Midwest Rail Publications, 1967.

Swingle, Calvin F. *Modern American Railway Practice.* Chicago: National Institute of Practical Mechanics, 1908.

Talbot, F. A. *Railway Wonders of the World.* 2 vols. London: Cassell and Company, 1914.

Taber, Thomas Townsend III. *The Delaware, Lackawanna & Western Railroad, Part One.* Williamsport, PA: Thomas Townsend Taber III, 1980.

Thompson, Gregory Lee. *The Passenger Train in the Motor Age.* Columbus, OH: Ohio State University, 1993.

Thompson, Slason. *Short History of American Railways.* Chicago: Bureau of Railway News and Statistics, 1925.

———. *The Railway Library: 1912.* Chicago: Bureau of Railway News and Statistics, 1913.

Trewman, H. F. *Electrification of Railways.* London: Sir Isaac Pitman & Sons, 1920.

Turner, Gregg M., and Melancthon W. Jacobus. *Connecticut Railroads.* Hartford, CT: The Connecticut Historical Society, 1989.

Vance, James E. Jr. *The North American Railroad.* Baltimore: The Johns Hopkins University Press, 1995.

Vauclain, Samuel M. *Optimism.* Philadelphia: privately published, 1924.

Vauclain, Samuel M., and Earl Chapin May. *Steaming Up!* New York: Brewer & Warren, 1930.

Walker, Mike. *Steam Powered Video's Comprehensive Railroad Atlas of North America: North East U.S.A.* Feaversham, UK: Steam Powered Publishing, 1993.

Warren, J. G. H. *A Century of Locomotive Building by Robert Stephenson & Co. 1823–1923.* Newcastle upon Tyne, UK: Andrew Reid & Company Ltd., 1923.

Waters, L. L. *Steel Trails to Santa Fe.* Lawrence, Kansas, 1950.

Weller, John, L. *The New Haven Railroad: Its Rise and Fall.* New York: Hastings House, 1969.

Westing, Frederic. *Apex of the Atlantics.* Milwaukee: Kalmbach Publishing, 1963.

———. *Penn Station: Its Tunnels and Side Rodders.* Seattle: Superior Publishing, 1977.

———. *The Locomotives That Baldwin Built.* Seattle: Superior Publishing, 1966.

Westing, Frederic, and Alvin F. Staufer. *Erie Power.* Medina, OH: Wayner, 1970.

White, John H. Jr. *A History of the American Locomotive: Its Development, 1830–1880.* Baltimore: Dover, 1968.

———. *Early American Locomotives.* Toronto: Dover Publications, 1979.

Williams, Harold A. *The Western Maryland Railway Story.* Baltimore: Western Maryland Railway Co., 1952.

Wilner, Frank N. *The Amtrak Story.* New York: Simmons-Boardman, 1994.

Wilson, Neill C., and Frank J. Taylor. *Southern Pacific: The Roaring Story of a Fighting Railroad.* New York: McGraw-Hill, 1952.

Wilson, O. Meredith. *The Denver and Rio Grande Project: 1870–1901.* Salt Lake City: Howe Brothers, 1982.

Winchester, Clarence. *Railway Wonders of the World.* 2 vols. London: Amalagated Press, 1935.

Wiswessar, Edward H., P.E. *Steam Locomotives of the Reading and P&R Railroads.* Sykeville, MD: Greenberg Publishing, 1988.

Withers, Paul, K. *Norfolk Southern Locomotive Directory 2001.* Halifax, PA: Withers Publishing, 2001.

Wright, Richard K. *Southern Pacific Daylight.* Thousand Oaks, CA: RKW Publication, 1970.

Young, William S. *Starrucca, the Bridge of Stone.* Aiken, SC: published privately, 2000.

Zimmermann, Karl R. *Erie Lackawanna East.* New York: Quadrant Press, 1975.

———. *The Remarkable GG1.* New York: Quadrant Press, 1977.

Periodicals

American Railroad Journal and Mechanics' Magazine (published in the 1830s and 1840s)

Baldwin Locomotives, Philadelphia (no longer published)

CTC Board, Ferndale, Washington

Diesel Era, Halifax, Pennsylvania

Diesel Railway Traction, supplement to *Railway Gazette* (UK) (merged into *Railway Gazette*)

Extra 2200 South, Cincinnati, Ohio

Jane's World Railways, London

Locomotive Cyclopedia, New York, 1922–1947 (no longer published)

Moody's Analyses of Investments, Part I—Steam Railroads, New York

Official Guide to the Railways, New York

Pacific RailNews, Waukesha, WI (no longer published)

Railroad History, formerly *Railway and Locomotive Historical Society Bulletin*, Boston

Railway Age, Chicago and New York

Railway and Locomotive Engineering, New York (no longer published)

Railway Gazette, New York, 1870–1908 (no longer published)

Railway Mechanical Engineer 1925–1952 (no longer published)

Shoreliner, Grafton, MA

Southern Pacific Bulletin, San Francisco

The Car and Locomotive Cyclopedia, Omaha, NE

The Railway Gazette, London.

TRAINS Magazine, Waukesha, WI

Vintage Rails, Waukesha, WI (no longer published)

Brochures, Timetables, Rule Books

American Locomotive Co. and General Electric Co. *Operating Manual Model RS-3.* Schenectady, NY: GE Transportation, 1951.

Amtrak public timetables, 1971 to 2011.

Baldwin Locomotive Works. *Baldwin-Westinghouse Diesel-Electric Locomotives General Specifications for Standard Units.* Philadelphia: Baldwin Locomotive Works, 1950.

Baldwin Locomotive Works. *Eight-Coupled Locomotives for Freight Service. Record No. 99.* Philadelphia: Baldwin Locomotive Works, 1920.

Baldwin Locomotive Works. *Exhibit at the Panama-Pacific International Exposition in San Francisco, California.* Published in conjunction with the exhibit of the same name. Philadelphia: Baldwin Locomotive Works, 1915.

Baldwin Locomotive Works. *6,000 HP Diesel Electric Road Freight Locomotives.* Philadelphia: Baldwin Locomotive Works, 1949.

Baldwin Locomotive Works. *Steam Locomotive Performance.* Philadelphia: Baldwin Locomotive Works, 1940.

Baldwin Locomotive Works. *Triple Articulated Compound Locomotive for the Erie Railroad Company. Record No. 81.* Philadelphia: Baldwin Locomotive Works, 1915.

Bearce, W. D. *Steam-Electric Locomotive.* Erie, PA: 1939.

Boston & Albany Railroad. *Time-Table No. 174.* Boston: Boston & Albany, 1955.

Boston & Albany Railroad. *Facts about the Boston & Albany R.R.* Boston: Boston & Albany, 1933.

Burlington Northern Santa Fe Corporation annual reports 1996–2004.

Burlington Northern Santa Fe Railway. *Grade profiles*. No date.

Burlington Northern Santa Fe Railway. *System Map*. Fort Worth, TX: BNSF, 2003.

Canadian National. *2007 Annual Report*. Montreal: Canadian National, 2007.

Canadian National. *Current Issues, Diesel Unit Data*. Montreal: Canadian National, circa 1970.

Central Vermont Railway. *Timetable 65, Northern and Southern Division*. St. Albans, VT: Central Vermont Railway, 1965.

Chicago, Milwaukee, St. Paul & Pacific public timetables 1943–1966.

Conrail. *Pittsburgh Division, System Timetable No. 5*. Philadelphia: Conrail, 1997.

CSX Transportation. *Baltimore Division, Timetable No. 2*. Jacksonville, FL: CSX, 1987.

Delaware, Lackawanna & Western. *A Manual of the Delaware, Lackawanna & Western*. Hoboken, NJ: Delaware, Lackawanna & Western, 1928.

Erie Railroad. *Erie Railroad its Beginnings and Today*. Erie, PA: Erie Railroad, 1951.

General Code of Operating Rules. 4th ed. 2000.

General Electric. *Dash 8 Locomotive Line*. Schenectady, NY: GE Transportation, no date.

General Electric. *A New Generation for Increased Productivity*. Erie, PA: General Electric, 1987.

General Electric. *GENESIS Series*. Schenectady, NY: GE Transportation, 1993.

General Motors. *Electro-Motive Division, Diesel Locomotive Operating Manual No. 2312 for Model GP7 with Vapor Car Steam Generator*. 2nd ed. La Grange, IL: GM, 1950.

General Motors. *Electro-Motive Division Model F3 Operating Manual No. 2308B*. La Grange, IL: GM, 1948.

General Motors. *Electro-Motive Division Model F7 Operating Manual No. 2310*. La Grange, IL: GM, 1951.

General Motors. *Electro-Motive Division F40PH-2C Operator's Manual*. La Grange, IL: GM, 1988.

General Motors. *Electro-Motive Division Model 567B Engine Maintenance Manual*. La Grange, IL: GM, 1948.

General Motors. *Electro-Motive Division Operating Manual No. 2300*. La Grange, IL: GM, 1945.

General Motors. *Electro-Motive Division SD45 Operator's Manual*. La Grange, IL: GM, 1977.

General Motors. *Electro-Motive Division SD70M Operator's Manual*. La Grange, IL: GM, 1994.

General Motors. *Electro-Motive Division SD80MAC Locomotive Operation Manual*. La Grange, IL: GM, 1996.

New York Central System. *Rules for the Government of the Operating Department*. New York: New York Central, 1937.

New York Central System public timetables 1943–1968.

Northeast Operating Rules Advisory Committee. *NORAC Operating Rules*. 7th ed. 2000.

Pennsylvania Railroad public timetables 1942–1968.

Richmond, Fredericksburg & Potomac Railroad Company. *Timetable No. 31*. Richmond, VA: RF&PR, 1962.

Santa Fe public timetables 1943–1964.

Southern Pacific Company. *Pacific System Time Table No. 17, Coast Division*. San Francisco: Southern Pacific, 1896.

Southern Pacific Company public timetables 1930–1958.

Southern Pacific Company. *Your Daylight Trip*. San Francisco: Southern Pacific, 1939.

Steamtown National Historic Site. *The Nation's Living Railroad Museum*. No date.

Reports, Papers, and Unpublished Works

Clemensen, A. Berle. *Historic Research Study: Steamtown National Historic Site Pennsylvania*. Denver: U.S. Department of the Interior, 1988.

Chappell, Gordon. *Flanged Wheels on Steel Rails: Cars of Steamtown*. Unpublished manuscript.

Johnson, Ralph P. *The Four Cylinder Duplex Locomotive as Built for the Pennsylvania Railroad*. Paper presented in New York, May 1945.

———. *Railroad Motive Power Trends*. Paper presented November 1945. Published in Philadelphia.

Meyer, C. W. *Comments on Ralph P. Johnson's Paper*, November 29, 1945. Presented November 1945. Published in Philadelphia.

Warner, Paul T. *The Story of the Baldwin Locomotive Works*. Philadelphia, 1935.

Warner, Paul T. *Compound Locomotives*. Paper presented in New York, April 14, 1939.

Internet Sources

www.aar.org
www.ble.org
www.bnsf.com
www.cn.ca
www.cpr.ca
www.csx.com
www.fra.dot.gov
www.guilfordrail.com
www.gwrr.com
www.kcsouthern.com
www.montanarail.com
www.nscorp.com
www.railamerica.com
www.uprr.com
www.vermontrailway.com
www.wsorrailroad.com

INDEX

ACKNOWLEDGMENTS

This book has benefited from a culmination of research gathered for many projects. My work on previous books and locomotive projects has produced a vast amount of information and experience relating to locomotives in North America, much of which has been blended together here. All of this has its roots in my early railway interest. It was my father who first brought me trackside, put a camera in my hand, and took me on my first train rides (and on a great many more since). I was about eight when he first brought me to Tucker's Hardware in Warren, Massachusetts. It was there I came to know Bob Buck. Like mine, Bob's interest in locomotives stemmed to his formative experiences. Growing up in Warren within sight of the Boston & Albany, he had many memorable experiences watching and riding on B&A's steam locomotives in their final years. Bob's interest took him far and wide, and he had the good fortune to experience in person many of the locomotives—steam, diesel, and electric—portrayed here. Many of his photos appear in this book. Over the years, he transformed his family hardware store into a great hobby shop, and he eventually sold the hardware business to focus on his first love, trains. His contagious enthusiasm and knowledge for locomotives never waned; he inspired generations of locomotive enthusiasts, educating them on the details and virtues of his favorite engines, while criticizing machines that he felt suffered from bad design, inappropriate machinery, or poor appearance. In recent years, Bob was an invaluable resource in my quest for information, images, and insight, and at every meeting he would lend me carefully stocked manila envelopes filled with photos, drawings, maps, timetables, and detailed railroad information, news, and history. Yet Bob's foremost skill was in making connections between people; many of my friends who've helped me over the years I met through the kindness and wisdom of Bob Buck. Sadly, Bob passed away on his 82nd birthday, shortly after I began work on this book.

I could not have produced either the text or photos without help. Over the years, countless railroaders, industry professionals, railway historians, librarians, technology enthusiasts, and photographers have guided me; answered my unending list of questions; and directed me toward valued information sources. In addition, many have traveled with me, lending their eyes and ears in the study of locomotives at work. Thanks to: Mike Abalos, Howard Ande, Jim Beagle, Ed Beaudette, F. L. Becht, Marshall Beecher, Kurt Bell, Robert Bentley, Travis Berryman, Dan Bigda, Mike Blaszak, Scott Bontz, Jim Boyd, Philip Brahms, Chris Burger, Joe Burgess, Brian Burns, Dave Burton, Steve Carlson, Paul Carver, Tom Carver, David Clinton, George C. Corey, Mike Danneman, Tom Danneman, Brandon Delaney, Tim Doherty, Oliver Doyle, Doug Eisele, Ken Fox, Michael L. Gardner, Colin Garratt, Chris Goepel, Phil Gosney, Sean Graham-White, Dick Gruber, John Gruber, J. J. Grumblatt Jr., Don Gulbrandsen, Chris Guss, Mark Healy, David Hegarty, Paul Hammond, John P. Hankey, Mark Hemphill, Tim Hensch, Mark Hodge, Will Holloway, Gerald Hook, T. S. Hoover, Thomas M. Hoover, Brian L. Jennison, Clark Johnson, Jr., Danny Johnson, Bill Keay, Tom Kline, George W. Kowanski, Blair Kooistra, Bob Krambles, Dennis LeBeau, Mark Leppert, Bill Linley, Don Marson, Fred Matthews, Norman McAdams, Denis McCabe, Patrick McKnight, Joe McMillan, George Melvin, Hal Miller, David Monte Verde, Doug Moore, Dan Munson, Vic Neves, Claire Nolan, Colm O'Callaghan, Mel Patrick, John Peters, John E. Pickett, Howard Pincus, Candace Pitarys, George S. Pitarys, Markku Pulkkinen, Joe Quinlan, Paul Quinlan, Peter Rausch, Rich Reed, Hal Reiser, Doug Riddell, Peter Rigney, Jon Roma, Brian Rutherford, Dean Sauvola, Mike Schafer, J. D. Schmid, Jim Shaughnessy, Gordon Smith, Scott Snell, Joe Snopek, Carl Swanson, Richard Steinheimer, Vic Stone, Carl Swanson, David Swirk, Tom Tancula, Emile Tobenfeld, Justin Tognetti, Harry Vallas, Otto M. Vondrak, John H. White Jr., Craig Willett, Matthew Wronski, Norman Yellin, Pat Yough, Nick Zmijewski, and Walter Zullig.

Special thanks those who assisted in production of this book. Chris Guss wrote sections on select Midwestern short lines, provided tech support and caption help, and lent photos from the Mike Abalos collection; Pat Yough located important photos and helped with technical facts and details; George C. Corey assisted with steam data; Kenneth Buck helped scan and caption Bob Buck's color work; George W. Kowanski and Rich Red advised me on Penn Central; and the staff at the Irish Railway Record Society in Dublin located books, rare documents, and other important sources. My parents, Richard Jay Solomon and Maureen Solomon, helped with logistical support during my lengthy travels and helped copy edit drafts of the text. A book like this relies on the keen eye of photographers to capture the spirit of the locomotive. Many photographers lent photographs from their collections, and each is credited by their appropriate images. In scouring railroad literature for facts, I've sometimes found inconsistencies while spotting the occasional mistake or typo. In this book, I've gone to great lengths to procure good information, while double checking sources and trying to ensure that the facts and photos are the best available. Yet no work is perfect; if mistakes should appear, these are my own and not those of the many people who helped me along the way.

My editor Dennis Pernu deserves the credit for helping to refine this book idea. Thanks to everyone at Quayside Publishing for their roles in production. Special thanks to Kenneth, Russell, and Sylvia Buck for helping me with Bob's archive and allowing me the use of his photographic collection.

Dedication

In memory of Robert A. Buck—who loved locomotives

CONTENTS

NORTH AMERICAN
LOCOMOTIVES

A Railroad-by-Railroad Photohistory

BRIAN SOLOMON

CRESTLINE